A Mary Austin Reader

Edited by

ESTHER F.
LANIGAN

The University of Arizona Press   Tucson

A
Mary
Austin
Reader

The University of Arizona Press
© 1996
The Arizona Board of Regents
All Rights Reserved
♾ This book is printed on acid-free, archival-quality paper.
Manufactured in the United States of America
First printing, 1996
Library of Congress Cataloging-in-Publication Data
Austin, Mary Hunter, 1868–1934.
    A Mary Austin reader / edited by Esther F. Lanigan.
        p. cm.
    Includes bibliographical references (p.   ).
    ISBN 0-8165-1619-7 (cloth : alk. paper). —
    ISBN 0-8165-1620-0 (paper : alk. paper)
    1. Indians of North America—West (U.S.)—Literary collections. 2. West (U.S.)—
Literary collections. I. Lanigan, Esther F. II. Title.
PS3501.U8A6 1996   95-41730
818'.5209—dc20   CIP
British Cataloguing-in-Publication Data
A catalogue record for this book is available from the British Library.

The editor gratefully acknowledges permission to reprint the following copyrighted
material:

Stories from *One-Smoke Stories* by Mary Austin. Copyright 1934 by Mary Austin, ©
renewed 1961 by School of American Research. Selections from *Starry Adventure* by
Mary Austin. Copyright 1931 by Mary Austin, © renewed 1959 by Mary C.
Wheelwright. Selections from *Earth Horizon* by Mary Austin. Copyright 1932 by Mary
Austin, © renewed 1960 by School of American Research. Reprinted by permission of
Houghton Mifflin Co. All rights reserved.

For Charles—always—for his support of me and of Mary

Contents

Acknowledgments

The editor wishes to acknowledge the Huntington Library and its staff for help in making possible this anthology of Mary Austin's writings: in particular, Sara Hodson, of American literary manuscripts, for clarifying matters of content and permission and also Jennifer Watts, curator of photographs of the Huntington, for help with the images used here.

I also thank Joanne O'Hare, senior editor of the University of Arizona Press, for her receptivity to the idea of *A Mary Austin Reader* when it was first proposed and for her encouragement throughout the project. Ruth Wild typed the manuscript, and I thank her for saving me from many embarrassing errors through her years of experience working with me on Mary Austin's texts.

Finally, I owe a debt of gratitude to Howard Lamar, Yale University Sterling Professor of History Emeritus, who led me to Mary Hunter Austin more than a decade ago.

Editorial Note

Mary Austin's spelling errors, in both common words and proper names, have invariably been noted by recent editors and scholars of her work. Why her irregular spelling was not corrected by editors of her published work in her own time is unknown. Because errors occur with such frequency, I have decided not to regularize the spelling and to give readers the original Mary Austin as faithfully as possible.

A Mary Austin Reader

1

Introduction

Mary Austin's literary career, enduring until her death in 1934, spanned four decades during which she wrote some thirty book-length works and more than two hundred essays, novels, dramas, short stories, poems, and articles. Her work primarily drew upon her impressions of the indigenous peoples and terrains of California, Arizona, and New Mexico. Paradoxically, while the writer derived her imaginative inspiration from the stark beauties of the American West, most of her income depended on the East Coast literary establishment, those editors and publishers whom she often criticized, even as they conferred legitimacy on her work by buying and publishing her writings.

At the turn of the century, and well beyond, the eastern literary magazines were filled with material about the West. Indeed, the West became an exoticized element of the American scene, and readers devoured fiction, travelogues, and memoirs describing its romantic inhabitants and its immense beauties. More recently, Austin and other Anglo writers of her time and place have been reevaluated by critics who have viewed them as insensitive exploiters of the native people of the West. To a degree, this criticism speaks to Austin's work, but the greater actuality seems to be that in the context of her times, she labored tirelessly to render her experience of the Far West and Southwest with realistic accuracy. Richard Drinnon in his 1980 book *Facing West: The Metaphysics of Indian-Hating and Empire-Building* is one such critic who sees at once Austin's exploitive role, as a member of the Anglo elite, as well as her genuine contribution to the portrayal of the West in her writings.

Because of her writing about the American West, Austin has finally come into her own as a notable writer in our own time, with biographies, new editions, and inclusion in anthologies that confer legitimacy to her work. Along with women writers who are now considered among the best American writers of the East, Austin ranks among the major writers of the American West.

Born in Carlinville, Illinois, in 1868, Austin was the daughter of Susannah Graham Hunter and a retired Civil War captain, George Hunter, who had emigrated from England with his brother. Captain Hunter, who had a love of books and wrote for the local press, had been in poor health following his valiant service in the war; his death in 1878 was one of the great tragedies of Austin's life. Throughout her life Mary's father remained the model for her of a literary man, and she recalls in her autobiography that she sought to emulate his "virile style" in her own writing (*Earth Horizon,* 30). Perhaps she thought that if he had survived he would have nurtured her own literary career, the kind of intellectual nurturance that Mary's mother seems to have been ill-equipped to give her.

After Captain Hunter's death, Susannah, a stalwart of the local Women's Christian Temperance Union, supplemented her meager widow's pension by nursing Carlinville's sick and dying. She relied upon Mary to assume household duties, including the care of her younger brother George. Added to this strain was the grief and guilt Mary experienced when her younger sister died of diphtheria after nursing Mary back to health from the same illness.

Susannah, grief-stricken from her double tragedy and left with a scant pension and three children, seems to have distanced herself from Mary just when the young girl most needed maternal solace. Apparently failing to recognize Mary's grief, Susannah left her daughter to struggle with these family deaths without comfort. Mary believed her mother actually blamed her for not dying instead of her sister, Jennie; consequently Mary Austin suffered survivor's guilt from her girlhood through her life. At the same time that her mother was heaping domestic tasks on the bereft ten-year-old, Mary perceived her older brother Jim to have found a favored status in the family. Many years later the writer faulted her mother, writing of the many rebuffs she recalled from the years of girlhood and young womanhood. Remembering the emotional barrenness of her youth, and the closeness she longed for during those years, Austin wrote, "I had, at least, learned to do without it [love]."[1]

What increasingly provided Mary with a connection to a world from which she felt cut off was her writing, and she wrote short pieces in high school and in college, a struggle because of Mary's illness during her years at Carlinville's normal school and subsequently Blackburn College. She claims that her time away from college was due partially to the cultural ideas of her time that proscribed a rigorous education for women as antithetical to the widely held medical beliefs about the frailty of women's bodies, in particular their reproductive systems. Austin experienced mounting dissatisfaction with her family, culminating in her own neurasthenic breakdowns; yet she earned her degree from Illinois' Blackburn College in 1888. The summer following graduation, the Hunter family decided to go West—as had thousands of Midwesterners who had read widely published accounts of post–Gold

Rush California in the popular periodicals of the day. James Hunter, as head of the family, persuaded his widowed mother that California, with its generous land-grant policy, would offer the family opportunities for advancement that Carlinville, Illinois, could not.

To prepare for the family's arrival, James preceded Susannah, Mary, and George to the coast, with his mother's assurances that the family would join him after Mary's graduation. Only reluctantly was Mary a party to the emigration plan, seeing nothing in California that Illinois did not already offer her. However, Jim and Susannah prevailed, and Mary emigrated West by railroad with her mother and younger brother—first for visits with relatives and friends in San Francisco and Los Angeles. Later, with brother Jim at the helm, the Hunters traveled by wagon to a bleak homestead in the extreme southern tip of the San Joaquin Valley of California, where in the late 1880s and early 1890s they eked out a subsistence on the dry land.

What California lacked in material fortune for the Hunter family, it more than gave back to the nascent writer from the moment she beheld the land before her. Mary recorded her initial impressions of the family's journey into the San Joaquin in a manuscript she sent back to her alma mater, titled "One Hundred Miles on Horseback." Although little known, this work remains one of the writer's most lyrical celebrations of the land and deserves to be read; hence, it is the first reading of this book. In her short piece, Mary Hunter speaks of the strangeness to the Easterner's eye of the variegated scenery she observed from her seat on the family's newly purchased "prairie schooner." Through her youthful account, available here for the first time since its publication in 1889 and a limited-edition printing in 1963, readers can experience at an almost one-hundred-year remove the wonderment of an emigrant to California. Assuredly, many viewed the land with astonishment, but few could express their awe as eloquently as the young Mary Hunter.

The Hunters were inexperienced farmers, and the dry soil of their homestead differed greatly from the fertile land of Illinois; not surprisingly, they failed at the homesteading venture. Susannah Hunter ultimately moved to the town of Bakersfield, east of the homesteads she and Jim had claimed, and Mary took tutoring jobs to pay her own way during these financially difficult years. By the time she left home, first to tutor for a dairyman's family and then to teach in a small school, she had begun to write the serious prose that the rugged new land inspired.

The conventional solution for young women living in straitened circumstances was marriage, an alternative Mary assumed would gain

Portrait of Mary Hunter and Wallace Stafford Austin, ca. 1891. (Courtesy of the Huntington Library, San Marino, California)

her a measure of independence, perhaps even respect. In 1891 she married Stafford Wallace Austin, a mining engineer of good family and a Berkeley education but with poor prospects, having already tried and failed at many undertakings including viticulture. By 1892, she was the mother of a child, Ruth Austin, born mentally disabled. This proved particularly devastating because Austin had assumed she would produce a wunderkind.[2]

Marriage had intervened just as Mary Hunter Austin was finding her true voice and vocation in writing. Like her contemporary Charlotte Perkins Gilman (1860–1935), whose marriage and maternity also were eclipsed by the urge to seek fulfillment as a writer, Austin found the daily pressures of married life with Wallace, then with the baby, enervating and frustrating. In addition, she was teaching school. Indeed, she claims in her autobiography *Earth Horizon* that she had not realized when she married that the duties of wife and mother were incompatible with her commitment to writing (239–41). It seems important to include in this anthology Austin's first-published California fiction from this troubled period: "The Mother of Felipe" (1892) and

"The Conversion of Ah Lew Sing" (1897)—until recently available only in rare book editions or in issues of often-inaccessible periodicals such as the *Overland Monthly*. Looking for approval, she asked her mother's opinion of her work. "I think you could have made more of it," Susannah reportedly said to her daughter (*Earth Horizon*, 240).

Austin had begun gathering material for these and other stories in the early California years under the tutelage of General Edward Fitzgerald Beale, owner of the vast Rancho Tejon, through whose introductions she began to meet and write about the people of California. The young emigrant was an avid note-taker, and she jotted down all that interested her for later use. Even when she had her baby to tend, she would often wander around the desert carrying Ruth in a backpack-style pouch, something she learned from the Indians of the Mojave area.

If learning and filling one's life with altogether new friendships and experiences of a hitherto unimaginably different terrain constituted happiness, Austin's earliest days in California appear to have been busy and fulfilling. However, her unhappy marriage—with its required subservience to Wallace Austin's frequent job and residence changes—caused her great tension as she tried to write and care for Ruth. Not until 1900 was she able to launch her career with the help of California literary friends, among them Charles Lummis, whose prestigious literary and artistic circle she was invited to join. Although sometimes crotchety, and a critic of what he considered the writer's carelessness in her use and spelling of Spanish names and places, Lummis gave Austin encouragement on her extended visits to his home El Alisal near Los Angeles, when she could get away from Wallace and, sometimes, Ruth. Austin also received support and solace from Lummis's second wife, Eve, to whom she dedicated her first book, *The Land of Little Rain* (1903), praising her as "The Comfortress of Unsuccess."

Perhaps Mary Austin's best-known book of naturist essays, *The Land of Little Rain* demonstrates most fully her dedication to the task of representing in language the land and the people that she met in her early days in the desertlands, and her ability to imaginatively assimilate their stories into her writing. Austin was thirty-five when she produced *The Land of Little Rain*, the book that rightfully established her place in American letters and introduced her as a writer with a unique voice and vision of the West. Since one of the book's strengths for most readers lies in the unity of Austin's sketches, the decision of which essays to include here proved difficult. Austin specialists may disagree with my selection of excerpts from this or any other of the prodigious author's writings, but my central concern in compiling this anthology has been to accommodate readers coming to Austin for the first time rather than to provide an overview for scholars who know her work well. In brief, I wish to convey some of the excitement I felt when I first read Mary Austin. The work I have selected from *The Land of Little Rain* and other texts suggests not only the ways that Austin stresses the cultural diversity and stark landscape of the West but the ways she stretched herself as a writer to meet this challenge.

The three essays I have selected from *The Land of Little Rain* are those that seem to best describe the region of California that Austin explored during her early ramblings through "the streets of the mountains," including the Tejon. In the first and title essay, "The Land of Little Rain," Austin introduces the topography she will write about throughout the book. To a great extent, the writer gives us an inscape, her narrative voice infused with wonder as she encounters the richly variegated flora and fauna of the immense desert. For her the desert is a seductive, sphinx-like landscape of "lotus charm" to which people return "bewitched" by its mystical secrets and "tempted to try the impossible" (*Land of Little Rain*, 16–17). By making the desert powerfully female, Austin seizes a quality that marked all of her nature writing: the mystical femaleness of a land that ravishes all who would traverse her, causing them to lose themselves, whether consciously or not, in what the narrator refers to in the first sentence as "the Country of Lost Borders," an idea she would develop later in the introductory chapter to her 1909 book of stories *Lost Borders*. In *Lost Borders* she again feminizes the land in a passage referring to the desert metaphorically as female and sphinx-like: "deep-breasted, broad in the hips, tawny, with tawny hair . . . 'possessing' . . . such a countenance as should make men serve without desiring her, such a largeness to her mind as it should make their sins of no account, passionate, but not necessitous, patient—" (10–11). Throughout her books about the land she deploys a narrative voice that is nothing short of oracular. Although *The Land of Little Rain* is now widely read in many editions, the title chapter here introduces the seductive character of the desert in Austin's work. Austin's desert, where borders are blurred or "lost" as she writes, suggests her interpretation of the Mojave area as a locus of mystical, female experience for its native inhabitants and for herself.

Austin remains purposely ambiguous about specific Mojave locations in her first book; we know only that "the land of little rain" lies between the high Sierra south from Yosemite and to the south of many of the mountain ranges of Death Valley, continuing into the Mojave Desert. The place names she gives seldom correspond to the real names of places, as Ansel Adams found when he attempted to photograph the area in a later book using Austin's evocative title.

The Land of Little Rain initiates Mary Austin's readers into another important aspect of her work: the perilous journey into what feminist critic Elaine Showalter has termed "the wild zone."[3] As I have argued elsewhere, Austin, as a precursor of modern feminist ideas, situated her first work outside the confines of male authority, and she purposely engaged places and people outside of the institutionalized codes of patriarchy. Hence she transformed the Mojave and the places we know as Tehachapi, Walker Pass, and Red Rock Canyon into sanctuaries of consciousness, mystery, and uncultivated grandeur, and she did so as a woman who took unto herself the ritual power invested in naming.

This brings us to the question of whether or not Austin was a feminist. Clearly, we see glimmers of Austin's feminism, idiosyncratic though it was, in all of her writings. Certainly she played no formal, organizational role in the women's movement of her day; nonetheless, in her articles and fiction, and especially in her autobiographical writings and letters, she persuades readers that she sees fundamental inequities between the status of men and women in her era, especially in the white middle class. In one of her stories, "A Case of Conscience," for example, about a Shoshone woman whose English common-law "husband" tries (unsuccessfully) to take their child away to England, in essence deserting his "wife" as an unfit mother of their daughter, Austin vigorously comments not only on the abuses of patriarchy but also on the fear of miscegenation. By transforming such social topics into fiction, Austin occupies a unique place among the Anglo women writers of her day.

Ideas of eco-feminism infuse her earliest writing in *The Land of Little Rain*. If Austin figures the land itself as inscrutably, mystically female, then her notable essay on a Paiute woman, "The Basket Maker," emerges as a study of the human female powerful enough to match the landscape. The Indian woman Seyavi encapsulates within her being a self-sufficiency in her artistry that Austin invites us to admire—even if as outsiders we cannot emulate the basket woman's devotion to the "wonders of technical precision" (169) that she creates in baskets crafted from the willows near her camp (*campoodie*). Austin praises the elderly, blind basket maker who nourishes her spirit in the inhospitable terrain. Because the blind woman knows the desert's secret ways, she possesses "the certainty that having borne herself courageously," persisting despite the rigors of *campoodie* life, her spirit in the next world will expand, perhaps because of all she has endured in the course of her long, hard life. Perhaps the writer saw that she and Seyavi had more in common than is apparent at first glance: both possess a love of their art. The basket maker thematizes a recurrent tension in Austin's writing: that of the woman who lacks an affiliation with a man but who manages "much more easily . . . without a man than might at first be supposed" (164).

While "The Basket Maker" suggests the writer's ideological concerns about women surviving without men, the final essay, "The Little Town of Grape Vines," renders in exquisite detail the folkways of a pueblo celebrating the Sixteenth of September, the anniversary of the liberation of Old Mexico. I include this essay about a typical Mexican pueblo, so different from the other two, because of Austin's lifelong engagement with the creativity she discovered in both American Indian and Hispanic cultures. Even if Austin's essay presents this town as something of a picture postcard, a little too quaint for modern tastes, she praises a way of life that she found superior to that of urban America, whose inhabitants "breed in an environment of asphalt pavements," (279) hence missing the joyous earthiness enjoyed by the dwellers of the adobe community Austin makes vivid for her readers.

The essays from *The Land of Little Rain,* which were first serialized in the *Atlantic Monthly,* also demonstrate Austin's ability to evoke the West that popular magazines wanted to present to an interested public, a picturesque West—inviting and friendly. Significantly, the success of the *Atlantic* series proved crucial to Austin's sale of the book manuscript to Houghton Mifflin, who published her next three books: *The Basket Woman* (1904), *Isidro* (1905), and *The Flock* (1906).

Simultaneous with modest literary success in the early 1900s came the breakdown of her marriage. The couple's incompatibility had been exacerbated by the birth of Ruth, their mentally handicapped and only child, in 1892. In 1905, seeing no other way to continue her writing career—a creative existence that had become increasingly important to her even as life turned increasingly harsh—Austin alone assumed the heart-rending responsibility for institutionalizing Ruth in a public sanitarium for "the feeble minded" in Santa Clara. When asked about her child, Austin usually said, "I have lost her," leaving the impression that Ruth had died. In fact, she lived until the flu epidemic of 1918 took her life some four years after Mary and Wallace Austin finally obtained a legal divorce. Austin seems never to have reconciled herself to the guilt of taking the path that she did with Ruth; nor could she accept the insensitivity of her family's reaction to the child. Mrs. Hunter's initial condemnation of her for Ruth's retardation was one that Mary could neither forgive nor forget: "I don't know what you have done, daughter, to have such a judgement upon you," she said when she realized Ruth's disability (*Earth Horizon*, 257).

Certainly Mary Austin's life was tragic in many aspects, but despite her personal problems she persevered with her writing, even when matters with Ruth and Wallace looked most grim. Like many creative individuals, Austin often could be less than pleasant to those she felt were intellectually inferior to herself or to those who ignored her intellectual contributions. She sometimes chafed under the stress of addressing women's clubs, the major source of her lecture income, but she was not alone in this.

Austin's manner and sometimes contentious personality might account for the lack of recognition given her by publishers and the larger public. Many people, including her acquaintances, called her "eccentric" or "queer"—terms the writer tossed off publicly while brooding about them privately.[4] Nonetheless, she resented the attention given the best-selling novels of her friends Jack London and Sinclair Lewis while her own novels—specifically, *No. 26 Jayne Street* (1920)—sold only modestly. Austin was particularly annoyed with London and Lewis because she believed they were giving the American public only stereotypes of women in the characters of their books, whereas her fiction contained fully realized women. She longed to gain a reputation as a successful "domocentric" novelist, as she termed her approach to the novel. In terms of regionalism, she was impatient with any writer who used the Southwest merely as a backdrop. Even her equally prickly friend, Willa Cather, did not escape criticism when she celebrated the French archbishop's construction of a Gothic cathedral in the center of Santa Fe in her novel *Death Comes for the Archbishop*. Austin, a champion of recuperating Spanish architecture in Santa Fe and a founder of the Colonial Arts Society, found the French influence of the real Bishop Lamy's Gothic-style cathedral in Santa Fe reprehensible. Oddly enough, she claimed (and Cather denied) that part of the novel was written in Austin's Santa Fe home, Casa Querida (Beloved House), when Cather visited to do final research on Santa Fe. Indeed Cather wrote on the flyleaf of Austin's gift copy: "For Mary Austin, in whose lovely study I wrote the last chapters of this book. She will be my sternest critic—and she has a right to be. I will always take a calling down from my betters" (gift copy of *Death Comes for the Archbishop* located in the Huntington Library).

Austin was fond of the dictionary and labored intensely for the exact word. Her novels and articles consistently engage contemporary readers with ideas that have great currency today: ideas about ecology and environmentalism, feminism and revised gender arrangements, especially in marriage. Her novels often suggest why romance fails in life and in fiction, unlike the works of her best-selling friends. This is why her fiction has undergone a renaissance of sorts in the last decade and why I include excerpts from two of her novels here: *Starry Adventure* and the recently discovered novella *Cactus Thorn*.

I urge those who wish to know Austin's many other interesting novels to read her romantic mission novel about Hispanic California, *Isidro;* her novel about socialism in New York, *No. 26 Jayne Street;* and her novel about a woman rancher dealing with the issue of California water rights, *The Ford.* Although she was envious of Jack London's, Sinclair Lewis's, and even Willa Cather's success in capturing larger public acclaim, her works consistently underscore forward-thinking notions about American culture at large.

Perhaps her most well known novel, *A Woman of Genius* (1912), whose female protagonist is a creative woman of the theater, will be missed in this volume. Because it has been reprinted elsewhere with an excellent afterword by Nancy Porter, I have not included any excerpts from it here. Instead, I have chosen essays that amplify the modern ideas in many of Austin's novels, particularly her thoughts about genius (a "hot" topic of her time) and a woman's place in the modern world of the 1910s and 1920s, a world in which the writer deemed herself a "feminist." These themes register in the content of her early novels and make them worth reading in their entirety today.

Some critics judge Austin's most successful venture in novel writing to be the 1931 publication of *Starry Adventure,* a vibrant novel about the New Mexican culture in which she had immersed herself since her permanent move to Santa Fe in the mid-1920s. Chapters from *Starry Adventure* and her novella *Cactus Thorn* (recently brought to publication by Austin scholar Melody Graulich) are included here to evidence Austin's continuing project of constructing a new form of regional realism, one that self-consciously concerns itself with the emerging geopolitical and cultural issues of her era. For example, Austin knew a great deal about the encroachment of Anglo elites upon indigenous Hispanic and Indian groups, and these insider perspectives served her western fictions well. She was also familiar with details of Indian ceremonial dances, Hispanic Penitente rituals, and other folk events that seemed—in her time and in ours—foreign, even exotic, to most Americans, and it is possible to trace how her work from 1900 to 1934 becomes an ongoing argument against those American intellectuals who, in Austin's opinion, erred in seeking their literary and artistic energy in Europe while a rich indigenous folk culture lay relatively unexplored in the American West. Austin sought to represent her perceptions of the West in subtle tones, and she stayed away from the genre of "the Western" as we know it, leaving this profitable literary territory to later mythologists of the romantic American West.

The celebration of nature always figures significantly in Austin's writing, and she returned to this form in the early 1920s in *The Land of Journeys' Ending* (1923), a well-received naturist book and companion volume of sorts to *The Land of Little Rain*, written almost twenty-five years before. The later book tours the Southwest through diverse essays about Papago Indians, kachinas, *santos*, rivers, canyons, camels, and cacti. Her prodigious writing during the first third of this century addressing the topics of ecology and the preservation of indigenous culture, feminism, and American culture suggests the remarkable timeliness of her work for modern readers.

Part of the desert's appeal for Austin appears to have been its elemental quality of collapsing or shifting gender differences. Included here are two short tales from the 1909 collection *Lost Borders* (referred to above) that illustrate the tenuous relationships between men and women in the desert: "A Case of Conscience" and "The Woman at the Eighteen-Mile." As is true of many writers who write both novels and short stories (Flannery O'Connor comes to mind), Austin's short stories seem her stronger suit. Hence, stories from two of her other collections—*The Basket Woman* (1904) and *One-Smoke Stories* (1934)—appear here to further delineate other major themes in her work: the integrity of indigenous Americans and the variousness of the American scene. In these fictions Austin's themes anticipate the problems of life in modernity that our most contemporary writers grapple with.

The exceptional power of observation revealed in Austin's fiction is no less present in her books that compass the history and culture of California. Her 1917 novel *The Ford* focuses on water rights, a topic of major interest to Austin due to her experiences with Wallace Austin and his involvement in the Owens River controversy. (The importance of the Owens River was that its water was used in the early 1900s for the greening of Los Angeles by unscrupulous development interests.) *The Flock* (1906), one of her finest works, is an earlier, sustained meditation on the history and habits of sheep and those who herd them. I have chosen to excerpt *The Flock*, based on Austin's personal observations and research before and around 1900, as the better example of her ability to write exceptional prose, rivaling that of canonized literary nature writers, for example Thoreau in the East or John Muir in the West. Because I have found so much to admire of the writer's style and perception in *The Flock*, I have included from it a rich historical account in the first chapter of the flocks coming to California, as well as the interesting theories of "flock mind" she expounds upon in the chapter entitled "The Flock."

Austin spent her professional life studying and writing about native peoples of the West and their contacts with outsiders. Her text from the 1930 edition of *Taos Pueblo* (a collaboration with her young photographer friend Ansel Adams) about the matriarchal society of the Tewa Indians seems crucial to understanding Austin's later career, and this anthology includes excerpts from that important and not widely accessible book. The text enunciates her ideas on the strength of the women of Taos Pueblo, where she and Adams (to whom she referred as "my illustrator") spent a great deal of time in the 1920s, often staying at Los Gallos, the home of Mabel Dodge Luhan.[5] The text of *Taos Pueblo* mated with Adams's remarkable photographs also restates Austin's belief in the Southwest as the touchstone of the American people. "One must have lived in Taos, revisited it from time to time, to realize how interest, curiosity, research, mere tourist determination not to miss anything that other people talk about are repolarized in contact with the living issue of our common past, this still kindling coal of the primitive hearth society" (n.p.). It is likely that Austin's use of "primitive" here was meant not to degrade or trivialize, but rather to celebrate a civilization overlooked by Eurocentric America.

Because Austin was a frequent contributor of essays to the mainstream and intellectual periodicals of her day, it seems only fair to let the writer have her say here. The theory of fiction that Austin elaborated in her 1923 essay "Sex in American Literature," published in the *Bookman*, provides a representative example of how Austin faced off against major writers on the literary issues of her day, particularly the image of women in fiction. She also wrote numerous articles on approaches to modern fiction, the artistic life, the creative process, the link between writing and genius, feminism, American Indian crafts and folkways, political issues (especially those affecting Indians and water rights), and many other topics.[6] Journalism, in fact, provided a steady flow of income for Austin. Many of her essays recount her enthusiasm for major writers in England and elsewhere—her conversations with playwright and social critic George Bernard Shaw, novelist Joseph Conrad, feminist writer May Sinclair, and Maria Stopes, whose book *Married Love* (1918), a revolutionary primer on birth control and marriage, enjoyed great success in America.

We can further trace how Austin came to her remarkably contemporary feminist ideas not only in her autobiography but in her journalism. She was invited by the editors of *The Nation* to contribute, along with sixteen other notable women of her day—including Genevieve Taggard, Crystal Eastman, and Inez Haynes Irwin—to a series that appeared throughout the years 1926 and 1927 entitled "These Modern Women." She chose to write an anonymous article for the series in which she briefly describes the obstacles she faced in the process of becoming a writer, first as a daughter of midwestern America, where she felt her ideas and ambitions diminished by her mother and brothers and the culture at large, and later as a self-styled "radical" who "found many reasons for being feminist in the injustices and impositions endured by women under the general idea of their intellectual inferiority to men" (*The Nation*, July 20, 1927, 58).

In her own life she had experienced numerous slights as a young girl, principally her mother's unveiled resentment that her younger sister, Jennie, instead of Mary had died of diphtheria in 1878 (the same year her father had died, probably of tuberculosis contracted when he was an Army officer fighting in the South). She also tells of her beleaguered girlhood after her father's death, when she was burdened with the majority of domestic work in the Hunter household, her older brother excused because he was male. Although she excelled in academic work, it was his academic achievements that received attention from their mother.

Also a poet of some note, although seldom anthologized or read in our time, Austin published in the major literary periodicals of her era, including *Poetry: A Magazine of Verse*. Included here is a sampling of her verse, much of which re-expresses Indian songs and chants. Those who wish to find out more about her controversial theory of American verse will want to turn to the 1930 text *The American Rhythm* (not included here), in which she argues that a certain indigenous rhythm based on the drumbeat pulses through all of the verse of American, if not European, culture. Although she herself was not proficient in Indian languages, she claimed much of her poetry was a "translation" from Indian dialects, and she crusaded for "Indian" poetry to be taught in the public schools. In her own time she was widely recognized as an expert on what she called "Amerind" verse.

Austin spoke with authority of her life experiences in her writings and on the frequent and exhausting lecture tours she was often forced to undertake when her writing did not generate sufficient income. She spent a great deal of time traveling on the railroad from East to West and back again for most of her professional life. She took some time out in the early 1920s for an excursion with friends through Arizona; the resulting book was *The Land of Journeys' Ending* (1924). Given high praise by critics, the book was singled out by Lawrence Powell in his *Southwestern Classics* as a great contribution to the literature of the region, and "the ripest, richest book of all the many that she wrote" (95). Austin claims in the preface to *The Land of Journeys' Ending* that her final naturist effort is "a book of prophecy of the progressive ac[c]ulturation of the land's people" as well as "a book of topography" (xxviii). Austin conceived her career as one of endless work and book production even when away from her desk or the lecture platform.

We receive some intimation of how difficult her life as a writer was in her widely acclaimed autobiography, *Earth Horizon*, excerpts of which are given in this volume's final selections. Only recently has *Earth Horizon*, published shortly before her death, been accessible to readers except in an expensive library edition or through rare-book dealers.[7] Because no selection of readings from Austin's works could suggest her literary range without including something of it, I have included the first and last sections. Here readers must turn to find Austin's conclusions about her life and career, ideas that begin the modern period in American women's writing. As such, her autobiography represents the essential contribution that Mary Hunter Austin made to American letters in her own time, a surprisingly modern legacy for readers of our own time.

Whether writing the accompanying text to the photographs of Ansel Adams, as she did in 1930, or short stories about the Hispanics, American Indians, or Anglo opportunists in the land of "lost borders"; whether telling us stories about those who lived on the margins of the far West, as in *One-Smoke Stories* (1934), or about her own life and times as in her remarkable autobiography, Mary Austin boldly confronted the people, the land, and the issues that continue to vibrate in the American scene. In this volume, I hope to place before the reader a range of Mary Austin's texts, works that have not previously been accessible as well as those recently revived, to better acquaint "the common reader" with this extraordinary American writer's major work.

2

"One Hundred Miles on Horseback"

For most modern American readers, the prospect of seeing land with little or no human presence, uncluttered by human intervention—large buildings, highways, signs—is an unimaginable experience. Yet this was precisely young Mary Hunter's experience in October 1888, when she and her family journeyed into the San Joaquin Valley by stagecoach.

An altogether different landscape than the more verdant farmlands she knew from Illinois, the country struck her with its canyons, *arroyos*, and mountain ranges. Her response to the land is perhaps surprising given her reluctance to emigrate to California with her mother and brothers, but this stark area called up from the twenty-year-old woman a reactive, lyrical prose that served as a catalyst for her future writing. In her autobiography *Earth Horizon*, she recalls the mystical presence of "a lurking, evasive Something, wistful, cruel, ardent; something that rustled and rank that hung half-remotely, insistent on being noticed" (187). The young writer had found her subject, and she could not record fast enough her varied sensory impressions, each registered with wonder during the journey to the Hunter homestead: the San Fernando Valley, shepherds tending flocks of sheep, herds of cattle, gold seekers, scores of adobe dwellings, chaparral, wild mountain flowers, and the howls of coyotes that punctuated the eight-day journey. The trip culminated in their passage through Tejon Pass and into the San Joaquin Valley, where they finally reached their squalid homestead in the midst of so much stark, natural beauty. The appearance of her account, even in so inconsequential a publication as *The Blackburnian*, her former college publication, marked the beginning of her distinguished literary career.[1]

One Hundred Miles on Horseback

Those whose lives have been spent in the prairie lands of Illinois can have little conception of the pleasure of a journey on horseback through the most picturesque part of California.

To us, weird with two thousand miles of hot and dusty railroad travel, and two days and nights of anguish in a Pacific coast steamer the prospect was delightful beyond comparison.

The point of starting was the "boom stricken" city of Pasadena, the point to be reached lay in the southern extremity of the San Joaquin valley, one hundred miles to the north. Between the two points rose three mountain ranges with their outlying foot hills and intervening valleys.

Our outfit, including the saddle horse and white topped "prairie schooner" drawn by a team of sturdy bronchos, appurtenances of the "mover" would have done credit to a Pike county Missourian.

Leaving Pasadena at noon we passed northward, through the most beautiful portion of the city, out toward the suburban town of Garvanza in the Eagle Rock valley. A drizzling rain, forerunner of the rainy season, compelled me to abandon my equestrian ambitions and make an inglorious retreat to the canvas shelter of the wagon. In this fashion we completed the afternoon journey through the Eagle Rock valley, one of the many similar valleys opening out on the southern slope of the Sierra Madre mountains.

The valley is populous and fertile, rich in vineyards and orchards. The peach and apricot orchards were shedding their dull leaves, with only here and there a touch of gold or crimson where breath of frost from the mountains had reached them. An autumn landscape in California is strangely devoid of color, and this silent succumbing to a process of nature made us homesick for the glory of the October hills of Illinois.

The second day's journey lay through the San Fernando valley, so named by the founders of the old Spanish mission of San Fernando.

Brown and sere the fields look now after the abundant harvest of barley and oats has been garnered. Thousands of sheep and cattle feed on the surrounding foot hills and the sight of the outlandish looking Mexican shepherds with their flocks and faithful dogs recalled vividly well known scriptural scenes and places. Alternating with the fertile strips were long, stony stretches, marking the "wash" of some mountain steam, and covered with brown tangled "chapparal," bristling with the dried stalks of that species of the yucca known as the "Spanish Bayonet."

Many of the stalks reach the height of fifteen or twenty feet in the spring are crowned with hundreds of fragrant, wax-like blossoms.

These stony places are the favorite haunts of the prickly pear, and here they raised their impenetrable barriers on every side. We gathered some of the rich purple fruit and found it not unpleasant to the taste, very much the flavor of watermelon, but slightly more acid.

Here as elsewhere in California, we noticed the absence of singing birds. The shrill pipe of the quail or the whirring wings of the chapparal cock were the only sounds that broke the silence. An occasional jack rabbit familiarly known as the "narrow gauge mule" hops across the road solemnly flapping an ear as a mute protest at our intrusion.

In the fertile portions of the valley we were much interested in the curious homes of the ground squirrel. They live in communities, the color of their fur varying according to the color of the soil they inhabit.

The valley was entirely treeless except that in some few well watered regions the willow and live oak flourished. We "foraged" in the large vineyards for which the valley is famous, but with indifferent success, for the first crops had been converted into wine or raisins, and the second growth was inferior in size and flavor.

We passed the second night at San Fernando. Although noted in local papers as a growing city, San Fernando is but a small village of some two or three hundred buildings, chief among which are an immense hotel (vacant) and a new Methodist Theological Seminary, in the first year of its existence.

The old mission of San Fernando is situated some two or three miles from the town and is probably one of the best preserved missions in the state.

Starting at sunrise the next morning our road followed the line of the railroad over the foothills into the mouth of the San Fernando pass. Soon after entering the hills the two roads separate, the railroad passing through the range by means of a tunnel, while the wagon road goes over the summit.

For a short distance the road rises gently, following the windings of a mountain stream, then suddenly the ascent becomes steep and the canyon walls narrow to within a few feet of the wheel track.

We passed over the summit without accident and found the descent on the other side comparatively easy. The north side of the mountains is usually heavily wooded with live oaks, willow, sycamore and higher up a few straggling pines.

A day's journey in front of us lay the second range of the Sierra Madre or "mother mountains" lifting their bare wind-swept peaks and wrinkled sides without a break, as far as the eye could see, and behind lay the range just crossed, apparently as impassable. The remainder of the day's travel alternated well cultivated fields and wooded pasture lands with long stretches of sand. Frequently we were obliged to give the right of way to the fierce looking Mexican shepherds and their flocks. Stopping at Newhall for supplies we saw two Mexican hunters bringing in half a dozen deer for shipment to the Los Angeles markets.

We camped that night at the first bit of natural green grass we had seen in California. It is known as salt grass and is found in the neighborhood of alkali springs. It has a decidedly salty taste and resembles what is known at home as "goose grass."

Growing about the spring we found the round green "tule" reeds. Those who have read "Ramona" will remember that it was in a hut thatched with these reeds that she and [Alessandro] began their housekeeping. During the night the coyotes came close up to the camp and howled, and growled, and barked, and shrieked like so many demons. There seems to be no limit to the hideous noises these animals can produce.

About nine o'clock next morning we entered the mouth of the San Francisquito canyon. The canyon walls rose higher and narrower as we proceeded, sometimes swelling gently until the hills were rounded to a perfect dome, covered with greasewood and enlivened by the dark red satin smooth stems, and olive green foliage of the manzanita; sometimes bare and ragged cliffs with strata turned, and twisted, and folded back upon itself, bearing on its face the marks of primeval fire and flood.

It is not possible for the mind to conceive of a force that could throw the elements of the solid earth into such confusion as is here displayed.

Opening out of the main canyon are innumerable smaller cross-canyons. In each one of these some Mexican or Indian has built his hut of adobe or tule, planted his grape-vine and set up his hive of bees. The houses are low and thatched, ornamented with strings of red pepper and skins of wild animals fastened on the walls of the house to dry, and all overflowing with dogs and children in dirty but picturesque confusion. Occasionally, somewhat back from the house, a little white wooden cross gleaming over a mound of earth made pathetically human a scene that might have been disgusting or merely amusing.

The greater part of the honey shipped from California comes from the San Francisquito canyon.

All along the canyon we saw traces of the gold seekers.

About the middle of the afternoon we began the ascent of what is known as the long grade. The canyon becomes so narrow that there is no room for a wagon road at the bottom, consequently the road is forced to climb the side of the mountains. For a distance of two miles it rises gradually, winding about the side of the mountain while far below it the stream rushes and roars and tumbles, flashing in tiny cascades or foaming in angry eddies. Up, up the road winds, a yellow line along the steep slope of the canyon wall, every curve apparently terminating in a sheer precipice, but the point being reached behold on the rounded front of the next hill the road lies far above. It rises in this spiral line from the bottom of the canyon to a point one thousand feet above, where looking up one can see only blue sky pierced by peaks more deeply blue, and down the almost vertical canyon wall one can scarcely see the tops of the tall trees that hide the brawling stream.

There is something indescribably awesome, traveling thus in the fast deepening twilight through these narrow gorges where the mountains close in upon us so silently and mysteriously that one unfamiliar with such scenes would declare that there is no outlet in either direction.

On previous nights the petticoated members of our party had camped in the wagon, but tonight, wrapped in our blankets, Indian fashion, we lay peacefully down under the bright stars of California in the shadow of her majestic mountains and—snored.

The next day being Sunday we rested a part of the day, but owing to the difficulty of finding suitable camping places, were obliged to break camp about three o'clock in the afternoon.

The ascent known as the Tejunga pass is long and steep and on account of the altitude and the lateness of the hour, the air was quite chilly, but the summit once reached we were fully repaid for our pains. Below us lay the green panorama of the canyon, while round about us peak after peak rose into view, violet, purple, and rose, outlined against the flaming gold of the sunset sky. The whole arch of the heavens was suffused with flowing rose color save where the ridge on which we stood intercepted the waning light, leaving a broad band of deepest blue along the eastern horizon, where the stars were already gleaming.

On the next to the last day of our journey we took dinner at "Hell," a supply station and hostelry, known sometimes as "Gorman's," situated just at the head of the valley. Bob McCord, from Nova Scotia, familiarly known as "Old Three-finger," one of the *habitues* of the place, a miner, a veritable "forty-niner" looking as if he had just stepped out of one of Bret Harte's stories was there on a periodical "drunk." He was very urgent in his entreaties for the man of our family to "come take one more drink and swear off."

The Tejon canyon, through which the remainder of the journey lay, is very beautiful. Never have I seen such magnificent trees as the live oaks that crowded each other in the canyon and on the hills. Festoons of grapevines hung from the willows across the noisy stream, and heavy garlands of mistletoe dropped from the branches of oak and sycamore.

On the afternoon of the eighth day we came out on the north side of the Tehachapi mountains in the valley of the San Joaquin. Here it is that I write, here where the tarantulas sun themselves on our front porch, the owls hoot on our roof at night, and gray coyotes come trotting up under our very windows. The mountains curve out about us from east to west, and below us on the slope we can catch the blue gleam of a lake. Scarcely a day or night but some member of the family calls us to "come and look"; sometimes at some new glory of cloud and sun on the mountains, sometimes at a herd of antelope feeding close to the house, or an eagle cleaving the air with swift wings, or the red light of an engine climbing down the long slope of the mountains thirty miles away; or at some new freak of the sense-deceiving mirage that makes flowing rivers or still lakes where yesterday was dry land.

We are twenty-five miles from town, but only seven miles from the famous Tejon ranch, where the oranges are now getting ripe and yellow and the olives purpling under the December sun.

But time and space compel me to postpone even the merest mention of the wild and romantic delights of the life of a pioneer in the "pampas" of the San Joaquin until some better opportunity.

3

The
Land
of
Little
Rain

To a great extent we are initiated into Mary Austin's inner world through *The Land of Little Rain*, into the places that Austin deemed sacred during her first years in California, a land quite different from the rich farm country of her girlhood in Illinois. A naturist even as a child, Austin knew that California inspired her imagination as had no other American place. When she looked at the mesas, the ranges, and the vastness of a then mainly unclaimed land (as the federal government viewed land grants), she felt moved to write about nature using an approach altogether unlike the northeastern American naturists who preceded her. In her first book she combined many rhetorical techniques, including autobiography and anthropomorphization, as critic William J. Scheick points out in an essay critical of Austin's egotism and Anglocentrism.[1] Specifically, her gaze fell on the Owens Valley, where her husband had taken a position supervising an irrigation project on Owens Lake.

Not content to stay at home before she found a teaching position, she spent her days wandering the land she was to immortalize. Nothing, it seems, escaped Austin's notice on her meanderings in the country "between the high Sierras south from Yosemite—west and south over a very great assemblage of broken ranges beyond Death Valley, and on illimitably into the Mojave Desert" (ix–x).[2] She asked readers to picture her writing her sketches in a "brown house under the willow-tree" at the foot of the Kearsarge (xi). For readers of the *Atlantic Monthly*, where many of these essays were first serialized, such descriptions of the writer in her brown house near a mountain in the far West suggested an idyllic existence.

Three readings from this significant naturist text appear here: the title essay, "The Land of Little Rain," in which the writer orients us to the diversity of desert vegetation and animal habitation; "The Little Town of Grape Vines," its final essay, and one that summarizes the celebratory eating and singing among the inhabitants of a town, the exact location of which our narrator refuses to give us: "Where it lies, how to come at it, you will not get from me; rather would I show you the heron's nest in the tulares" (265). Perhaps the most important essay for many readers is "The Basket Maker." Here we glimpse a self-portrait of the writer in Austin's empathic portrait of Seyavi, the craftswoman who "learned the sufficiency of mother-wit, and how much more easily one can do without a man than might at first be supposed" (164). In Austin's essay, Seyavi is the artist who "made baskets for love and sold them for money, in a generation that preferred iron pots for utility" (168–69). "The Basket Maker" is only one essay in *The Land of Little Rain* that reveals Austin was not just interested in the landscape. An amateur ethnographer, she often stopped to talk with strangers—Indian, Hispanic, or Anglo—about their stories and those of others. She wrote down her impressions in a small notebook and allowed them to marinate before it came time to write her essays for the *Atlantic Monthly*, whose editors and readers pronounced them "charming." Later she gathered them to make the book upon which, to a large extent, her literary reputation rests.

Why this is so might say something about the way she was typecast as a naturist writer rather than a talented fiction writer, even though she wrote several novels and collections of short fiction. Her publishers and public wanted to see her as a writer walking through the desert and making pronouncements as she did in *The Land of Little Rain;* they distinctly did not want to see her as the Edith Wharton of the Far West, or even as its Willa Cather. This puzzled and perplexed Austin, who wanted most of all to become a successful novelist.

Reading *The Land of Little Rain* today, almost a century after it was published, we hear a stark, biblical, almost mystical cadence precisely suited to the land she described. This tone and language (the markers of Austin's idiosyncratic, unique style) often failed to accommodate the requirements of the social novel. Her point of view, at once distanced and immediate, and an oracular tone constitute important elements of her style in her desert essays, altogether different from the tone of the drawing room employed by Edith Wharton or Henry James who furnish the interiors of their fictions. She persuades us that she is one with the desert, that she knows its ways and has listened to its voices.

At the same time, however, we are given to understand that only the narrator/writer is privileged to experience the land as she has. An aura of performance hovers over *The Land of Little Rain,* conveying a sense of intense drama, as in the narrator's warning that "To underestimate one's thirst, to pass a given landmark to the right or left, to find a dry spring where one looked for running water—there is no help for any of these things" (9). She also chooses her adjectives with deliberation—yuccas are "tormented," creosote "immortal," the men who dwell in the desert "bewitched." In the essay "Scavengers," she tells of "a very squalid tragedy,—that of the dying brutes [cattle] and the scavenger birds" (49). Ultimately, though, it is the story of the people who live in this treacherous and compelling land, who have experienced the desert in its beauty and terror, that gives Austin's prose its singular quality.

In "Shoshone Land," Austin gives us a romantic, reverential image of Indian life. "When the rain is over and gone they [the Shoshones] are stirred by the instinct of those that journeyed eastward from Eden, and go up each with his mate and young brood like birds to old nesting places" (90). Because of passages such as this one, Austin sometimes suffers rebukes from modern critics who find her observations of American Indian life simplistic, essentialist, colonizing, or worse, as when she writes "Every Indian woman is an artist" (168). Perhaps it might better serve to say that although Austin's Anglo perspective appears unnecessarily limited, particularly to modern sensibilities, she was a writer of her times and sincerely admired the indigenous cultures that she tried to represent in several of the fourteen essays included in *The Land of Little Rain.*

The Land of Little Rain

East away from the Sierras, south from Panamint and Amargosa, east and south many an uncounted mile, is the Country of Lost Borders.

Ute, Paiute, Mojave, and Shoshone inhabit its frontiers, and as far into the heart of it as a man dare go. Not the law, but the land sets the limit. Desert is the name it wears upon the maps, but the Indian's is the better word. Desert is a loose term to indicate land that supports no man; whether the land can be bitted and broken to that purpose is not proven. Void of life it never is, however dry the air and villainous the soil.

This is the nature of that country. There are hills, rounded, blunt, burned, squeezed up out of chaos, chrome and vermilion painted, aspiring to the snow-line. Between the hills lie high level-looking plains full of intolerable sun glare, or narrow valleys drowned in a blue haze. The hill surface is streaked with ash drift and black, unweathered lava flows. After rains water accumulates in the hollows of small closed valleys, and, evaporating, leaves hard dry levels of pure desertness that get the local name of dry lakes. Where the mountains are steep and the rains heavy, the pool is never quite dry, but dark and bitter, rimmed about with the efflorescence of alkaline deposits. A thin crust of it lies along the marsh over the vegetating area, which has neither beauty nor freshness. In the broad wastes open to the wind the sand drifts in hummocks about the stubby shrubs, and between them the soil shows saline traces. The sculpture of the hills here is more wind than water work, though the quick storms do sometimes scar them past many a year's redeeming. In all the Western desert edges there are essays in miniature at the famed, terrible Grand Cañon, to which, if you keep on long enough in this country, you will come at last.

  Since this is a hill country one expects to find springs, but not to depend upon them; for when found they are often brackish and unwholesome, or maddening, slow dribbles in a thirsty soil. Here you find the hot sink of Death Valley, or high rolling districts where the air has always a tang of frost. Here are the long heavy winds and breathless calms on the tilted mesas where dust devils dance, whirling up into a wide, pale sky. Here you have no rain when all the earth cries for it, or quick downpours called cloud-bursts for violence. A land of lost rivers, with little in it to love; yet a land that once visited must be come back to inevitably. If it were not so there would be little told of it.

  This is the country of three seasons. From June on to November it lies hot, still, and unbearable, sick with violent unrelieving storms; then on until April, chill, quiescent, drinking its scant rain and scanter snows; from April to the hot season again, blossoming, radiant, and seductive. These months are only approximate; later or earlier the rain-laden wind may drift up the water gate of the Colorado from the Gulf, and the land sets its seasons by the rain.

  The desert floras shame us with their cheerful adaptations to the seasonal limitations. Their whole duty is to flower and fruit, and they do it hardly, or with tropical luxuriance, as the rain admits. It is recorded in the report of the Death Valley expedition that after a year of abundant rains, on the Colorado desert was found a specimen of Amaranthus ten feet high. A year later the same species in the same place matured in the drought at four inches. One hopes the land may breed like qualities in her human offspring, not tritely to "try," but to do. Seldom does the desert herb attain the full stature of the type. Extreme aridity and extreme altitude have the same dwarfing effect so that we find in the high Sierras and in Death Valley related species in miniature that reach a comely growth in mean temperatures. Very fertile are the desert plants in expedients to prevent evaporation, turning their foliage edgewise toward the sun, growing silky hairs, exuding viscid gum. The wind, which has a long sweep, harries and helps them. It rolls up dunes about the stocky stems, encompassing and protective,

Portrait by Charles Lummis of the young Mary Austin in the early 1900s. (Courtesy of the Southwest Museum, Los Angeles. Photo #24280)

and above the dunes, which may be, as with the mesquite, three times as high as a man, the blossoming twigs flourish and bear fruit.

There are many areas in the desert where drinkable water lies within a few feet of the surface, indicated by the mesquite and the bunch grass (*Sporobolus airoides*). It is this nearness of unimagined help that makes the tragedy of desert deaths. It is related that the final breakdown of that hapless party that gave Death Valley its forbidding name occurred in a locality where shallow wells should have saved them. But how were they to know that? Properly equipped it is possible to go safely across that ghastly sink, yet every year it takes its toll of death, and yet men find there sun-dried mummies, of whom no trace or recollection is preserved. To underestimate one's thirst, to pass a given landmark to the right or left, to find a dry spring where one looked for running water—there is no help for any of these things.

Along springs and sunken watercourses one is surprised to find such water-loving plants as grow widely in moist ground, but the true desert breeds its own kind, each in its particular habitat. The angle of the slope, the frontage of a hill, the structure of the soil determines the plant. South-looking hills are nearly bare, and the lower tree-line higher here by a thousand feet. Cañons running east and west will have one wall naked and one clothed. Around dry lakes and marshes the herbage preserves a set and orderly arrangement. Most species have well-defined areas of growth, the best index the voiceless land can give the traveler of his whereabouts.

If you have any doubt about it, know that the desert begins with the creosote. This immortal shrub spreads down into Death Valley and up to the lower timber-line, odorous and medicinal as you might guess from the name, wandlike, with shining fretted foliage. Its vivid green is grateful to the eye in a wilderness of gray and greenish white shrubs. In the spring it exudes a resinous gum which the Indians of those parts know how to use with pulverized rock for cementing arrow points to shafts. Trust Indians not to miss any virtues of the plant world!

Nothing the desert produces expresses it better than the unhappy growth of the tree yuccas. Tormented, thin forests of it stalk drearily in the high mesas, particularly in that triangular slip that fans out eastward from the meeting of the Sierras and coastwise hills where the first swings across the southern end of the San Joaquin Valley. The yucca bristles with bayonet-pointed leaves, dull green, growing shaggy with age, tipped with panicles of fetid, greenish bloom. After death, which is slow, the ghostly hollow network of its woody skeleton, with hardly power to rot, makes the moonlight fearful. Before the yucca has come to flower, while yet its bloom is a creamy cone-shaped bud of the size of a small cabbage, full of sugary sap, the Indians twist it deftly out of its fence of daggers and roast it for their own delectation. So it is that in those parts where man inhabits one sees young plants of *Yucca arborensis* infrequently. Other yuccas, cacti, low herbs, a thousand sorts, one finds journeying east from the coastwise hills. There is neither poverty of soil nor species to account for the sparseness of desert growth, but simply that each plant requires more room. So much earth must be preëmpted to extract so much moisture. The real struggle for existence, the real brain of the plant, is underground; above there is room for a rounded perfect growth. In Death Valley, reputed the very core of desolation, are nearly two hundred identified species.

Above the lower tree-line, which is also the snow-line, mapped out abruptly by the sun, one finds spreading growth of piñon, juniper, branched nearly to the ground, lilac and sage, and scattering white pines.

There is no special preponderance of self-fertilized or wind-fertilized plants, but everywhere the demand for and evidence of insect life. Now where there are seeds and insects there will be birds and small mammals and where these are, will come the slinking sharp-toothed kind that prey on them. Go as far as you dare in the heart of a lonely land, you cannot go so far that life and death are not before you. Painted lizards slip in and out of rock crevices, and pant on the white hot sands. Birds, hummingbirds even, nest in the cactus scrub; woodpeckers befriend the demoniac yuccas; out of the stark, treeless waste rings the music of the night-singing mockingbird. If it be summer and the sun well down, there will be a burrowing owl to call. Strange, furry tricksy things dart across the open places, or sit motionless in the conning towers of the creosote. The poet may have "named all the birds without a gun," but not the fairy-footed, ground-inhabiting, furtive, small folk of the rainless regions. They are too many and too swift; how many you would not believe without seeing the footprint tracings in the sand. They are nearly all night workers, finding the days too hot and white. In mid-desert where there are no cattle, there are no birds of carrion, but if you go far in that direction the chances are that you will find yourself shadowed by their tilted wings. Nothing so large as a man can move unspied upon in that country, and they know well how the land deals with strangers. There are hints to be had here of the way in which a land forces new habits on its dwellers. The quick increase of suns at the end of spring sometimes overtakes birds in their nesting and effects a reversal of the ordinary manner of incubation. It becomes necessary to keep eggs cool rather than warm. One hot, stifling spring in the Little Antelope I had occasion to pass and repass frequently the nest of a pair of meadowlarks, located unhappily in the shelter of a very slender weed. I never caught them sitting except near night, but at midday they stood, or drooped above it, half fainting with pitifully parted bills, between their treasure and the sun. Sometimes both of them together with wings spread and half lifted continued a spot of shade in a temperature that constrained me at last in a fellow feeling to spare them a bit of canvas for permanent shelter. There was a fence in that country shutting in a cattle range, and along its fifteen miles of posts one could be sure of finding a bird or two in every strip of shadow; sometimes the sparrow and the hawk, with wings trailed and beaks parted, drooping in the white truce of noon.

If one is inclined to wonder at first how so many dwellers came to be in the loneliest land that ever came out of God's hands, what they do there and why stay, one does not wonder so much after having lived there. None other than this long brown land lays such a hold on the affections. The rainbow hills, the tender bluish mists, the luminous radiance of the spring, have the lotus charm. They trick the sense of time, so that once inhabiting there you always mean to go away without quite realizing that you have not done it. Men who have lived there, miners and cattle-men, will tell you this, not so fluently, but emphatically, cursing the land and going back to it. For one thing there is the divinest, cleanest air to be breathed anywhere in God's world. Some day the world will understand that, and the little oases on the windy tops of hills will harbor for healing its ailing, house-weary broods. There is promise there of great wealth in ores and earths, which is no wealth by reason of being so far removed from water and workable conditions, but men are bewitched by it and tempted to try the impossible.

You should hear Salty Williams tell how he used to drive eighteen and twenty-mule teams from the borax marsh to Mojave, ninety miles, with the trail wagon full of water barrels. Hot days the mules would go so mad for drink that the clank of the water bucket set them into an uproar of hideous, maimed noises, and a tangle of harness chains, while Salty would sit on the high seat with the sun glare heavy in his eyes, dealing out curses of pacification in a level, uninterested voice until the clamor fell off from sheer exhaustion. There was a line of shallow graves along that road; they used to count on dropping a man or two of every new gang of coolies brought out in the hot season. But when he lost his swamper, smitten without warning at the noon halt, Salty quit his job; he said it was "too durn hot." The swamper he buried by the way with stones upon him to keep the coyotes from digging him up, and seven years later I read the penciled lines on the pine headboard, still bright and unweathered.

But before that, driving up on the Mojave stage, I met Salty again crossing Indian Wells, his face from the high seat, tanned and ruddy as a harvest moon, looming through the golden dust above his eighteen mules. The land had called him.

The palpable sense of mystery in the desert air breeds fables, chiefly of lost treasure. Somewhere within its stark borders, if one believes report, is a hill strewn with nuggets; one seamed with virgin silver; an old clayey water-bed where Indians scooped up earth to make cooking pots and shaped them reeking with grains of pure gold. Old miners drifting about the desert edges, weathered into the semblance of the tawny hills, will tell you tales like these convincingly. After a little sojourn in that land you will believe them on their own account. It is a question whether it is not better to be bitten by the little horned snake of the desert that goes sidewise and strikes without coiling, than by the tradition of a lost mine.

And yet—and yet—is it not perhaps to satisfy expectation that one falls into the tragic key in writing of desertness? The more you wish of it the more you get, and in the mean time lose much of pleasantness. In that country which begins at the foot of the east slope of the Sierras and spreads out by less and less lofty hill ranges toward the Great Basin, it is possible to live with great zest, to have red blood and delicate joys, to pass and repass about one's daily performance an area that would make an Atlantic seaboard State, and that with no peril, and, according to our way of thought, no particular difficulty. At any rate, it was not people who went into the desert merely to write it up who invented the fabled Hassay[a]mpa, of whose waters, if any drink, they can no more see fact as naked fact, but all radiant with the color of romance. I, who must have drunk of it in my twice seven years' wanderings, am assured that it is worth while.

For all the toll the desert takes of man it gives compensation, deep breaths, deep sleep, and the communion of the stars. It comes upon one with new force in the pauses of the night that the Chaldeans were a desert-bred people. It is hard to escape the sense of mastery as the stars move in the wide clear heavens to risings and settings unobscured. They look large and near and palpitant; as if they moved on some stately service not needful to declare. Wheeling to their stations in the sky, they make the poor world-fret of no account. Of no account you who lie out there watching, nor the lean coyote that stands off in the scrub from you and howls and howls.

The Basket Maker

"A man," says Seyavi of the campoodie, "must have a woman, but a woman who has a child will do very well."

That was perhaps why, when she lost her mate in the dying struggle of his race, she never took another, but set her wit to fend for herself and her young son. No doubt she was often put to it in the beginning to find food for them both. The Paiutes had made their last stand at the

border of the Bitter Lake; battle-driven they died in its waters, and the
land filled with cattle-men and adventurers for gold: this while Seyavi
and the boy lay up in the caverns of the Black Rock and ate tule roots
and fresh-water clams that they dug out of the slough bottoms with
their toes. In the interim, while the tribes swallowed their defeat, and
before the rumor of war died out, they must have come very near to the
bare core of things. That was the time Seyavi learned the sufficiency of
mother wit, and how much more easily one can do without a man than
might at first be supposed.

To understand the fashion of any life, one must know the land it is
lived in and the procession of the year. This valley is a narrow one, a
mere trough between hills, a draught for storms, hardly a crow's flight
from the sharp Sierras of the Snows to the curled, red and ochre,
uncomforted, bare ribs of Waban. Midway of the groove runs a burrowing, dull river, nearly a hundred miles from where it cuts the lava
flats of the north to its widening in a thick, tideless pool of a lake.
Hereabouts the ranges have no foothills, but rise up steeply from the
bench lands above the river. Down from the Sierras, for the east ranges
have almost no rain, pour glancing white floods toward the lowest land,
and all beside them lie the campoodies, brown wattled brush heaps,
looking east.

In the river are mussels, and reeds that have edible white roots, and
in the soddy meadows tubers of joint grass; all these at their best in the
spring. On the slope the summer growth affords seeds; up the steep the
one-leafed pines, an oily nut. That was really all they could depend
upon, and that only at the mercy of the little gods of frost and rain. For
the rest it was cunning against cunning, caution against skill, against
quacking hordes of wild-fowl in the tulares, against pronghorn and bighorn and deer. You can guess, however, that all this warring of rifles and
bowstrings, this influx of overlording whites, had made game wilder
and hunters fearful of being hunted. You can surmise also, for it was a
crude time and the land was raw, that the women became in turn the
game of the conquerors.

There used to be in the Little Antelope a she dog, stray or outcast,
that had a litter in some forsaken lair, and ranged and foraged for them,
slinking savage and afraid, remembering and mistrusting humankind,
wistful, lean, and sufficient for her young. I have thought Seyavi might
have had days like that, and have had perfect leave to think, since she
will not talk of it. Paiutes have the art of reducing life to its lowest ebb
and yet saving it alive on grasshoppers, lizards, and strange herbs; and

that time must have left no shift untried. It lasted long enough for Seyavi to have evolved the philosophy of life which I have set down at the beginning. She had gone beyond learning to do for her son, and learned to believe it worth while.

In our kind of society, when a woman ceases to alter the fashion of her hair, you guess that she has passed the crisis of her experience. If she goes on crimping and uncrimping with the changing mode, it is safe to suppose she has never come up against anything too big for her. The Indian woman gets nearly the same personal note in the pattern of her baskets. Not that she does not make all kinds, carriers, water-bottles, and cradles,—these are kitchen ware,—but her works of art are all of the same piece. Seyavi made flaring, flat-bottomed bowls, cooking pots really, when cooking was done by dropping hot stones into water-tight food baskets, and for decoration a design in colored bark of the procession of plumed crests of the valley quail. In this pattern she had made cooking pots in the golden spring of her wedding year, when the quail went up two and two to their resting places about the foot of Oppapago. In this fashion she made them when, after pillage, it was possible to reinstate the housewifely crafts. Quail ran then in the Black Rock by hundreds,—so you still find them in fortunate years,—and in the famine time the women cut their long hair to make snares when the flocks came morning and evening to the springs.

Seyavi made baskets for love and sold them for money, in a generation that preferred iron pots for utility. Every Indian woman is an artist,—sees, feels, creates, but does not philosophize about her processes. Seyavi's bowls are wonders of technical precision, inside and out, the palm finds no fault with them, but the subtlest appeal is in the sense that warns us of humanness in the way the design spreads into the flare of the bowl. There used to be an Indian woman at Olancha who made bottle-neck trinket baskets in the rattlesnake pattern, and could accommodate the design to the swelling bowl and flat shoulder of the basket without sensible disproportion, and so cleverly that you might own one a year without thinking how it was done; but Seyavi's baskets had a touch beyond cleverness. The weaver and the warp lived next to the earth and were saturated with the same elements. Twice a year, in the time of white butterflies and again when young quail ran neck and neck in the chaparral, Seyavi cut willows for basketry by the creek where it wound toward the river against the sun and sucking winds. It never quite reached the river except in far-between times of summer flood, but it always tried, and the willows encouraged it as much as they could. You nearly always found them a little farther down than the trickle of eager water. The Paiute fashion of counting time appeals to me more than any other calendar. They have no stamp of heathen gods nor great ones, nor any succession of moons as have red men of the East and North, but count forward and back by the progress of the season; the time of *taboose*, before the trout begin to leap, the end of the piñon harvest, about the beginning of deep snows. So they get nearer the sense of the season, which runs early or late according as the rains are forward or delayed. But whenever Seyavi cut willows for baskets was always a golden time, and the soul of the weather went into the wood. If you have ever owned one of Seyavi's golden russet cooking bowls with the pattern of plumed quail, you would understand all this without saying anything.

Before Seyavi made baskets for the satisfaction of desire,—for that is a house-bred theory of art that makes anything more of it,—she danced and dressed her hair. In those days, when the spring was at flood and the blood pricked to the mating fever, the maids chose their flowers, wreathed themselves, and danced in the twilights, young desire crying out to young desire. They sang what the heart prompted, what the flower expressed, what boded in the mating weather.

"And what flower did you wear, Seyavi?"

"I, ah,—the white flower of twining (clematis), on my body and my hair, and so I sang:—

"I am the white flower of twining,

Little white flower by the river,

Oh, flower that twines close by the river;

Oh, trembling flower!

So trembles the maiden heart."

So sang Seyavi of the campoodie before she made baskets, and in her later days laid her arms upon her knees and laughed in them at the recollection. But it was not often she would say so much, never understanding the keen hunger I had for bits of lore and the "fool talk" of her people. She had fed her young son with meadowlarks' tongues, to make him quick of speech; but in late years was loath to admit it, though she had come through the period of unfaith in the lore of the clan with a fine appreciation of its beauty and significance.

"What good will your dead get, Seyavi, of the baskets you burn?" said I, coveting them for my own collection.

Thus Seyavi, "As much good as yours of the flowers you strew."

Oppapago looks on Waban, and Waban on Coso and the Bitter Lake, and the campoodie looks on these three; and more, it sees the beginning of winds along the foot of Coso, the gathering of clouds behind the high ridges, the spring flush, the soft spread of wild almond bloom on the mesa. These first, you understand, are the Paiute's walls, the other his furnishings. Not the wattled huts is his home, but the land, the winds, the hill front, the stream. These he cannot duplicate at any furbisher's shop as you who live within doors, who, if your purse allows, may have the same home at Sitka and Samarcand. So you see how it is that the homesickness of an Indian is often unto death, since he gets no relief from it; neither wind nor weed nor sky-line, nor any aspect of the hills of a strange land sufficiently like his own. So it was when the government reached out for the Paiutes, they gathered into the Northern Reservation only such poor tribes as could devise no other end of their affairs. Here, all along the river, and south to Shoshone Land, live the clans who owned the earth, fallen into the deplorable condition of hangers-on. Yet you hear them laughing at the hour when they draw in to the campoodie after labor, when there is a smell of meat and the steam of the cooking pots goes up against the sun. Then the children lie with their toes in the ashes to hear tales; then they are merry, and have the joys of repletion and the nearness of their kind. They have their hills, and though jostled are sufficiently free to get some fortitude for what will come. For now you shall hear of the end of the basket maker.

In her best days Seyavi was most like Deborah, deep bosomed, broad in the hips, quick in counsel, slow of speech, esteemed of her people. This was that Seyavi who reared a man by her own hand, her own wit, and none other. When the townspeople began to take note of her—and it was some years after the war before there began to be any towns—she was then in the quick maturity of primitive women; but when I knew her she seemed already old. Indian women do not often live to great age, though they look incredibly steeped in years. They have the wit to win sustenance from the raw material of life without intervention, but they have not the sleek look of the women whom the social organization conspires to nourish. Seyavi had somehow squeezed out of her daily round a spiritual ichor that kept the skill in her knotted fingers long after the accustomed time, but that also failed. By all counts she would have been about sixty years old when it came her turn to sit in the dust on the sunny side of the wickiup, with little strength left for anything but looking. And in time she paid the toll of the smoky huts and became blind. This is a thing so long expected by the Paiutes that when it comes they find it neither bitter nor sweet, but tolerable because common.

There were three other blind women in the campoodie, withered fruit on a bough, but they had memory and speech. By noon of the sun there were never any left in the campoodie but these or some mother of weanlings, and they sat to keep the ashes warm upon the hearth. If it were cold, they burrowed in the blankets of the hut; if it were warm, they followed the shadow of the wickiup around. Stir much out of their places they hardly dared, since one might not help another; but they called, in high, old cracked voices, gossip and reminder across the ash heaps.

Then, if they have your speech or you theirs, and have an hour to spare, there are things to be learned of life not set down in any books, folk tales, famine tales, love and long-suffering and desire, but no whimpering. Now and then one or another of the blind keepers of the camp will come across to where you sit gossiping, tapping her way among the kitchen middens, guided by your voice that carries far in the clearness and stillness of mesa afternoons. But suppose you find Seyavi retired into the privacy of her blanket, you will get nothing for that day. There is no other privacy possible in a campoodie. All the processes of life are carried on out of doors or behind the thin, twig-woven walls of the wickiup, and laughter is the only corrective for behavior. Very early the Indian learns to possess his countenance in impassivity, to cover his head with his blanket. Something to wrap around him is as necessary to the Paiute as to you your closet to pray in.

So in her blanket Seyavi, sometime basket maker, sits by the unlit hearths of her tribe and digests her life, nourishing her spirit against the time of the spirit's need, for she knows in fact quite as much of these matters as you who have a larger hope, though she has none but the certainty that having borne herself courageously to this end she will not be reborn a coyote.

The Little Town of Grape Vines

There are still some places in the west where the quails cry *"cuidado"*; where all the speech is soft, all the manners gentle; where all the dishes have *chile* in them, and they make more of the Sixteenth of September than they do of the Fourth of July. I mean in particular El Pueblo de Las Uvas. Where it lies, how to come at it, you will not get from me; rather would I show you the heron's nest in the tulares. It has a peak behind it, glinting above the tamarack pines, above a breaker of ruddy hills that have a long slope valley-wards and the shoreward steep of waves toward the Sierras.

Below the Town of the Grape Vines, which shortens to Las Uvas for common use, the land dips away to the river pastures and the tulares. It shrouds under a twilight thicket of vines, under a dome of cottonwood-trees, drowsy and murmurous as a hive. Hereabouts are some strips of tillage and the headgates that dam up the creek for the village weirs; upstream you catch the growl of the arrastra. Wild vines that begin among the willows lap over to the orchard rows, take the trellis and roof-tree.

There is another town above Las Uvas that merits some attention, a town of arches and airy crofts, full of linnets, blackbirds, fruit birds, small sharp hawks, and mockingbirds that sing by night. They pour out piercing, unendurably sweet cavatinas above the fragrance of bloom and musky smell of fruit. Singing is in fact the business of the night at Las Uvas as sleeping is for midday. When the moon comes over the mountain wall new-washed from the sea, and the shadows lie like lace on the stamped floors of the patios, from recess to recess of the vine tangle runs the thrum of guitars and the voice of singing.

At Las Uvas they keep up all the good customs brought out of Old Mexico or bred in a lotus-eating land; drink, and are merry and look out for something to eat afterward; have children, nine or ten to a family, have cock-fights, keep the siesta, smoke cigarettes and wait for the sun to go down. And always they dance; at dusk on the smooth adobe floors, afternoons under the trellises where the earth is damp and has a fruity smell. A betrothal, a wedding, or a christening, or the mere proximity of a guitar is sufficient occasion; and if the occasion lacks, send for the guitar and dance anyway.

All this requires explanation. Antonio Sevadra, drifting this way from Old Mexico with the flood that poured into the Tappan district after the first notable strike, discovered La Golondrina. It was a generous lode and Tony a good fellow; to work it he brought in all the Sevadras, even to the twice-removed; all the Castros who were his wife's family, all the Saises, Romeros, an[d] Eschobars,—the relations of his relations-in-law. There you have the beginning of a pretty considerable town. To these accrued much of the Spanish California float swept out of the southwest by eastern enterprise. They slacked away again when the price of silver went down, and the ore dwindled in La Golondrina. All the hot eddy of mining life swept away from that corner of the hills, but there were always those too idle, too poor to move, or too easily content with El Pueblo de Las Uvas.

Nobody comes nowadays to the town of the grape vines except, as we say, "with the breath of crying," but of these enough. All the low sills run over with small heads. Ah, ah! There is a kind of pride in that if you did but know it, to have your baby every year or so as the time sets, and keep a full breast. So great a blessing as marriage is easily come by. It is told of Ruy Garcia that when he went for his marriage license he lacked a dollar of the clerk's fee, but borrowed it of the sheriff, who expected reëlection and exhibited thereby a commendable thrift.

Of what account is it to lack meal or meat when you may have it of any neighbor? Besides, there is sometimes a point of honor in these things. Jesus Romero, father of ten, had a job sacking ore in the Marionette which he gave up of his own accord. "Eh, why?" said Jesus, "for my fam'ly."

"It is so, señora," he said solemnly, "I go to the Marionette, I work, I eat meat—pie—frijoles—good, ver' good. I come home sad'day nigh' I see my fam'ly. I play lil' game poker with the boys, have lil' drink wine, my money all gone. My fam'ly have no money, nothing eat. All time I work at mine I eat, good, ver' good grub. I think sorry for my fam'ly. No, no señora, I no work no more that Marionette, I stay with my fam'ly." The wonder of it is, I think, that the family had the same point of view.

Every house in the town of the vines has its garden plot, corn and brown beans and a row of peppers reddening in the sun; and in damp borders of the irrigating ditches clumps of *yerba santa*, horehound, catnip, and spikenard, wholesome herbs and curative, but if no peppers then nothing at all. You will have for a holiday dinner, in Las Uvas, soup with meat balls and chile in it, chicken with chile, rice with chile, fried beans with more chile, enchilada, which is corn cake with a sauce of chile and tomatoes, onion, grated cheese, and olives, and for a relish chile *tepines* passed about in a dish, all of which is comfortable and corrective to the stomach. You will have wine which every man makes for himself, of good body and inimitable bouquet, and sweets that are not nearly so nice as they look.

There are two occasions when you may count on that kind of a meal; always on the Sixteenth of September, and on the two-yearly visits of Father Shannon. It is absurd, of course, that El Pueblo de Las Uvas should have an Irish priest, but Black Rock, Minton, Jimville, and all that country round do not find it so. Father Shannon visits them all,

waits by the Red Butte to confess the shepherds who go through with
their flocks, carries a blessing to small and isolated mines, and so in the
course of a year or so works around to Las Uvas to bury and marry and
christen. Then all the little graves in the *Campo Santo* are brave with
tapers, the brown pine headboards blossom like Aaron's rod with paper
roses and bright cheap prints of Our Lady of Sorrows. Then the Señora
Sevadra, who thinks herself elect of heaven for that office, gathers up
the original sinners, the little Elijias, Lolas, Manuelitas, Josés, Felipés,
by dint of adjurations and sweets smuggled into small perspiring palms,
to fit them for the Sacrament.

I used to peek in at them, never so softly, in Doña Ina's living-room;
Raphael-eyed little imps, going sidewise on their knees to rest them
from the bare floor, candles lit on the mantel to give a religious air, and a
great sheaf of wild bloom before the Holy Family. Come Sunday they
set out the altar in the schoolhouse, with the fine-drawn altar cloths, the
beaten silver candlesticks, and the wax images, chief glory of Las Uvas,
brought up mule-back from Old Mexico forty years ago. All in white
the communicants go up two and two in a hushed, sweet awe to take the
body of their Lord, and Tomaso, who is priest's boy, tries not to look
unduly puffed up by his office. After that you have dinner and a bottle
of wine that ripened on the sunny slope of Escondito. All the week
Father Shannon has shriven his people, who bring clean conscience to
the betterment of appetite, and the Father sets them an example. Father Shannon is rather big about the middle to accommodate the large
laugh that lives in him, but a most shrewd searcher of hearts. It is
reported that one derives comfort from his confessional, and I for my
part believe it.

The celebration of the Sixteenth, though it comes every year, takes
as long to prepare for as Holy Communion. The señoritas have each a
new dress apiece, the señoras a new *rebosa*. The young gentlemen have
new silver trimmings to their sombreros, unspeakable ties, silk hand-
kerchiefs, and new leathers to their spurs. At this time when the peppers glow in the gardens and the young quail cry *"cuidado,"* "have a
care!" you can hear the *plump, plump* of the *metate* from the alcoves of
the vines where comfortable old dames, whose experience gives them
the touch of art, are pounding out corn for tamales.

School-teachers from abroad have tried before now at Las Uvas to
have school begin on the first of September, but got nothing else to stir
in the heads of the little Castros, Garcias, and Romeros but feasts and
cock-fights until after the Sixteenth. Perhaps you need to be told that

this is the anniversary of the Republic, when liberty awoke and cried in the provinces of Old Mexico. You are aroused at midnight to hear them shouting in the streets, *"Vive la Libertad!"* answered from the houses and the recesses of the vines, *"Vive la Mexico!"* At sunrise shots are fired commemorating the tragedy of unhappy Maximilian, and then music, the noblest of national hymns, as the great flag of Old Mexico floats up the flag-pole in the bare little plaza of shabby Las Uvas. The sun over Pine Mountain greets the eagle of Montezuma before it touches the vineyards and the town, and the day begins with a great shout. By and by there will be a reading of the Declaration of Independence and an address punctured by *vives;* all the town in its best dress, and some exhibits of horsemanship that make lathered bits and bloody spurs; also a cock-fight.

By night there will be dancing and such music! old Santos to play the flute, a little lean man with a saintly countenance, young Garcia whose guitar has a soul, and Carrasco with the violin. They sit on a high platform above the dancers in the candle flare, backed by the red, white, and green of Old Mexico, and play fervently such music as you will not hear otherwhere.

At midnight the flag comes down. Count yourself at a loss if you are not moved by that performance. Pine Mountain watches whitely overhead, shepherd fires glow strongly on the glooming hills. The plaza, the bare glistening pole, the dark folk, the bright dresses, are lit ruddily by a bonfire. It leaps up to the eagle flag, dies down, the music begins softly and aside. They play airs of old longing and exile; slowly out of the dark the flag drops down, bellying and falling with the midnight draught. Sometimes a hymn is sung, always there are tears. The flag is down; Tony Sevadra has received it in his arms. The music strikes a barbaric swelling tune, another flag begins a slow ascent,—it takes a breath or two to realize that they are both, flag and tune, the Star Spangled Banner,—a volley is fired, we are back, if you please, in California of America. Every youth who has the blood of patriots in him lays ahold on Tony Sevadra's flag, happiest if he can get a corner of it. The music goes before, the folk fall in two and two, singing. They sing everything, America, the Marseillaise, for the sake of the French shepherds hereabout, the hymn of Cuba, and the Chilian national air to comfort two families of that land. The flag goes to Doña Ina's, with the candlesticks and the altar cloths, then Las Uvas eats tamales and dances the sun up the slope of Pine Mountain.

You are not to suppose that they do not keep the Fourth, Washington's Birthday, and Thanksgiving at the town of the grape vines. These make excellent occasions for quitting work and dancing, but the Sixteenth is the holiday of the heart. On Memorial Day the graves have garlands and new pictures of the saints tacked to the headboards. There is great virtue in an *Ave* said in the Camp of the Saints. I like that name which the Spanish speaking people give to the garden of the dead, *Campo Santo,* as if it might be some bed of healing from which blind souls and sinners rise up whole and praising God. Sometimes the speech of simple folk hints at truth the understanding does not reach. I am persuaded only a complex soul can get any good of a plain religion. Your earthborn is a poet and a symbolist. We breed in an environment of asphalt pavements a body of people whose creeds are chiefly restrictions against other people's way of life, and have kitchens and latrines under the same roof that houses their God. Such as these go to church to be edified, but at Las Uvas they go for pure worship and to entreat their God. The logical conclusion of the faith that every good gift cometh from God is the open hand and the finer courtesy. The meal done without buys a candle for the neighbor's dead child. You do foolishly to suppose that the candle does no good.

At Las Uvas every house is a piece of earth—thick walled, whitewashed adobe that keeps the even temperature of a cave; every man is an accomplished horseman and consequently bow-legged; every family keeps dogs, flea-bitten mongrels that loll on the earthen floors. They speak a purer Castilian than obtains in like villages of Mexico, and the way they count relationship everybody is more or less akin. There is not much villainy among them. What incentive to thieving or killing can there be when there is little wealth and that to be had for the borrowing! If they love too hotly, as we say "take their meat before grace," so do their betters. Eh, what! shall a man be a saint before he is dead? And besides, Holy Church takes it out of you one way or another before all is done. Come away, you who are obsessed with your own importance in the scheme of things, and have got nothing you did not sweat for, come away by the brown valleys and full-bosomed hills to the even-breathing days, to the kindliness, earthiness, ease of El Pueblo de Las Uvas.

The Flock

4

When Mary Austin published her favorably received book *The Flock* in 1906, she was already recognized as the author of *The Land of Little Rain, Isidro,* and *The Basket Woman*. She had earned a reputation as one who knew the folkways of the Mexican, Basque, and French herdsmen whose skills were integral to the sheep business that flourished in the San Joaquin Valley of California's Sierra Nevada. As if to prove her affinity with those about whom she writes—the shepherds, the herdsmen, the ranchers, and the dogs who aid the shepherds—she dedicates the book "to the people of the book."

The selections here present Austin's interest in the history of Hispanic California, the introduction during the eighteenth and early nineteenth centuries of large sheep herds into the territory, and the role of the sheep business in fueling the antipathy that naturally developed between the owners of cattle and those of sheep, each seeking precious resources to feed and water the animals. The writer invents a new form of pastoral, a melange of discursive forms—part history, part anecdotal narrative, part folklore, part meditation—to tell the story of the flocks and their management. Austin called this a narrative of "flock-mind," the notion of momentum found in the flock, a consciousness of group action known intimately to the herdsmen, dogs, and goats who guide and guard the sheep toward their goal of finding green feeding ground amid what Austin commentator Melody Graulich has called "the wild disorder of the ranges." Austin demonstrates her knowledge of sheep and their habits, of herdsmen and their skills, and of the sociohistorical problems that plagued sheep ranching in California.

Austin got much of her information from walking and riding with General William Beale of the vast Ranchos Tejon; Jimmy Rosemeyre, "the real repository of the tradition of the Tejon" (223); and José Jesús Lopez, who tutored her in the ways of the sheep and the lore of the Tejon. "You should have seen," our narrator tells us admiringly, "Don José Jesús letting his cigarette die out between his fingers as he told the story of his Long Drive" (239).[1] Nor does Austin's fascination with flocks and shepherds end with this book; in the stories of *Lost Borders*, they again emerge prominently, as when she, in the guise of the Walking Woman, meets up with Filon, the shepherd, during a sandstorm in the Tehachapi: "We kept the flock together," reports the narrator of the book, whether we see her as the fictional Walking Woman or the young writer Mary Austin.[2]

Imbuing the flock with a quasi-mystical "Primal Impulse," an instinctual intelligence that passes down through the ages, Austin endows the herders with prescience to read the "flock-mind" against such marauders as coyotes and bears, and against the rigors of the desert and the drought of the soil that the flock must traverse. In a book that reflects upon the diurnal and nocturnal rhythms of shepherding, it seems appropriate that the writer in the persona of a commentator uses an oracular tone to conclude that "nothing contributes more to the sense of human inconsequence than the unhoused nights of shepherding." The narrator continues in the tones of a seer, "But in the Wild the night moves forward at an impulse flowing from unknowable control" (262–63).

The Coming of the Flocks

A great many interesting things happened about the time Rivera y Moncada brought up the first of the flocks from Velicatá. That same year Daniel Boone, lacking bread and salt and friends, heard with prophetic rapture the swaying of young rivers in the Dark and Bloody Ground; that year British soldiers shot down men in the streets of Boston for beginning to be proud to call themselves Americans and think accordingly; that year Junípero Serra lifted the cross by a full creek in the Port of Monterey;—coughing of guns by the eastern sea, by the sea in the west the tinkle of altar bells and soft blether of the flocks.

All the years since Oñate saw its purple hills low like a cloud in the west, since Cabrillo drifted past the tranquil reaches of its coast, the land lay unspoiled, inviolate. Then God stirred up His Majesty of Spain to attempt the dominion of Alta California by the hand of the Franciscans. This sally of the grey brothers was like the return of Ezra to upbuild Jerusalem; "they strengthened their hands with vessels of silver," with bells, with vestments and altar cloths, with seed corn and beasts collected from the missions of Baja California. This was done under authority by Rivera y Moncada. "And," says the Padre in his journal, "although it was with a somewhat heavy hand, it was undergone for God and the King."

Four expeditions, two by land and two by sea, set out from Old Mexico. Señor San José being much in the public mind at that time, on account of having just delivered San José del Cabo from a plague of locusts, was chosen patron of the adventure, and Serra, at the request of his majesty, sang the Mass of Supplication. The four expeditions drew together again at San Diego, having suffered much, the ships' crews from scurvy and the land parties from thirst and desertion. It was now July, and back a mile from the weltering bay the bloom of cacti pricked the hot, close air like points of flame.

Señor San José, it appeared, had done enough for that turn, for though Serra, without waiting for the formal founding of Mission San Diego de Alcalá, dispatched Crespi and Portolá northward, their eyes were holden, and they found nothing to their minds resembling the much desired Port of Monterey, and the Mission prospered so indifferently that their return was to meet the question of abandonment. The good Junípero, having reached the end of his own devising, determined to leave something to God's occasions, and instituted a *novena*. For nine days Saint Joseph was entreated by prayers, by incense, and candle smoke; and on the last hour of the last day, which was March 19, 1770, there appeared in the far blue ring of the horizon the white flick of a sail bringing succor. Upon this Serra went on the second and successful expedition to Monterey, and meantime Don Fernando de Rivera y Moncada had gone south with twenty soldiers to bring up the flocks from Velicatá.

Over the mesa from the town, color of poppies ran like creeping fire in the chamisal, all the air was reeking sweet with violets, yellow and paling at the edges like the bleached, fair hair of children who play much about the beaches. Don Fernando left Velicatá in May—O, the good land that holds the record of all he saw!—the tall, white, odorous Candles-of-Our Lord, the long, plumed reaches of the chamisal, the tangle of the *meghariza*, the yellow-starred plats of the *chili-cojote*, reddening berries of rhus from which the Padres were yet to gather wax that God's altars might not lack candles, the steep barrancas clothed with deer-weed and *toyon*, blue hills that swam at noon in waters of mirage. There was little enough water of any sort on that journey, none too much of sapless feed. Dry camp succeeded to dry camp. Hills neared them with the hope of springs and passed bone-dry, inhospitably stiff with cactus and rattle weed. The expedition drifted steadily northward and smelled the freshness of the sea; then they heard the night-singing mocking bird, wildly sweet in the waxberry bush, and, still two days from San Diego, met the messengers of Governor Portolá going south with news of the founding of Monterey. This was in June of 1770. No doubt they at San Diego were glad when they heard the roll of the bells and the blether of the flock.

Under the Padres' careful shepherding the sheep increased until, at the time of the secularization, three hundred and twenty thousand fed in the Mission purlieus. Blankets were woven, serapes, and a coarse kind of cloth called *jerga,* but the wool was poor and thin; probably the home government wished not to encourage a rival to the exports of Spain. After secularization of 1833, the numbers of sheep fell off in California, until, to supply the demand for their coarse-flavored mutton, flocks were driven in from Mexico. These "mustang sheep" were little and lean and mostly black, sheared but two and one half pounds of wool, and were so wild that they must be herded on horseback. About this time rams were imported from China without materially improving the breed. Then the rush westward in the eager fifties brought men whose trade had been about sheep. Those who had wintered flocks on New England hill pastures began to see possibilities in the belly-deep grasses of the coast ranges. In '53, William W. Hollister brought three hundred ewes over the emigrant trail and laid the foundation of a fortune. But think of the fatigues of it, the rivers to swim, the passes to attempt, the watch fires, the far divided water holes, the interminable lapsing of days and nights,—and a sheep's day's journey is seven miles! No doubt they had some pressing, and comfortable waits in fat pastures, but it stands on the mere evidence of the fact, that Hollister was a man of large patience. During the next year Solomon Jewett, the elder, shipped a flock by way of Panama, and the improvement of the breeds began. The business throve from the first; there are men yet to tell you they have paid as high as twelve dollars for a well-fatted mutton.

The best days of shepherding in California were before the Frenchmen began to appear on the mesas. Owners then had, by occupancy, the rights to certain range, rights respected by their neighbors. Then suddenly the land was overrun by little dark men who fed where feed was, kept to their own kind, turned money quickly, and went back to France to spend it. At evening the solitary homesteader saw with dread their dust blurs on his horizon, and at morning looked with rage on the cropped lands that else should have nourished his own necessary stock; smoke of the burning forests witnessed to heaven against them. Of this you shall hear further with some particularity. Those who can suck no other comfort from the tariff revision of the early eighties may write to its account that it saved us unmeasured acreage of wild grass and trees.

Portrait signed by Brian Maura, dated 1906. (Courtesy of the Huntington Library, San Marino, California)

What more it did is set down in the proper place, but certainly the drop in prices drove out of the wool industry those who could best be spared from it. Now it could be followed profitably by none but the foreseeing and considering shepherd, and to such a one dawned the necessity of conserving the feed, though he had not arrived altruistically at wanting it conserved for anybody else. So by the time sheep-herding had recovered its status as a business, the warrings and evasions began again over the withdrawal of the forest reserves from public pasturing. Here in fact it rests, for though there be sheep-owners who understand the value of tree-covered water-sheds, there are others to whom the unfair discrimination between flocks and horned cattle is an excuse for violation; and just as a few Cotswolds can demoralize a bunch of tractable merinos, so the unthinking herder brings the business to disesteem.

What I have to do here is to set down without prejudice, but not without sympathy, as much as I have been able to understand of the whole matter kindled by the journey up from Velicatá in the unregarded spring of 1770, and now laid to the successors of Don Fernando de Rivera y Moncada.

I suppose of all the people who are concerned with the making of a true book, the one who puts it to the pen has the least to do with it. This is the book of Jimmy Rosemeyre and José Jesús Lopez, of Little Pete, who is not to be confounded with the Petit Pete who loved an antelope in the Ceriso,—the book of Noriega, of Sanger and the Manxman and Narcisse Duplin, and many others who, wittingly or unwittingly, have contributed to the performances set down in it. Very little, not even the virtue of being uniformly grateful to the little gods who have constrained me to be of the audience, can be put to the writer's credit. All of the book that is mine is the temper of mind which makes it impossible that there should be any play not worth the candle.

By two years of homesteading on the borders of Tejon, by fifteen beside the Long Trail where it spindles out through Inyo, by all the errands of necessity and desire that made me to know its moods and the calendar of its shrubs and skies, by the chances of Sierra holidays where there were always bells jangling behind us in the pines or flocks blethering before us in the meadows, by the riot of shearings, by the faint winy smell in the streets of certain of the towns of the San Joaquin that apprises of the yearly inturning of the wandering shepherd, I grew aware of all that you read here and of much beside. For if I have not told all of the story of Narcisse Duplin and what happened to the Indian who worked for Joe Espelier, it is because it concerned them merely as men and would as likely have befallen them in any other business.

Something also I had from the Walking Woman, when that most wise and insane creature used to come through by Temblor, and a little from pretty Edie Julien interpreting shyly in her father's house, but not much, I being occupied in acquiring a distaste for my own language hearing her rippling French snag upon such words as "spud" and "bunch" and "grub." In time I grew to know the owner of flocks bearing the brand of the Three Legs of Man, and as I sat by his fire, touching his tempered spirit as one half draws and drops a sword in its scabbard for pleasure of its fineness, becoming flock-wise I understood why the French herders hereabout give him the name of the Best Shepherd. I met and talked with the elder Beale after he had come to the time of life when talking seems a sufficient occupation, and while yet there was color and glow as of the heart wood breaking in the white ash of remembrance. But, in fact, the best way of knowing about shepherding is to know sheep, and for this there was never an occasion lacking. In this land of such indolent lapping of the nights and days that neither the clock nor the calendar has any pertinence to time, I call on the eye of my mind, as it were, for relief, looking out across the long moon-colored sands, and say:—

"Do you see anything coming, Sister Anne?"

"I see the dust of a flock on the highway."

Well, then, if from the clutch of great Tedium (of whom more than his beard is blue) there is no rescue but such as comes by way of the flock, let us at least miss no point of the entertainment.

The Flock

The earliest important achievement of ovine intelligence is to know whether its own notion or another's is most worth while, and if the other's, which one. Individual sheep have certain qualities, instincts, competencies, but in the man-herded flocks these are superseded by something which I shall call the flock-mind, though I cannot say very well what it is, except that it is less than the sum of all their intelligences. This is why there have never been any notable changes in the management of flocks since the first herder girt himself with a wallet of sheepskin and went out of his cave dwelling to the pastures.

Understand that a flock is not the same thing as a number of sheep. On the stark wild headlands of the White Mountains, as many as thirty Bighorn are known to run in loose, fluctuating hordes; in fenced pastures, two to three hundred; close-herded on the range, two to three thousand; but however artificially augmented, the flock is always a conscious adjustment. As it is made up in the beginning of the season, the band is chiefly of one sort, wethers or ewes or weanling lambs (for the rams do not run with the flock except for a brief season in August); with a few flock-wise ones, trained goats, the *cabestres* of the Mexican herders, trusted bell-wethers or experienced old ewes mixed and intermeddled by the herder and the dogs, becoming invariably and finally coördinate. There are always Leaders, Middlers, and Tailers, each insisting on its own place in the order of going. Should the flock be rounded up suddenly in alarm it mills within itself until these have come to their own places.

If you would know something of the temper and politics of the shepherd you meet, inquire of him for the names of his leaders. They should be named for his sweethearts, for the little towns of France, for the generals of the great Napoleon, for the presidents of Republics,—though for that matter they are all ardent republicans,—for the popular heroes of the hour. Good shepherds take the greatest pains with their leaders, not passing them with the first flock to slaughter, but saving them to make wise the next.

There is much debate between herders as to the advantage of goats over sheep as leaders. In any case there are always a few goats in a flock, and most American owners prefer them; but the Frenchmen choose bell-wethers. Goats lead naturally by reason of a quicker instinct, forage more freely, and can find water on their own account. But wethers, if trained with care, learn what goats abhor, to take broken ground sedately, to walk through the water rather than set the whole flock leaping and scrambling; but never to give voice to alarm as goats will, and call the herder. Wethers are more bidable once they are broken to it, but a goat is the better for a good beating. Echenique has told me that the more a goat complains under his cudgelings the surer he is of the brute's need of discipline. Goats afford another service in furnishing milk for the shepherd, and, their udders being most public, will suckle a sick lamb, a pup, or a young burro at need.

It appears that leaders understand their office, and goats particularly exhibit a jealousy of their rights to be first over the stepping-stones or to walk the teetering log-bridges at the roaring creeks. By this facile reference of the initiative to the wisest one, the shepherd is served most. The dogs learn to which of the flock to communicate orders, at which heels a bark or a bite soonest sets the flock in motion. But the flock-mind obsesses equally the best trained, flashes as instantly from the Meanest of the Flock.

Suppose the sheep to scatter widely on a heather-planted headland, the leader feeding far to windward. Comes a cougar sneaking up the trail between the rooted boulders toward the Meanest of the Flock. The smell of him, the play of light on his sleek flanks startles the unslumbering fear in the Meanest; it runs widening in the flock-mind, exploding instantly in the impulse of flight.

Danger! flashes the flock-mind, and in danger the indispensable thing is to run, not to wait until the leader sniffs the tainted wind and signals it; not for each and singly to put the occasion to the proof; but to run—of this the flock-mind apprises—and to keep on running until the impulse dies faintly as water-rings on the surface of a mantling pond. In the wild pastures flight is the only succor, and since to cry out is to interfere with that business and draw on the calamity, a flock in extremity never cries out.

Consider, then, the inadequacy of the flock-mind. A hand-fed leader may learn to call the herder vociferously, a cosset lamb in trouble come blatting to his heels, but the flock has no voice other than the deep-mouthed pealings hung about the leader's neck. In all that darkling lapse of the time since herders began to sleep by the sheep with their weapons, affording a protection that the flock-mind never learns to invite, they have found no better trick than to be still and run foolishly. For the flock-mind moves only in the direction of the Original Intention. When at shearings or markings they run the yearlings through a gate for counting, the rate of going accelerates until the sheep pass too rapidly for numbering. Then the shepherd thrusts his staff across the opening, forcing the next sheep to jump, and the next, and the next, until, Jump! says the flock-mind. Then he withdraws the staff, and the sheep go on jumping until the impulse dies as the dying peal of the bells.

By very little the herder may turn the flock-mind to his advantage but chiefly it works against him. Suppose on the open range the impulse to forward movement overtakes them, set in motion by some eager leaders that remember enough of what lies ahead to make them oblivious to what they pass. They press ahead. The flock draws on. The momentum of travel grows. The bells clang soft and hurriedly; the sheep forget to feed; they neglect the tender pastures; they will not stay to drink. Under an unwise or indolent herder the sheep going on an accustomed trail will over-travel and under-feed, until in the midst of good pasture they starve upon their feet. So it is on the Long Trail you so often see the herder walking with his dogs ahead of his sheep to hold them back to feed. But if it should be new ground he must go after and press them skillfully, for the flock-mind balks chiefly at the unknown.

If a flock could be stopped as suddenly as it is set in motion, Sanger would never have lost to a single bear the five hundred sheep he told me of. They were bedded on a mesa breaking off in a precipice two hundred feet above the valley, and the bear came up behind them in the moonless watch of night. With no sound but the scurry of feet and the startled clamor of the bells, the flock broke straight ahead. The brute instinct had warned them asleep but it could not save them awake. All that the flock-mind could do was to stir them instantly to running, and they fled straight away over the headland, piling up, five hundred of them, in the gulch below.

In sudden attacks from several quarters, or inexplicable man-thwarting of their instincts, the flock-mind teaches them to turn a solid front, revolving about in the smallest compass with the lambs in the midst, narrowing and in-drawing until they perish by suffocation. So they did in the intricate defiles of Red Rock, where Carrier lost two hundred and fifty in '74, and at Poison Springs, as Narcisse Duplin told me, where he had to choose between leaving them to the deadly waters, or, prevented from the spring, made witless by thirst, to mill about until they piled up and killed threescore in their midst. By no urgency of the dogs could they be moved forward or scattered until night fell with coolness and returning sanity. Nor does the imperfect gregariousness of man always save us from ill-considered rushes or strangulous in-turnings of the social mass. Notwithstanding there are those who would have us to be flock-minded.

It is probable that the obsession of this over-sense originates in the extraordinary quickness with which the sheep makes the superior intel-ligence of the leader serve his own end. A very little running in the open range proves that one in every group of sheep has sharper vision, quicker hearing, keener scent; henceforth it is the business of the dull sheep to watch that favored one. No slightest sniff or stamp escapes him; the order for flight finds him with muscles tense for running.

The worth of a leader in close-herded flocks is his ability to catch readily the will of the herder. Times I have seen the sheep feeding far from the man, not knowing their appointed bedding-place. The dogs lag at the herder's heels. Now as the sun is going down the man thrusts out his arm with a gesture that conveys to the dogs his wish that they turn the flock toward a certain open scarp. The dogs trot out leisurely, circling widely to bring up the farthest stragglers, but before they round upon it the flock turns. It moves toward the appointed quarter and pours smoothly up the hill. It is possible that the leaders may have learned the language of that right arm, and in times of quietude obey it without intervention of the dogs. It is also conceivable that in the clear silences of the untroubled wild the flock-mind takes its impulse directly from the will of the herder.

Almost the only sense left untouched by man-herding is the weather sense. Scenting a change, the sheep exhibit a tendency to move to higher ground; no herder succeeds in making his flock feed in the eye of the sun. While rain falls they will not feed nor travel except in extreme desperation, but if after long falling it leaves off suddenly, night or day, the flock begins to crop. Then if the herder hears not the bells nor wakes himself by the subtle sense which in the outdoor life has time to grow, he has his day's work cut out for him in the rounding-up. A season of long rains makes short fleeces.

Summers in the mountains, sheep love to lie on the cooling banks and lick the snow, preferring it to any drink; but if falling snow overtakes them they are bewildered by it, find no food for themselves, and refuse to travel while it lies on the ground. This is the more singular, for the American wild sheep, the Bighorn, makes nothing of a twenty foot fall; in the blinding swirl of flakes shifts only to let the drifts pile under him; ruminates most contentedly when the world is full of a roaring white wind. Most beasts in bad weather drift before a storm. The faster it moves the farther go the sheep; so if there arises one of those blowy days that announce the turn of the two seasons, blinding thick with small dust, at the end of a few hours of it the shepherd sees the tails of his sheep disappearing down the wind. The tendency of sheep is to seek lower ground when disturbed by beasts, and under weather stress to work up. When any of his flock are strayed or stampeded, the herder knows by the occasion whether to seek them up hill or down. Seek them he must if he would have them again, for estrays have no faculty by sense or scent to work their way back to the herd. Let them be separated from it but by the roll of the land, and by accident headed in another direction, it is for them as if the flock had never been. It is to provide against this incompetency that the shepherd makes himself markers, a black sheep, or one with a crumbled horn or an unshorn patch on the rump, easily noticeable in the shuffle of dust-colored backs. It is the custom to have one marker to one hundred sheep, each known by his chosen place in the flock which he insists upon, so that if as many as half a dozen stray out of the band the relative position of the markers is changed; or if one of these conspicuous ones be missing it will not be singly, because of the tendency of large flocks to form smaller groups about the best worth following.

I do not know very well what to make of that trait of lost sheep to seek rock shelter at the base of cliffs, for it suits with no characteristic of his wild brethren. But if an estray in his persistent journey up toward the high places arrives at the foot of a tall precipice, there he stays, seeking not to go around it, feeding out perhaps and returning to it, but if frightened by prowlers, huddling there to starve. Could it be the survival, not of a wild instinct,—it is too foolish to have been that,—but of the cave-dwelling time when man protected him in his stone shelters or in pens built against the base of a cliff, as we see the herder yet for greater convenience build rude corrals of piled boulders at the foot of an overhanging or insurmountable rocky wall? It is yet to be shown how long man halted in the period of stone dwelling and the sheep with him; but if it be assented that we have brought some traces of that life forward with us, might not also the sheep?

Where the wild strain most persists is in the bedding habits of the flock. Still they take for choice, the brow of a rising hill, turning outward toward the largest view; and never have I seen the flock all lie down at one time. Always as if by prearrangement some will stand, and upon their surrendering the watch others will rise in their places headed to sniff the tainted wind and scan the rim of the world. Like a thing palpable one sees the racial obligation pass through the bedded flock; as the tired watcher folds his knees under him and lies down, it passes like a sigh. By some mysterious selection it leaves a hundred ruminating in quietude and troubles the appointed one. One sees in the shaking of his sides a hint of struggle against the hereditary and so unnecessary instinct, but sighing he gets upon his feet. By noon or night the flock instinct never sleeps. Waking and falling asleep, waking and spying on the flock, no chance discovers the watchers failing, even though they doze upon their feet; and by nothing so much is the want to interrelation of the herder and the flock betrayed, for watching is the trained accomplishment of dogs.

The habit of nocturnal feeding is easily resumed, the sheep growing restless when the moon is full, and moving out to feed at the least encouragement. In hot seasons on the treeless range the herder takes advantage of it, making the longer siesta of the burning noon. But if the habit is to be resumed or broken off, it is best done by moving to new grounds, the association of locality being most stubborn to overcome.

Of the native instincts for finding water and knowing when food is good for them, herded goats have retained much, but sheep not a whit. In the open San Joaquin, said a good shepherd of that country, when the wind blew off the broad lake, his sheep, being thirsty, would break and run as much as a mile or two in that direction; but it seems that the alkaline dust of the desert range must have diminished the keenness of smell, for Sanger told me how, on his long drive, when his sheep had come forty miles without drink and were then so near a water-hole that the horses scented it and pricked up their ears, the flock became unmanageable from thirst and broke back to the place where they had last drunk. Great difficulty is experienced in the desert ranges in getting the flock to water situated obscurely in steep ravines; they panting with water need, but not even aware of its nearness until they have been fairly thrust into it. Then if one lifts up a joyous blat the dogs and the herder must stand well forward to prevent suffocation by piling up of the flock. You should have heard José Jesús Lopez tell how, when the ten thousand came to water in the desert after a day or two of dry travel, when the first of the nearing band had drunk he lifted up the water call; how it was taken up and carried back across the shouldering brutes to the nearest band behind, and by them flatly trumpeted to the next, and so across the mesa, miles and miles in the still, slant light.

When Watterson ran his sheep on the plains he watered them at a pump, and in the course of the season all the bands that bore the Three Legs of Man got to know the smell pertaining to that brand, drinking at the troughs as they drew in at sundown from the feeding-ground. But when for a price strange bands in passing drank there, he could in no wise prevail upon his own sheep to drink of the water they had left. The flocks shuffled in and sniffed at the tainted drink and went and lay down waterless. The second band drew alongside and made as if to refresh themselves at the troughs, but before they had so much as smelled of it:—

Ba-a-a, Ba-a-a-a! blatted the first flock, and the newcomers turned toward them and lay down. Comes another band and the second takes up the report, not having proved the event but accepting it at hearsay from the first.

Ba-a-a-a-d, Ba-a-a-a-d! blat the watchers, and when that has happened two or three times the shepherd gives over trying to make his sheep accept the leavings of the troughs, whatever the price of water, but turns it out upon the sand. Sheep will die rather than drink water which does not please them, and die drinking water with which they should not be pleased. Nor can they discriminate in the matter of poisonous herbs. In the northerly Sierras they perish yearly, cropping the azaleas; Julien lost three or four hundred when wild tobacco (*nicotiana attenuata*) sprang up after a season of flood water below Coyote Holes; and in places about the high mountains there are certain isolated meadows wherein some herb unidentified by sheepmen works disaster to the ignorant or too confiding herder. Such places come to be known as Poison Meadows, and grasses ripen in them uncropped year after year. Yet it would seem there is a rag-tag of instinct left, for in the desert regions where sheep have had a taste of Loco-weed (*astragalus*) which affects them as cocaine, like the devotees of that drug, they return to seek for it and become dopy and worthless through its excess; and a flock that has suffered from milkweed poisoning learns at last to be a little aware of it. Old tales of folklore would have us to understand that this atrophy of a vital sense is within the reach of history. Is it not told indeed, in Araby, that the exhilaration of coffee was discovered by a goatherd from the behavior of his goats when they had cropped the berries?

By much the same cry that apprises the flock of tainted drink they are made aware of strangers in the band. This is chiefly the business of yearlings, wise old ewes and seasoned wethers not much regarding it. One of the band discerns a smell not the smell of his flock, and bells the others to come on and inquire. They run blatting to his call and form a ring about the stranger, vociferating disapproval until the flock-mind wakes and pricks them to butt the intruder from the herd; but he persisting and hanging on the outskirts of the flock, acquaints them with his smell and becomes finally incorporate in the band. Nothing else but the rattlesnake extracts this note of protest from the flock. Him also they inclose in the noisy ring until the rattler wriggles to his hole, or the herder comes with his *makila* and puts an end to the commotion.

It is well to keep in mind that ordinarily when the flock cries there is nothing in particular the matter with it. The continuous blether of the evening round-up is merely the note of domesticity, ewes calling to their lambs, wethers to their companions as they revolve to their accustomed places, all a little resentful of the importunity of the dogs. In sickness and alarm the sheep are distressfully still, only milkweed poisoning, of all evils, forcing from them a kind of breathy moan; but this is merely a symptom of the disorder and not directed toward the procurement of relief.

It is doubtful if the herder is anything more to the flock than an incident of the range, except as a giver of salt, for the only cry they make to him is the salt cry. When the natural craving is at the point of urgency they circle about his camp or his cabin, leaving off feeding for that business; and nothing else offering, they will continue this headlong circling about a boulder or any object bulking large in their immediate neighborhood remotely resembling the appurtenances of man, as if they had learned nothing since they were free to find licks for themselves, except that salt comes by bestowal and in conjunction with the vaguely indeterminate lumps of matter that associate with man. As if in fifty centuries of man-herding they had made but one step out of the terrible isolation of brute species, an isolation impenetrable except by fear to every other brute, but now admitting the fact without knowledge, of the God of the Salt. Accustomed to receiving this miracle on open boulders, when the craving is strong upon them they seek such as these to run about, vociferating, as if they said, In such a place our God has been wont to bless us, come now let us greatly entreat Him. This one quavering bleat, unmistakable to the sheepman even at a distance, is the only new note in the sheep's vocabulary, and the only one which passes with intention from himself to man. As for the call of distress which a leader raised by hand may make to his master, it is not new, is not common to flock usage, and is swamped utterly in the obsession of the flock-mind.

But when you hear shepherds from the Pyrenees speak of the salt call it is no blether of the sheep they mean, but that long, rolling, high and raucous *Ru-u-u-u-u-u* by which they summon the flock to the lick. And this is most curious that no other word than this is recognized as exclusive to the sheep, as we understand "scat" to be the peculiar shibboleth of cats, and "bossy" the only proper appellate of cows. Ordinarily the herder does not wish to call the sheep, he prefers to send the dogs, but if he needs must name them he cries Sheep, sheep! or *mouton,* or *boreito,* as his tongue is, or apprises them of the distribution of salt by beating on a pan. Only the Basco, and such French as have learned it from him, troubles his throat with this searching, mutilated cry. If it should be in crossing the Reserve when the rangers hurry him, or on the range when in the midst of security, suddenly he discovers the deadly milkweed growing all abroad, or if above the timber-line one of the quick, downpouring storms begins to shape in the pure aerial glooms, at once you see the herder striding at the head of his flock drawing them on with the uplifted, *Ru-u-u-uuuuu!* and all the sheep running to it as [if] it were the Pied Piper come again.

Suppose it were true what we have read, that there was once an Atlantis stationed toward the west, continuing the empurpled Pyrenees. Suppose the first of these Pyrenean folk were, as it is written, just Atlantean shepherds straying farthest from that happy island, when the seas engulfed it; suppose they should have carried forward with the inbred shepherd habit some roots of speech, likeliest to have been such as belonged to shepherding—well then, when above the range of trees, when the wild scarps lift rosily through the ineffably pure blue of the twilight earth, suffused with splendor of the alpen glow, when the flock crops the tufted grass scattering widely on the steep, should you see these little men of long arms leaping among the rocks and all the flock lift up their heads to hear the ululating *Ru–u–ubru–u–uuu!* would not all these things leap together in your mind and seem to mean something? Just suppose!

Short Stories

5

The stories I have chosen are those that best illustrate Austin's range as a writer. Often she presents her tales in the first person, with the narrator/Austin speaking in the voice of one who has received the tale through gossip during her desert wanderings. Because she insinuates us into this gossip, we feel complicitous in the telling of the tale. An example of such a narrative strategy appears in "The Coyote-Spirit and the Weaving Woman," a story in the collection *The Basket Woman* (1904). The narrator intimates that she knows the myths of the desert inhabitants, as when she instructs the reader, "Now a Coyote-Spirit, from having been a man, is continually thinking about men and wishing to be with them, and, being a coyote and of the wolf's breed, no sooner does he have his wish than he thinks of devouring" (48). Further, Austin herself sets up the preface of *The Basket Woman* to vouch for the veracity of the narrator: "I know the story of the Coyote-Spirit is true," writes Austin, "because the Basket Woman told it to me, and evidently believed it. She said she had seen the Coyote Spirits in Saline Valley and at Fish Lake."[1] Or, in "The Man Who Lied About a Woman," the narrator begins by absorbing us into the universal "everybody." In the first line of the tale, the narrator says, "Everybody knew that the girl who passed for the daughter of Tizessína was neither her daughter nor a Jicarilla Apache."[2]

This narrative style affords Austin the opportunity to reinforce the authenticity of her tales and the probity of her characters within the boundaries of the story-within-a-story framework, as in "A Case of Conscience." In this story the narrator tells how she pieced together a portion of the story from many oral sources. "When Indian women talk together, and they are great gossips, three things will surely come to the surface in the course of the afternoon—children, marriage, and the ways of whites."[3] In "The Woman at the Eighteen-Mile," one of the stories in *Lost Borders*, Austin's narrator tells the reader that she confirmed the story on a stage coach, this time from Anglo passengers. "Then I heard of the story again between Red Rock and Coyote holes, about moon-set, when the stage labored up the long gorge, waking to hear the voices of the passengers run on steadily with the girding of the sand and the rattle of harness-chains, run on and break and eddy around Dead Man's Springs, and back up in turgid pools of comment and speculation, falling in shallows of miner's talk, lost at last in the waste of ledges and contracts and forgotten strikes. Waking and falling asleep again, the story shaped itself of the largeness of the night." Finally after hearing it again from some strangers, the narrator confides, "But what I had heard of the story confirmed it exactly, the story I had so long sought" (95–96).

Many of Austin's stories were published in literary magazines—the *Atlantic Monthly*, the *Overland Monthly, Century, Sunset*, and the *American Mercury*—before she collected them into the volumes of *Lost Borders* and *One-Smoke Stories*. Thematically the stories demonstrate how Austin used the materials of her own life as well as the Californians—Anglos, Hispanics, and Indians—she met as a young woman, with whom she talked about the issues of marriage, ethnicity, and gender. The writer's first published story, "The Mother of Felipe," appeared in the *Overland Monthly* in November 1892, at the time of her daughter's birth. The theme of the story, a mother's love for her son, greater than any wife's or lover's, resonates in the last lines of the story. "Only in the hearts of mothers lives unconsolable regret." This powerful line underscores a theme that Austin would return to many times in her work. Rooted in her own life, the story foretells the writer's unhappy motherhood, for her only child was mentally disabled and institutionalized at an early age.

A later tale, "Frustrate," concerns a narrator who admits, "I had never been popular with young men." Although she succumbs to pressure and eventually marries Henry, the narrator concludes that her husband lacks the capacity to ever come to know or to understand her. Surely a commentary on her failed marriage to Stafford Wallace Austin, the man she unhappily married in 1891 shortly after emigrating to California with her family, "Frustrate" stands as an example of how Austin integrated life experiences into her fiction. "Frustrate" was published in *Century* magazine in 1912, two years before her divorce.

Published first in *Sunset* in 1918, "The Divorcing of Sina" has been criticized by several critics who have seen racism in the story's sometimes humorous narrative explanations of Paiute folkisms, and its inclusion of an incident that suggests wife abuse in an interracial marriage between a young Paiute woman and a white cowhand. Certainly Austin ironically addresses the vicissitudes that inhere in a marriage when the incorporation of two different cultural traditions lead to misunderstanding, but the aspect of racism remains open to question.

"A Case of Conscience," one of two stories from *Lost Borders* (1909) included here, narrates the tale of a smug Englishman married to a beautiful young Indian woman. The male character, overcome by "Anglo-Saxon prejudice," wishes to abandon his Indian lover and to take their child with him back to England, where he will be reared "properly" to be prepared to assume his aristocratic birthright. The Englishman underestimates the mother's bond to her child, however, and Austin ironically portrays the father's false consciousness about his progeny in the tale's resolution.

"The Woman at the Eighteen-Mile" tells the story of an indomitable woman of the Mojave Desert area of Death Valley, "a good woman with great power and possibilities of passion" (100). The central figure becomes the avatar of Austin's strong female protagonists—perhaps even the writer's alter ego—for the desert woman demonstrates her equality to her man in every respect: "concerned in his work, running neck and neck with it . . . supplementing it not with the merely feminine trick of making him more complacent with himself, but with vital remedies and aids" (102). Yet, here too, Austin writes of the woman deceived, the woman who aligns herself with a man unequal to her passion and devotion. She endures, while he falls short of the mark.

Also included is "The Conversion of Ah Lew Sing," one of Austin's earliest San Francisco stories, later published in the 1934 collection *One-Smoke Stories*—so called because the telling of the tale was meant to occupy the inhalation of a corn-husk cigarette in the camp of the Navajo. A cautionary tale about a Chinese man who by his cunning steals the purchased bride of his friend, it seems an odd fit in a volume mainly containing tales about indigenous New Mexico and Shoshone land, the literary territory Austin calls "Amerind." Nonetheless, Austin defended its inclusion within a book about the many races who inhabited the Far West when she emigrated.

"The Man Who Lied About a Woman" seems a more typical tale from *One-Smoke Stories* in that it tells of a young Apache who, in boasting about his conquest of a beautiful maiden of the village, comes to eat his words in the ironic denouement. Readers might recall Kate Chopin's similar handling of the theme of miscegenation in her stories of the Louisiana Bayou.

In her short stories, unified by time and setting, Austin seems more successful than in the novel form, where the juggling of more characters over longer periods of time in several settings causes confusion in several of her narratives. The short stories gave her a literary form to deliver incisive, often ironic, lessons in man's inhumanity to woman, or to speak of woman's endurance.

The Mother of Felipe

That triangular portion of the great Mojave desert lying south of the curve of the Sierra Nevadas, where those mountains unite with the coast hills is known as Antelope Valley. A big, barren, windy country, rising from the level of the desert in long, undulating slopes that face abruptly toward the mountains.

In the open places rise weird phalanxes of yucca palms, and among the hills little dark pools hide their treacherous margins in unwholesome grasses, and the white leprous crest of alkali. A country to be avoided by the solitary traveler, with its hard, inhospitable soil, and its vast monotony of contour and color. A country sublime in its immensity of light, and soft unvarying tints,—fawn, and olive, and pearl, with glistening stretches of white sand, and brown hollows between the hills, out of which the gray and purple shadows creep at night. A country laid visibly under the ban of eternal silence.

Crossing the valley, forming the third side of the triangle, runs the long road that leads from San Diego and the south to the open country along the Sacramento and the San Joaquin. Coming over the rise of the hill where this road turns away from Elizabeth Lake, rode in the early October morning a little train of horsemen, followed by half a dozen nondescript vehicles from which the faces of women and children peered through a confusion of household goods.

They were of the class commonly styled "Greasers," a mixed origin plainly visible in the dark hue of the skin, the crisp, coarse hair, the high-arched foot and the Madonna-like outlines of the women's heads. The dust of travel lay thick on the wide sombreros of the men and in the creases of their heavy saddles. The horses and women showed the fatigue of a long journey. Still they went forward briskly. There was the vigor of youth in the clear air. The grease of the breakfast shone on the children's faces. There was much animated conversation among the men and gay sallies from the young women; but whenever unusual

laughter was provoked it was checked by sighs and shrugs of com-
miseration, and the women glanced sympathetically at the last wagon
in the train.

It was driven by a woman, whose form betrayed the shapeless
middle-age common to her class. The strong patience of the hills was in
her eyes and mouth. Whenever a smooth bit of road permitted her to
take her eyes from the horses she looked back into the wagon, where on
a rude bed, under an improvised covering of calico bed-quilts, lay a
young man in the delirium of fever. He had been ailing for some time,
and three days ago the fever seized him with an intermittent force that
sapped his strength visibly, like the shaking of an hour-glass.

The mother had urged the expedition forward with all possible
speed. They were still many days distant from a physician to make him
well, or a priest if he should die. "Mother of God! if he should die!" A
sudden spasm of anxiety contracted her oval, unwrinkled face into the
semblance of shrunken old age. Had she not daily prayed to the Virgin
that he might live to comfort her, now that his father was dead. *Ave
Santisima!* He was her only son. For what sin would the good God
punish her?

There was the heavy gold bracelet the *Inglés* had given her,—and
Felipe's father had been so angry. She, she had been a vain, foolish
thing, but, Santa Maria, what can you expect when one is young? The
bracelet had been given to the priest, and she and her husband had been
very happy together. Mother of Christ! how proud he had been when
Felipe was born! That was because she had prayed to the Virgin for a
son. She had burned a wax candle before the Virgin for each month of
her pregnancy, and they had burned quite clear and evenly down to the
end; not one had flickered or gone out. Ave Maria!—and Felipe was
such a son,—there was never another like him. Now if he would get
well, she would give the Virgin the gold beads her husband had bought
her. True, she had intended the beads for Felipe's wife,—but if he
should die, what then? Ay, Jesu Christi! He must not die.

At noon the travelers halted before a brackish spring that oozed
stealthily out of the hillside. The horses drank thirstily of the warm,
turbid stream that flowed across the road; the men shook their damp,
crisp hair, pressed close to the head in a shining crease where the heavy
sombrero rested. The women gathered sympathetically around the
mother of Felipe, chattering together in their soft dialect, with little
nods and shrugs, and pious ejaculations in quick, bird like accents. For
only one of these the mother drew back the calico curtain; this was

Benita, Felipe's betrothed. The girl rested one round arm on the rim of the wheel, and laid her hand on the young man's forehead. She leaned forward lazily; her dress fell away untidily from her brown throat, revealing the beauty of the warm, young curves within. She remained silently stroking her lover's forehead, while the elder women questioned and suggested volubly.

The halt at noon was short; the expedition hoped to cross the mountains before night, and the ascent was long and difficult.

A dry, warm wind was blowing; the horses strained in their collars, the sick man tossed and moaned continually.

The hills were higher and more desolate, and seemed endowed with some infernal mechanism, shutting in silently behind, and opening out noiselessly before, giving up the road grudgingly, as if the very secret of the earth went with it.

There is always a wind at the summit of the hills. There is full daylight there, too, until the night falls suddenly. It is as if the wind blew against the shadows that would have crept up from the valley, beating them back and back from the high places until night falls.

There is hope, too, at the summit of the hill. Who has not drawn it in with deep breaths of the scentless wind? Felipe forgot his delirious dreams, turned easily on his side and slept, and Benita and the mother comforted each other.

The two women rode down the grade together. Antonio Lesalda, Benita's father, walked beside the wagon, saying, "It is a good country that we come to. There is much food there for the horses, and wood, and a good spring that I know of, coming out of the rocks at the foot of the last grade. It will be better for Felipe if we rest there three days. Besides the hunting is good. My father and Mateo Gonzales killed three bears there in one week. It will not be long now, but it is soon dark in the cañon."

The women spoke to each other seldom. It was inexplicable to Benita that her lover should be ill. Luis and Pablo had not so much strength in their whole bodies as was in Felipe's right arm, and she could hear them laughing now with that Gonzales girl. Felipe could not be very sick. How soundly he slept. Her father was right,—they would rest for three days, and the men would get him fresh meat to eat, and he would be strong again. "Now, what are they laughing at there, I wonder!"

The elder woman glanced furtively at the girl's face between her mumbled prayers.

"She is so young, how will she bear it if he should die?" she thought. "Jesu! What am I saying! If he sleeps, all will be well, and I will live with them,—but the Virgin shall have the gold beads."

At the foot of the mountains the men came to unharness the horses. This they did quietly, for the mother had fallen on her knees, rosary in hand. She could not do this before. It took both her hands to drive. The horses wallowed in the rank grass, the children ran about to gather sticks for the fire. "See that you go not too far, or the bears will get you," cried Antonio teasingly. The women busied themselves about the supper. Benita sat beside Felipe and held his hand. He had recognized her, and she felt now more than ever that she loved him. She began to be touched by the fierce anxiety the mother displayed in every tone and movement.

When all had been made safe for the night, the mother of Felipe went a little apart from the camp to pray. After the children were asleep the other women joined her, each for a little while,—moving sidewise while they prayed, to rest their knees from the hard stones.

There was no motion in the hills and the moon was shining. Benita felt her heart in her mouth. The click of the rosary sounded, as loud to her as the "*shriek, shriek*" of the night birds. The mother mumbled on,—"The Virgin will surely hear me,—she also is a mother,—he is my only son,—and I will burn my candles."

"Come," said Benita, "you must sleep. See how wet the grass is."

In the morning Felipe was dead.

The travelers had camped in a broad, sandy basin, strewn with boulders, cut across the deep irregular gullies, now concealed by a coarse rank growth of weeds and grass,—the dry bed of a mountain torrent.

The mother would not consent that Felipe should be buried here. "How shall I find my son if he be buried here?" she thought.

"It is well," said Antonio to the men. "It is hard to dig here, we will go on."

When they had come to a little rise of ground overlooking Lastac Lake, Antonio drew rein. "Shall it not be here?"

The woman shook her head.

Again in a little while,—"Shall it not be here?"

"Not yet. Not yet."

They were now well into the Cañon de Los Vinos. Great oaks lined the water-courses, and climbed half way up the hills. There were still green places by the springs, and running water. The cavalcade drew out from the roadside. "It must be here, Señora," said Antonio authoritatively.

The women sobbed vehemently, Benita loudest of all. The mother did not weep. She seemed suddenly to have fallen into the inscrutable old age that overtakes women of her race. She could look no older, and appeared never to have been young.

When it was over, some one cut Felipe's name on the oak under which they buried him.

At high noon the diminished party of wanderers passed slowly and with effort over the barrier that rears itself across the cañon's mouth like the outer rim of the world, dropping down into the vast, dim valley of the San Joaquin, hazy with the mists of its marshes, and the floating phantoms of mirage where the quivering light strikes back from the long vistas of its unsheltered sands.

After ten years the mother of Felipe no longer mourned openly for her son, but her face had forgotten any other expression than the look of inscrutable old age she had carried away from his grave. It had become as fixed as the contour of the hills or as the purpose in her heart.

Mass had been said for her son's soul; his body must not always lie in unblessed ground. After ten years God gave her an opportunity. Her brother's son and one of the men that had buried Felipe had affairs that took them within a few hours' journey of the Cañon de Los Vinos. It is not in the hearts of these people to deny a consolation to old age. They had little faith in the success of her undertaking: many trees had been cut down, the old wagon trail was obliterated, and the present stage road had been made on the other side of the cañon.

The mother felt no uncertainty. She had marked the place too well for that. A feverish excitement stirred her dull pulses. Yonder, under the blazed oak Felipe was lying,—his face was turned a little to one side,—the cross was on his breast.

Antonio had marked out the grave by the shadow of the straight, thick trunk, three paces from the foot of the tree. The men stepped off the distance, and began to dig. Presently they perceived that they had made a mistake. Felipe had been buried in the early morning, and it was now noon. They selected a new place more carefully, and began again.

Conversation flagged when they were knee deep; at waist deep, perspiration broke out suddenly. They threw down their shovels, and began to poke in the loosened earth with sticks, never with their hands.

First there was a collar bone, then an arm and a hand. The men threw the bones out upon the grass, shaking their hands free of the earth that clung to them. The mother of Felipe gathered the bones into her apron, stooping painfully. Age overcame her power of quick motion, moveover she was fat. Tears ran from her sunken eyes, and hung in the creases of her withered cheeks. Patches of damp mould clung to the unwholesome relics; these she wiped off upon the grass and on her dress.

The diggers finished their task quickly. She sat down upon the grass hugging the ghastly bundle to her breast, unwilling to allow it to be placed in the box prepared for it. She took up handfuls of the discolored earth and wept over it.

This purpose accomplished she had one other desire. She wished to see Benita. Antonio Lesalda, in pursuance with his nomadic instincts, had drifted back from the north into these very mountains and made his home in one of those innumerable triangular openings between the hills. This much she knew from floating bits of information that had reached her. She knew also that his wife was dead, and that Benita was still with him. The heart of the mother was very tender toward the woman who also mourned for her son. "We will not forget Felipe," the two women had sobbingly protested to each other at parting.

They found Lesalda's place with little difficulty, and Benita was very glad to see them. She put down her baby that she might discharge the duties of hospitality. When the youngster rolled over on the floor and cried she put both hands under his arms and dragged him into a sitting posture, chattering with short-breathed volubility.

"Did they not know she was married? Yes,—for five years, and she had three children. Her husband was in Los Angeles with the horses. Such a good man and so handsome,—but they would see; he would surely be home in a day or two. What? They must go on tonight!"

Benita was genuinely sorry for this; visitors were rare with her. The old woman had made her decision suddenly. The mother of her son would not stay in a house that had forgotten him. She had never contemplated the possibility of Benita's marriage; the fact came to her with all the shock of a flagrant desertion. She was almost dumb under the fire of Benita's good-natured questioning.

Now, what had she come for? For Felipe? "Ah! poor Felipe! But you should have stayed with me, and my father would have gone with the men. It is not for women to be digging in the graves of the dead."

An hour later the mother of Felipe, looking back from the last curve of the winding road, saw Benita balancing the baby with her fat hands while the bare, brown legs wavered through the intricacies of three short paces.

The treasured box of grisly relics had not been disturbed. Only in the hearts of mothers lives unconsolable regret.

The Conversion of Ah Lew Sing

Ah Lew Sing was the proprietor of a vegetable garden between the stockyard and the railroad bridge, on the farther side of the Summerfield Canal. He was the lankest, obliquest-eyed celestial that ever combined an expression of childlike innocence with the appearance of having fallen into a state of permanent disrepair.

Previous to his conversion, his ideas, if he had any, in regard to the Deity were hazy in the extreme; but his convictions on the subject of devils were concise and dogmatic. There were about three hundred according to Ah Lew Sing's computation; all of the most malevolent type. If the potatoes rotted, if the celery rusted, if the cabbages failed to head, and the blight got his early peas, Ah Lew Sing was at no loss where to lay the blame. All of these things frequently happened, notwithstanding he burned punk at the four corners of his fields and at all the foot-bridges that crossed his irrigating ditches, which were so narrow and low that no sort of devil could cross without wetting his feet, a thing to which Chinese devils are very much averse.

But in spite of the devils and a brisk competition in the vegetable trade, Ah Lew Sing was able to put by a moiety of his earnings which he further increased by judicious speculation with his friends Choc Sin, Sam Kee, and Foo Chou, choice spirits all. Choc Sin was more ignorant and cunning than Ah Lew Sing; Sam Kee was worse than Choc Sin; and when Foo Chou could dupe his friends he did so; when he could not, he consoled himself that none of them would ever be able to fleece him. But in this he reckoned without Ah Lew Sing.

The speculations of Foo Chou were various, including by preference anything sufficiently lawless and dangerous to make other people afraid of doing it. One of these chances of fortune put him in possession of the person of Li Choi, whose father had previously sold her for a sixteenth interest in a tea store on Dupont Street. Li Choi had very small feet and very large earrings and smooth glistening bands of hair with an astonishing number of jade ornaments stuck in them. Foo

Chou expected to make as much as three hundred dollars on her, and Foo Chou was a judge of marketable women. But the cunningest of speculators comes to grief now and then, and Foo Chou made the mistake of his life when he brought his three friends to the close red-curtained room where his property was sequestered, and permitted them to gaze through the hole he had cut in the door to display the charms of Li Choi.

The eyes of Ah Lew Sing had no sooner beheld her than the heart of Ah Lew Sing was consumed by love. Forthwith he began to suffer the pangs of disappointed affection, for his potato crop, owing perhaps to the devils, perhaps to a superfluity of water, was a failure, and the purse of Ah Lew Sing did not contain a cash equivalent for so much loveliness. While he debated the possibility of inducing that hardened piece of rascality to abate the price for friendship's sake, Foo Chou was growing morose. No purchaser was forthcoming for the lovely Li Choi, and she was costing him dear for her keep, besides wasting her loveliness with secret tears.

It was not because of any lack of appreciation of her charms that Foo Chou had not espoused her himself. In the gambling dens of Summerfield's Chinatown, Foo Chou was known as the most inveterate and unluckiest gambler of them all, and no profitable villainies being at hand, nothing but a cash price for Li Choi could replenish his failing fortunes.

What maiden fears and childish terrors and dread of outraged womanhood were endured in that little red-curtained room no one knew. No one unless perhaps Ah Phoo, who was grandfather at large to all the little pig-tailed celestials in Chinatown. He might have heard her crying as he squatted under her window while his shaved and sandaled little charges made a skipping-rope of his grizzled queue, which was pieced out an extra length for their especial accommodation.

Foo Chou, coming one morning to take stock of his property, found a strange key in the door and the room empty. Great was the wrath of Foo Chou, and such the questioning and gesticulating and running to and fro that Grandfather Phoo had to move his charges quite two blocks away to escape being trodden upon. Later, word came to Foo Chou that his property had taken refuge at the mission, whose gray walls towered at least a story and a half above the shabby roofs that sheltered Chinatown.

Foo Chou and his kind looked with marked disfavor on the mission and its mistress whose success in luring profitable females from their rightful masters was regarded as an unwarrantable interference in trade. The friends of Foo Chou advised an appeal to the law for the recovery of his property. Not, of course, that the law of this enlightened country recognized the lovely Li Choi as a legal chattel, but any number of respectable merchants in Chinatown were ready to swear to being the husband, father, or brother, or otherwise legal guardian, praying her restoration to his loving protection. The thing had been done before, but Foo Chou deemed it inadvisable for several reasons, chief of which was the recollection of a recent encounter with the law on his own account in a little operation connected with the opium trade, in which Foo Chou had come hardly off.

For the present, until some better plan could be devised, Li Choi must remain where she was. True, she might be converted to Christianity, but she was safe against any other chance and cost him nothing. As for the Christianity, Foo Chou had never seen a case of it so bad it could not be cured with two or three judicious beatings; nevertheless, he must keep as close a watch as circumstances permitted over the recreant Li Choi. Obviously this must be done by deputy, since the villainous face of Foo Chou, if recognized, would bring about the very thing he feared, namely, the removal of Li Choi to a mission in another part of the State, where she might be hopelessly lost to her proprietor.

In his perplexity he bethought himself of the guileless front of his friend Ah Lew Sing. Then it was that Ah Lew Sing congratulated himself that he had never confessed his tender attachment to Foo Chou, and his smile was bland enough to have deceived the Father of Mischief himself, as he purchased a primer and joined the night class at the mission. Faithfully for a week he poured over the intricacies of c-a-t and d-o-g, but never once did he catch a glimpse of the bright eyes of Li Choi, nor hear the pat-pat of her entrancing little feet. Now the mission school is but a trap to catch converts, and that the shrewd celestial knows as well as anybody, and is wary to avoid its pitfalls, but the conversion of Ah Lew Sing dated from the day he discovered that the converts of both sexes participated in the religious exercises.

From that time his growth in grace was astonishing. Within a week it carried him from a back seat near the door to the front row of shining examples beside Li Choi, who in the grateful promptings of her simple heart believed whatever she thought would please Miss Campbell, the matron of the mission. When they stood around the organ and sang, "Oh, how I love Jesus," Li Choi looked at Miss Campbell and Ah Lew Sing looked at Li Choi. "Me velly happy," was Ah Lew Sing's unfailing testimony. So Ah Lew Sing kept watch over Li Choi while Foo Chou perfected his plans. If the law, he reasoned, did not recognize his proprietary interest in the person of Li Choi, it could not deny his right to the jade ornaments which had been no inconsiderable item of the purchase price.

Foo Chou meant to swear out a warrant for the arrest of Li Choi for the theft of certain earrings, hair ornaments, and armlets which she did feloniously abstract from the residence of Foo Chou. While the arrest was in progress, the friends of Foo Chou would rush to the rescue of the distressed Li Choi and bear her away from the cruel arms of the law. Foo Chou thought for a sufficient sum the constable might even permit himself to be knocked down in defense of his prisoner. Foo Chou for reasons before mentioned being averse to appearing on the scene in person, it was agreed that the rescue should be conducted by Choc Sin and Sam Kee and that Ah Lew Sing should convey the prisoner to the safe place in the country to which the wily Foo Chou should retire after arranging the arrest.

It must be said, to Foo Chou's credit, that he left the management of an affair of such importance in the hands of his friends with reluctance; however, there was no help for it and he trusted to his well-known reputation for blood-thirstiness to ensure the fidelity of Choc Sin, Sam Kee, and Ah Lew Sing. He meant to stay quietly in the country until the affair had had time to blow over and then he hoped to get safely off to Sacramento where the traffic in small feet and bright eyes was flourishing. The arrest took place exactly as prescribed. At an hour when all Chinatown smoked its pipe and the charges of Grandfather Phoo napped in the shade, the constable rapped at the door and presented his warrant for Li Choi. Miss Campbell demurred and was lost; for while she suspected the design of Foo Chou, still the thing might have been contrived to herd her away from her other charges, more than one of whom was the alleged property of some enterprising celestial. While she debated the tearful Li Choi was hurried out of reach. The rescue was the most successful affair of the kind ever carried out in Chinatown. When Sam Lee and Choc Sin crept out of the cellar in which they had lain quiet during the perfunctory search carried on by a profane but not over-zealous officer, they glowed with honest pride to find nothing else talked of in the tea shops and laundries. Ah Lew Sing was not molested by the officers, for nobody testified to the bundle of quilted petticoat which was hustled under the canvas cover of his vegetable wagon waiting innocently around the corner.

What happened in the interim between the rescue and the return of Foo Chou on the third day, exceedingly wroth at what he supposed to be the total failure of his plans, can never be accurately known; whether the heart of Ah Lew Sing, meditating long and tenderly on the charms of Li Choi, had yielded to an overwhelming temptation, or whether his childlike countenance covered more duplicity than even Foo Chou gave him credit for, is open to debate. Perhaps the demure Li Choi did not greatly resist the manifest destiny of her sex. It is not to be supposed that she was unaware of all those devoted glances when they stood up in Sunday School and shared the same Gospel hymn-book. Certainly Li Choi did not want to be handed over to Foo Chou, neither did she want to go to jail, and, although a Chinaman in a vegetable wagon is not exactly an ideal knight errant rescuing a distressed damsel, it might have appeared so to Li Choi. At any rate, he carried her away to his own domicile with a serene disregard of consequences that did credit to his courage.

But the courage paled visibly before the information brought by the friendly Ah Phoo that Foo Chou had learned the real state of affairs and was coming with a very big knife to kill Ah Lew Sing and cut off his queue and carry Li Choi away. All of which might have come to pass had not Ah Lew Sing consulted with his friend the flagman at the railroad crossing. "What you want to do to keep anybody from touching your wife is to get married, alle samee white man, sabee?"

Ah Lew Sing reflected, to get married "alle samee white man" might make Li Choi secure, but it might also make it somewhat difficult if he should ever wish to get rid of her. But then Ah Lew Sing did not believe he would ever want to get rid of Li Choi. Besides, Foo Chou was coming with his knife. The flagman scribbled a line on the back of an old letter, "You take this to City Hall, give him to Mr McGee, he fix him all right." Half an hour later, while Foo Chou was furiously searching the premises of Ah Lew Sing, the worthy was helping his pretty bride up the steps of the City Hall, her parasol awry and her embroidered sandals sadly the worse for their hasty flight across lots. Ah Lew Sing, in the swelling of commendable pride at having out-witted the most notorious highbinder in Chinatown, built him a house that was quite large enough to swing a cat in, and as gorgeous inside as a Joss house and quite as dingy without, with the wisdom of Confucius done in very large characters on very red paper pasted all about the front door.

Ah Lew Sing has returned to his old occupation of fighting devils. A three-hundred-dollar wife must be supported in a style to correspond with her worth; besides, there is a little Ah Lew Sing who is expected to grow up and become a mandarin with a green button on his hat and must be looked after accordingly.

Ah Lew Sing never went back to the mission, although Miss Campbell visited him as soon as she heard of the wedding and exhorted him to hold fast to the faith that he had. His wife goes sometimes and sits in her old seat, but it is simply an act of grateful remembrance like the packages of nice stale duck eggs and roasted watermelon seeds that find their way occasionally to Grandfather Phoo.

As for Foo Chou, he departed for regions unknown. He might have devised new rascalities to compensate for the loss of his property, but to be overreached by a mere vegetable gardener, a man who worked for a living! After that no self-respecting highbinder could hold up his head.

The Search for Jean Baptiste

I One bred to the hills and the care of dumb, helpless things must in the end, whatever else befalls, come back to them. That is the comfort they give him for their care and the revenge they have of their helplessness. If this were not so Gabriel Lausanne would never have found Jean Baptiste. Babette, who was the mother of Jean Baptiste and the wife of Gabriel, understood this also, and so came to her last sickness in more comfort of mind than would have been otherwise possible; for it was understood between them that when he had buried her, Gabriel was to go to America to find Jean Baptiste.

He had been a good son to them in his youth and good to look upon: a little short of stature,—no taller, in fact, than Babette, who was a head shorter than Gabriel—but broad in the shoulders and strong in the thighs beyond belief. But the strength of his thews and sinews had been Jean Baptiste's undoing. About the time he came to the age of a man and the fullness of his strength, he began to think too much of himself and his cleverness in breaking other people's collar-bones by pitching them over his shoulder.

The towns drew him; the hills had no power to hold. He left minding the sheep; he sought jolly companions, and went boisterously about with them from inn door to inn door. Finally the fame of his wrestling spread until there were few men in the province dared try a fall with him. From bragging he went to broiling, and at last fell into such grievous trouble that there was nothing for it but to slip away to America between the night and the morning.

Then Gabriel and Babette, who had not thought before to take stock of their years, began to understand that they were old, and at the time when they had looked to see children's children about their knees, Babette had slipped away to find the little ones who died before Jean Baptiste was born, and Gabriel was beginning his search for Jean Baptiste, the well beloved.

America is a wide land, but the places in it where men fare forth to the hills with sheep are known and limited; and when he had inquired where these were, there, because of the faith he had, went Gabriel Lausanne. He came, in the course of a year, to the shepherd world that lies within the Sierra Nevada and its outlying spurs. For it is known that the shepherds of the Sierras are strange, Frenchmen, Basques mostly, and a few Mexicans, but never an English-speaking one, from the Temblor Hills to the Minaretts.

Things went hardly with Gabriel at first, for he was new to the land and bewildered by its bigness; but once he had gotten a place to help at lambing-time his work was assured, for there was little he did not know about lambs. And finally he was given charge of a flock, and went wandering with it into the high glacier meadows, learning the haps and seasons of the hills. He got to know the trails and the landmark peaks, what meadows were free and what could be rented for a song, the trail of bear and wildcat, the chances of snow in August, and all shepherd's lore. He knew the brands of sheep as a man knows the faces of his neighbors, and from the signs of the trails how they fared that were ahead of him, and how to prosper his own.

All this time he had not left off inquiring for Jean Baptiste, though the manner in which he should do this gave much trouble of mind to Gabriel Lausanne. He thought it reasonable to suppose that Jean Baptiste had not kept his own name, lest the old wrong should find him out by means of it. And if it should come to his ears that inquiries were made concerning him, he might be more careful to hide himself, suspecting an enemy. In the end Gabriel had to content himself asking every man he met for news of his son, whom he loved dearly and would find.

"Jean Baptiste, your father loves you," he wrote upon the rocks; "Jean Baptiste, your father loves you," he cut painstakingly upon the blazed trunks of pines; and "Jean Baptiste!" he whispered nightly to the wide-open stars when he lay with his flocks wintering on the sunward slopes of the Little Antelope.

II So the years went over him, and his heart warmed toward the big new land where any meadow might hold his son, or any coyote-scaring fire might be Jean Baptiste's.

By as many shepherds as he met Gabriel Lausanne was respected for his knowledge of ailing sheep, and laughed at for his simple heart, but as yet he had not come up with the shepherds of Los Alamos. The Los Alamos grant covered thousands of acres of good pasturelands, but they counted their flocks and herds by tens of thousands, and reached out as far as they could or dared into the free forest-lands and the glacier meadows set between.

They sent out large flocks, strong and well shepherded; and what they could not get by the fair right of first comers, they took by force and wile. They wrested the best feeding-grounds from small shepherds by the sheer force of numbers, and when they met with bands strong and adventurous as their own, the shepherds cracked one another's heads merrily with their long staves, and the pasture went to the men with the thickest skulls.

They were bold rogues, those shepherds of Los Alamos. They would head their flocks away from the line of the Forest Reserve, un-der the ranger's eye, and as soon as his head was turned cut back to the forbidden pastures, and out again before he could come up with them.

They turned streams out of their courses, and left uncovered fires behind them to run unchecked in the wood, for the sake of the new feed that grew up in the burned districts. For them the forest existed only to feed sheep, and Los Alamos sheep at that.

There are shepherds in the Sierras who from long association grow into a considerable knowledge of woodcraft and have respect for the big trees, but not the shepherds of Los Alamos. No doubt there was much mischief charged to them which was not properly their own, but in any event they had never been loved, and were even dreaded because of that one of them who was called "The Mule."

Every shepherd has two names—the one he signs to his contract and the one he is known by. The Mule, so called because of a certain manner of surly silence and the exceeding breadth and strength of his back, had been picked up by Le Berge, the head shepherd, at a shearing, poorly clad and wholly at the end of his means. There was that in his look and the way in which he handled a sheep that made it plain that he had been born to it; and when he had plucked up a man who annoyed him and pitched him over his shoulder, Le Berge loved him as a brother. He hired him forth-with, though he had to discharge another man to make place for him. And now it was said that whoever came in the way of the shepherds of Los Alamos must try a fall with The Mule for the right of feeding-grounds; and the fame of his wrestling was such that timid shepherds kept well away from his trail.

III Gabriel Lausanne, keeping to the small meadows and treeless hills, had not yet fallen in with the flocks of Los Alamos. The fifth year of his shepherding there was no rain at all on the inland ranges. The foot-hill pastures failed early, and by the middle of July the flocks were all driven to the feeding-grounds of the high Sierras.

Gabriel came early to Manache, a chain of grassy, gentian-flowered plats strung on the thread of a snow-fed brook, large and open, and much frequented by shepherds. In Manache, if one waits long enough, one gets to know all the flocks and every shepherd ranging between Tahoe and Temblors. Gabriel, a little wearied at heart, purposed to stay the summer through in that neighborhood, moving only as the flock required.

Jean Baptiste he knew must come to the hills as surely as the swallow to the eves or the stork to her chimney, but he was perplexed by the thought that in the years that had passed so many changes had come to them both that they might unwittingly meet and pass each other. He wished that he might find other messengers than the wind and the rain-washed rocks and the fast-obliterating pines. And while Gabriel pondered these things with a sore heart, two thousand of the Los Alamos sheep poured down upon his meadow from the upper pass.

Their shuddering bleat, their jangling bells, sounded unseen among the tamarack pines all the half of one day before they found him. But when they came into the open and saw him feeding down the stream-side among the dwarf willows, the shepherds of Los Alamos promised themselves great sport.

Le Berge, walking lazily at the head of his flock, spoke a word to his dogs, and the dogs in their own fashion spoke to the flock, and straight-way the sheep began to pour steadily down the meadow and around the flock of Gabriel; for that was a way they of Los Alamos had—compelling small shepherds to keep their sheep parted out at their own cost.

"And what do you here, friend?" said Le Berge, when he had reached Gabriel.

"I feed my flock," answered the old man. "The pasture is free. Also I seek my son."

The under-shepherds came hurrying, expecting to be greatly entertained, and one called to another, "Hi, Mule, here is work for you!"

The man so called came slowly and in silence, a short man, but close-knit and broad in the shoulders, a wrestler by the look of him, and leaning upon his staff until his part of the entertainment should begin.

"Free is it," said Le Berge, still to Gabriel. "Yes, free to those who can hold it. By the turn of your tongue you should be from Bourdonne. Here, Mule, is a countryman of thine. Come teach him the law of the feeding-ground."

"I am an old man," said Gabriel, "and I wish no harm. Help me out with my flock and I will be gone. But you," he said to The Mule, "are you truly of Bourdonne? I am Gabriel Lausanne, and I seek my son, Jean Baptiste, whom I love. We also are of Bourdonne; it may be you can tell where he is to be found."

"Enough said," cried Le Berge. "Up with him, Mule."

IV And then the shepherds of Los Alamos looked with mouths agape to see that The Mule stood still, and the knuckles of the hand that grasped his staff were strained and white. The voice of Gabriel quavered on amid the bleating of the sheep:

"If you are surely of Bourdonne you will earn an old man's blessing; and say to him that his mother is dead, and his father has come to find him. Say to my son, 'Jean Baptiste, your father loves you.'" The old man stooped a little, that he might meet The Mule eye to eye.

"Jean Baptiste," he said again, and then his staff shook in his hands, though there was no wind, and his voice shook, too, with a sudden note of hope and doubt and wistful inquiry. "Jean Baptiste," he cried, "your father loves you! Jean Baptiste—"

Jean Baptiste, called The Mule, dropped his staff and wept with his face between his hands, and his whole strong frame shook with emotion, and his father fell on his neck and kissed him.

So Gabriel found his son.

V And now it is said that there are no better shepherds in the Sierras than the two Lausannes, the one famed for his skill with the lambs, the other for his knowledge of the feeding-grounds.

They will not be hired apart, and it is believed that it will be so until the end; for it is said at shearings, as a joke that is half believed, that when father Gabriel is too old to walk, The Mule will carry him.

They are a silent pair, and well content to be so; but as often as they come by Manache, when they sit by the twilight fire at the day's end, Gabriel puts out his hand to his son, saying softly, as of old habit, "Jean Baptiste, your father loves you"; and The Mule, patting the hand upon his arm, makes answer, "Ay, father; Jean Baptiste knows."

A Case of Conscience

Saunders was an average Englishman with a lung complaint. He tried Ashfork, Arizona, and Indio, and Catalina. Then he drifted north through the San Jacinta mountains and found what he was looking for. Back in England he had left so many of the things a man wishes to go on with, that he bent himself with great seriousness to his cure. He bought a couple of pack-burros, a pair of cayaques, and a camp kit. With these, a Shakespeare, a prayer-book, and a copy of *Ingoldsby Legends*, he set out on foot to explore the coast of Lost Borders. The prayer-book he had from his mother; I believe he read it regularly night and morning, and the copy of *Ingoldsby Legends* he gave me in the second year of his exile. It happened about that time I was wanting the *Ingoldsby Legends*, three hundred miles from a library, and book money hard to come by. Now there is nearly always a copy of *Ingoldsby Legends* in the vicinity of an Englishman. Englishmen think them amusing, though I do not know why. So I asked my friend, the barkeeper at the Last Chance, to inquire for it of the next Englishman who hit the town. I had to write the name out plainly so the barkeeper could remember it. The first who came was an agent for a London mining syndicate, and he left an address of a book-shop where it could be bought. The next was a remittance man, and of course he hadn't anything. If he had he would have put it in soak. That means he would have put the book up for its value in bad drink, and I write it as a part of our legitimate speech, because it says so exactly what had occurred: that particular Englishman had put everything, including his honor and his immortal soul, in soak. And the third was Saunders. He was so delighted to find an appreciator of the *Ingoldsby Legends* in the wilderness, that he offered to come to the house and render the obscure passages, and that was the beginning of my knowing about what went on later at Ubehebe.

Saunders had drifted about from water-hole to water-hole, living hardily, breathing the driest, cleanest air, sleeping and waking with the ebb and flow of light that sets in a mighty current around the world. He went up in summer to the mountain heads under the foxtail pines, and back in winter to watch the wild almond bloom by Resting Springs. He saw the Medicine dance of the Shoshones, and hunted the bighorn on Funeral Mountains, and dropped a great many things out of his life without making himself unhappy. But he kept the conscience he had brought with him. Of course it was a man's conscience that allowed him to do a great many things that by the code and the commandments are as wrong as any others, but in the end the wilderness was too big for him, and forced him to a violation of what he called his sense of duty.

In the course of time, Saunders came to a range of purplish hills lying west from Lost Valley, because of its rounded, swelling, fair twin peaks called Ubehebe (Maiden's Breast). It is a good name. Saunders came there in the spring, when the land is lovely and alluring, soft with promise and austerely virgin. He lingered in and about its pleasant places until the month of the Deer-Star, and it was then, when he would come up a week's journey to Lone Pine, for supplies, he began to tell me about Turwhasé, the gray-eyed Shoshone. He thought I would be interested, and I was, though for more reasons than Saunders at first supposed. There is a story current and confirmed, I believe, by proper evidence, that a man of one of the emigrant trains that suffered so much, and went so far astray in the hell trap of Death Valley, wandering from his party in search of water, for want of which he was partly crazed, returned to them no more and was accounted dead. But wandering in the witless condition of great thirst, he was found by the Shoshones, and by them carried to their campody in the secret places of the hills. There, though he never rightly knew himself, he showed some skill and excellences of the white man, and for that, and for his loose wit, which was fearful to them, he was kept and reverenced as a Coyote-man and a Medicine-maker of strange and fitful powers. And at the end of fifteen years his friends found him and took him away. As witness of his sojourning, there is now and then born to the descendants of that campody a Shoshone with gray eyes.

When Saunders began to tell me about Turwhasé, I knew to what it must come, though it was not until his mother wrote me that I could take any notice of it. Some too solicitous person had written her that Saunders had become a squaw-man. She thought he had married Turwhasé, and would bring home a handful of little half-breeds to inherit the estate.

She never knew how near Saunders came to doing that very thing, nor to say truth did I when I wrote her that her son was not married, and that she had nothing to fear; but with the letter I was able to get out of Saunders as much as I did not already know of the story.

I suppose at bottom the things a man loves a woman for are pretty much the same, though it is only when he talks to you of a woman not of his own class that he is willing to tell you what those things are. Saunders loved Turwhasé: first, because he was lonely and had to love somebody; then because of the way the oval of her cheek melted into the chin, and for the lovely line that runs from the waist to the knee, and for her soft, bubbling laughter; and kept on loving her because she made him comfortable.

I suppose the white strain that persisted in her quickened her aptitude for white ways. Saunders taught her to cook. She was never weary nor afraid. She was never out of temper, except when she was jealous, and that was rather amusing. Saunders told me himself how she glowed and blossomed under his caress, and wept when he neglected her. He told me everything I had the courage to know. When a man has gone about the big wilderness with slow death and sure camping on his trail, there is not much worth talking about except the things that are. Turwhasé had the art to provoke tenderness and the wish to protect, and the primitive woman's capacity for making no demands upon it. And this, in fine, is how these women take our men from us, and why, at the last, they lose them.

If you ask whether we discussed the ethics of Saunders' situation— at first there didn't appear to be any. Turwhasé was as much married as if Church and State had witnessed it; as for Saunders, society, life itself, had cast him off. He was unfit for work or marrying; being right-minded in regard to his lung complaint, he drank from no man's cup nor slept in any bed but his own. And if society had no use for him, how had it a right to say what he should do out there in the bloomy violet spaces at Maiden's Breast? Yet, at the last, the Englishman found, or thought he found, a moral issue.

Maiden's Breast—virgin land, clear sun, unsullied airs, Turwhasé. Isn't there a hint all through of the myth of the renewal of life in a virgin embrace? A great many myths come true in the big wilderness. Saunders went down to Los Angeles once in the year to a consulting physician to please his mother, not because he hoped for anything. He came back from one such journey looking like a sleepwalker newly awakened. He had been told that the diseased portion of his lung was all sloughed away, and if nothing happened to him in six months more of Ubehebe, he might go home! It was then Saunders' conscience began to trouble him, for by this time, you understand, Turwhasé had a child—a daughter, small and gold-colored and gray-eyed. By a trick of inheritance the eyes were like Saunders' mother's, and in the long idle summer she had become a plaything of which he was extremely fond. The mother, of course, was hopeless. She had never left off her blanket, and like all Indian women when they mature, had begun to grow fat. Oh, I *said* he had a man's conscience! Turwhasé must be left behind, but what to do about the daughter lay heavily on Saunders' mind.

It made an obstinate ripple in his complacency like a snag in the current of his thought, which set toward England. Out there by the water-holes, where he had expected to leave his bones, life had been of a simplicity that did not concern itself beyond the happy day. Now the old needs and desires awoke and cried in him, and along with them the old, obstinate Anglo-Saxon prejudice that makes a man responsible for his offspring. Saunders must have had a bad time of it with himself before he came to a decision that he must take the child to England. It would be hard on Turwhasé; if it came to that, it would be hard on him—there would be explanations. As matters stood he looked to make a very good marriage at home, and the half-breed child would be against him. All his life she would be against him. But then it was a question of duty. Duty is a potent fetish of Englishmen, but the wilderness has a word bigger than that. Just how Turwhasé took his decision about the child I never heard, but as I know Indian women, I suppose she must have taken it quietly at first, said no, and considered it done with; then, as she saw his purpose clear, sat wordless in her blanket, all its folds drawn forward as a sign of sullenness, her thick hair falling on either side to screen her grief; neither moved to attend him, nor ate nor slept; and at last broke under it and seemed to accept, put the child from her as though it was already not hers, and made no more of it.

If there was in this acquiescence a gleam in her gray eye that witnessed she had found the word, Saunders was not aware of it.

As to what he felt himself in regard to Turwhasé I am equally uninformed. I've a notion, though, that men do not give themselves time to feel in such instances; they just get it over with. All I was told was, that when at last he felt himself strong for it, Saunders put the child before him on the horse—she was then about two years old—and set out from Ubehebe. He went all of one day down a long box cañon, where at times his knees scraped the walls on either side, and over the tortuous roots of the mountain blown bare of the sand. The evening of the next day saw the contour of the Maiden's Breast purpling in the east, fading at last in the blurred horizon. He rode all day on glittering pale sands and down steep and utterly barren barrancas. All through that riding something pricked between his shoulders, troubled his sleep with expectancy, haunted him with a suggestion of impossible espionage. The child babbled at first, or slept in his arm; he hugged it to him and forgot that its mother was a Shoshone. It cried in the night and began to refuse its food. Great tears of fatigue stood upon its cheeks; it shook with long, quivering sobs, crying silently as Indian children do when they are frightened. Saunders' arm ached with the weight of it; his heart with the perplexity. The little face looked up at him, hard with inscrutable savagery. When he came to the Inyo range and the beaten trail, he distrusted his judgment; his notion of rearing the child in England began to look ridiculous. By the time he had cleared the crest and saw the fields and orchards far below him, it appeared preposterous. And the hint of following hung like some pestiferous insect about his trail.

In all the wide, uninterrupted glare no speck as of a moving body swam within his gaze. By what locked and secret ways the presence kept pace with him, only the vultures hung high under the flaring heaven could have known.

At the hotel at Keeler that night he began to taste the bitterness he had chosen. Men, white men, mining men, mill superintendents, well-dressed, competent, looked at the brat which had Shoshone written plainly all over it, and looked away unsmiling; being gentlemen, they did not so much as look at one another. Sanders [sic] gave money to the women at the hotel to keep his daughter all night out of his sight. Riding next day toward Lone Pine between the fenced lands, farms and farmhouses, schools, a church, he began to understand that there was something more than mere irresponsibility in the way of desert-faring men who formed relations such as this and left them off with the land, as they left the clothes they wore there and its tricks of speech.

He was now four days from Ubehebe. The child slept little that night; sat up in bed, listened; would whisper its mother's name over and over, questioning, expectant; left off, still as a young quail, if Saunders moved or noticed it. It occurred to him that the child might die, which would be the best thing for it.

Coming out of his room in the early morning he stumbled over something soft in a blanket. It unrolled of itself and stood up— Turwhasé! The child gave a little leap in his arms and was still, pitifully, breathlessly still. The woman stretched out her own arms, her eyes were red and devouring.

"My baby!" she said. "Give it to me!" Without a word Saunders held it out to her. The little dark arms went around her neck, prehensile and clinging; the whole little body clung, the lines of the small face softened with a sigh of unutterable content. Turwhasé drew up her blanket and held it close.

"Mine!" she said, fiercely. "Mine, not yours!"

Saunders did not gainsay her; he drew out all the money he had and poured it in her bosom. Turwhasé laughed. With a flirt of her blanket she scattered the coins on the ground; she turned with dignity and began to walk desertward. You could see by the slope of the shoulders under the blanket and the swing of her hips, as she went, that she was all Indian.

Saunders reached down to me from the platform of the train that morning for a last goodby. He was looking very English, smug and freshly shaven.

"I am convinced," he said, "that it really wouldn't have done, you know." I believe he thought he had come to that conclusion by himself.

What I like most about the speech of the campody is that there are no confidences. When they talk there of the essential performances of life, it is because they are essential and therefore worth talking about. Only Heaven, who made my heart, knows why it should have become a pit, bottomless and insatiable for the husks of other people's experiences, as if it were not, as I declare it, filled to the brim with the entertainment of its own affairs; as if its mere proximity were an advertisement for it, there must be always some one letting fall confidences as boys drop stones in wells, to listen afterward in some tale of mine for the faint, reverberating sound. But this is the mark of sophistication, that they always appear *as* confidences, always with that wistful back-stroke of the ego toward a personal distinction. "I don't know why I am telling you this—I shouldn't like to have you repeat it"—and then the heart loosening intimacy of speech and its conscious easement.

But in a campody it is possible to speak of the important operations of life without shamefacedness. Mid-afternoons of late fall and winter weather—for though you may speak to your brother man without curtailment, it is not well to do so in summer when the snakes are about, for the snakes are two-tongued and carry word to the gods, who, if they are to be of use to you, must not know too much of your affairs—in mid-afternoon then, when the women weave baskets and grind at the metate, and the men make nets and snares, there is good talk and much to be learned by it. Such times the sky is hard like polished turquoise set in the tawny matrix of the earth, the creek goes thinly over the stones, and the very waters of mirage are rolled back to some shut fountain in the skies; the *plump, plump!* of the metate beats on under the talk of the women like the comfortable pulse of not too insistent toil.

When Indian women talk together, and they are great gossips, three things will surely come to the surface in the course of the afternoon—children, marriage, and the ways of the whites. This last appears as a sort of pageant, which, though it is much of it sheer foolishness, is yet charged with a mysterious and compelling portent. They could never, for example, though they could give you any number of fascinating instances, get any rational explanation of the effect of their familiar clear space and desertness upon the white man adventuring in it. It was as if you had discovered in your parlor-furniture an inexplicable power of inciting your guest to strange behavior. And what in the conduct of men most interests women of the campody, or women anywhere for that matter, is their relation to women. If this, which appears to have rooted about the time the foundations of the earth were laid, is proved amenable to the lack of shade, scarcity of vegetation, and great spaces disinterested of men—not these of course, but the Power moving nakedly in the room of these things—it only goes to show that the relation is more incidental than we are disposed to think it. There is nothing in the weather and the distance between water-holes to affect a man's feeling for his children, as I have already explained to you in the case of Saunders and Mr. Wills. But there where the Borders run out, through all the talk of the women, white women, too, who get no better understanding of the thing they witness to, through the thin web of their lives moves the vast impersonal rivalry of desertness. But because of what I said in the beginning I can tell you no more of that than I had from Tiawa in the campody of Sacabuete, where there are no confidences.

The Man Who Lied About a Woman

Everybody knew that the girl who passed for the daughter of Tizessína was neither her daughter nor a Jicarilla Apache. Tizessína, being childless, had bought her, squalling, from a Navajo whose wife had died in giving birth, and she loved her inordinately, She was called Tall Flower after the hundred-belled white yucca, and carried herself always with the consciousness of superior blood. None of the Jicarilla youths, it seemed, were good enough for her. When Tizessína, who was as anxious as any real mother to see the girl well settled, asked her what she wanted, "I shall know when I see it," said Tall Flower, and continued to give the young men who walked with her the squashes. For she was the sort that every man desired and herself desired nothing. She laughed and went her way, and whatever she did Tizessína approved.

Nevertheless, she was disappointed when the girl hunched her shoulder to Natáldin, who, besides being the richest young man of the Apaches, was much sought after and would require careful handling. "But, my mother," laughed Tall Flower, "I shall handle him not at all."

This being her way with him, Natáldin, who was used to having marriageable girls go to a great deal of trouble on his account, was hurt in his self-esteem. To keep the other young men from finding out that with the daughter of Tizessína he had to take all the trouble himself, he took the manner when he walked with her of a lover who is already successful. He stuck a flower in his hat and swung his blanket from his shoulder until Tizessína herself began to nod and wink when the other women hinted.

Then suddenly Tall Flower went off overnight with her mother and two or three other women to Taos Pueblo to gather wild plums for drying. She went without letting Natáldin know, and, when the young men of Jicarilla found this out, they laughed and presented him with a large ripe squash. Nothing like this having happened to the young man before, he stiffened his lip and swung his shoulder. "And if I did not get the young woman," he said, "I got as much as I wanted of her."

No one liked to ask him what he meant by this, for to the others the girl had been as straight and as aloof as her name flower, and to take away a maiden's honor is a serious matter among the Jicarilla Apaches. But Natáldin, for the very reason that he had had not so much from Tall Flower as the touching of her littlest finger, salved his pride with looks and shrugs and by changing the subject when her name was mentioned. The truth was that he was afraid to talk of her, not for fear he might tell more than was seemly, but for fear somebody might find out what he had lately discovered, that if he did not have the daughter of Tizessína to be his wife, his life would be as a wild gourd, smooth without, but within a mouthful of bitter ashes.

The girl and her mother went not only to Taos Pueblo where the plum branches are bent over with bright fruit, but to Taos town, where a white man persuaded Tall Flower to be painted among the plum branches. Then they gathered *osha* in the hills toward Yellow Earth, where Tizessína, who was Government School taught, stayed for a month to cook for a camp of Government surveyors. In the month of the Cold Touching Mildly, they came to Jicarilla again.

Natáldin, who found Tall Flower more to be desired than ever, was in two minds how he should punish her, but unfortunately what was in his mind turned out to be so much less than what was in his heart that he ended by thinking only how he could persuade her to be his wife. Tizessína, he saw, was wholly on his side, but some strange fear of her daughter kept her silent. Natáldin would catch her looking at him as though she wished him to know something that she feared to tell. At other times Tizessína looked at Natáldin from behind a fold of her blanket as a wild thing watches a hunter from the rocks, while Tall Flower looked over and beyond them both. There was a dream in her eyes, and now and then it flowered around her mouth.

Presently there began to be other looks: matrons watching Tall Flower out of the tails of their eyes, young girls walking in the twilight with their arms about one another, looking the other way as she passed; young men look[ing] slyly at Natáldin, with laughs and nudges. Natáldin, who was sick to think that another had possessed her, where he had got the squash, denied nothing. If he remembered the punishment that is due to a man who lies about a woman, he reflected that a woman who has given herself to one lover is in no position to deny that she has given herself to two. But in fact he reflected very little. He was a man jabbing at an aching tooth in the hope of driving out one pain with another. It had been midsummer when Tizessína had taken her daughter to gather plums, and in the month of Snow Water, Tall Flower being far gone with child, the two women talked together in their house.

"I have heard," said Tizessína, "that Natáldin tells it about camp that he is the father of your child."

"Since how long?" said Tall Flower.

"Since before we had come to Taos town," said the mother, and repeated all she had heard.

"Then he has twice lied," said the girl.

"He is the richest man in Jicarilla, as well as a liar," said Tizessína, "and you will not get a husband very easily after this. I shall bring it to Council."

"What he does to another, that to him also," said the girl, which is a saying of the Apaches. "By all means take it to Council. But I shall not appear."

When Natáldin saw the *algucil* coming to call him before the Council, he was half glad, for now his tooth was about to come out. But he was sick when he saw that the girl was not there; only Tizessína, who stood up and said, "O my fathers! You know that my daughter is with child, and this one says that he is the father of it. This is established by many witnesses. Therefore, if he is the father, let him take my daughter to his house. But if he has lied, then let him be punished as is the custom for a man who has lied about a woman."

Said the Council, "Have you lied?" and Natáldin saw that he was between the bow and the bowstring.

"Only Tall Flowers knows if I have lied," he said, "and she does not appear against me. But I am willing to take her to my house, and the child also."

"So let it be," said the Council; and the young man's tooth was stopped, waiting to see whether it would come out or not.

But Tall Flower, when the judgment was reported to her, made conditions. "I will come to his house and cook for him and mend," she said, "but until after the child is born I will not come to his bed." And Natáldin, to whom nothing mattered except that now Tall Flower should be his wife, consented. Although he was tormented at times by the thought of that other who had had all his desire of her where Natáldin himself had got the squash, the young man salved his torment by thinking that, now the girl was his wife, nobody would be able to say that he has not also been her lover. He thought that when he told the daughter of Tizessína that he had lied to save her shame, she would never shame him by telling that he had lied. What nobody knows, nobody doubts; which is also a saying of the Jicarilla Apaches. Therefore, when he walked abroad with his young wife, Natáldin carried himself as a man who has done all that can be expected of him. As for Tizessína, she walked like the mother-in-law of the richest young man in Jicarilla, and Tall Flower walked between them, dreaming.

In due time, as he worked in his field Natáldin saw Tizessína and the neighbor women hurrying to his house, after which he worked scarcely at all, but leaned upon his hoe until the sun was a bowshot from its going down, and listened to the shaking of his own heart. As he came up the trail to his house at last, he saw his wife lying under the *ramada*, and beside her Tizessína with something wrapped in a blanket. "Let me see my son," he said, and wondered why the neighbor women rose and hurried away with their blankets over their faces, for with the first-born there should be compliments and present-giving. But when Tizessína turned back the blanket and showed him the child's face, he knew that after all he should not escape the punishment of a man who has lied about a woman. For the child was white!

The Woman at the Eighteen-Mile

I had long wished to write a story of Death Valley that should be its final word. It was to be so chosen from the limited sort of incidents that could occur there, so charged with the still ferocity of its moods that I should at length be quit of its obsession, free to concern myself about other affairs. And from the moment of hearing of the finding of Lang's body at Dead Man's Spring I knew I had struck upon the trail of that story.

It was a teamster who told it, stopping over the night at McGee's, a big, slow man, face and features all of a bluntness, as if he had been dropped before the clay was set. He had a big, blunt voice through which his words rolled, dulled along the edges. The same accident that had flattened the outlines of his nose and chin must have happened to his mind, for he was never able to deliver more than the middle of an idea, without any definiteness as to where it began or ended and what it stood next to. He called the dead man Long, and failed to remember who was supposed to have killed him, and what about.

We had fallen a-talking round the fire of Convict Lake, and the teamster had handed up the incident of Dead Man's Spring as the only thing in his experience that matched with the rooted horror of its name. He had been of the party that recovered the body, and what had stayed with him was the sheer torment of the journey across Death Valley, the aching heat, the steady, sickening glare, the uncertainty as to whether there was a body in the obliterated grave, whether it was Lang's body, and whether they would be able to prove it; and then the exhuming of the dead, like the one real incident in a fever dream. He was very sure of the body, done up in an Indian blanket striped red and black, with a rope around it like a handle, convenient for carrying. But he had forgotten what set the incident in motion, or what became of Lang after that, if it really were Lang in the blanket.

Then I heard of the story again between Red Rock and Coyote Holes, about moon-set, when the stage labored up the long gorge, waking to hear the voices of the passengers run on steadily with the girding of the sand and the rattle of harness-chains, run on and break and eddy around Dead Man's Spring, and back up in turgid pools of comment and speculation, falling in shallows of miner's talk, lost at last in a waste of ledges and contracts and forgotten strikes. Waking and falling asleep again, the story shaped itself of the largeness of the night; and then the two men got down at Coyote Holes an hour before dawn, and I knew no more of them, neither face nor name. But what I had heard of the story confirmed it exactly, the story I had so long sought.

Those who have not lived in a mining country cannot understand how it is possible for whole communities to be so disrupted by the failure of a lode or a fall in the price of silver, that I could live seven years within a day's journey of Dead Man's Spring and not come upon anybody who could give me the whole of that story. I went about asking for it, and got sticks and straws. There was a man who had kept bar in Tio Juan at the time, and had been the first to notice Whitmark's dealing with the Shoshone who was supposed to have stolen the body after it was dug up. There was a Mexican who had been the last to see Lang alive and might have told somewhat, but death got him before I did. Once, at a great dinner in San Francisco, a large, positive man with a square forehead and a face below it that somehow implied he had shaped it so butting his way through life, across the table two places down, caught at some word of mine, leaning forward above the bank of carnations that divided the cloth.

"Queer thing happened up in that country to a friend of mine, Whitmark—" But the toast-master cut *him* off. All this time the story glimmered like a summer island in a mist, through every man's talk about it, grew and allured, caressing the soul. It had warmth and amplitude, like a thing palpable to be stroked. There was a mine in it, a murder and a mystery, great sacrifice, Shoshones, dark and incredibly discreet, and the magnetic will of a man making manifest through all these; there were lonely water-holes, deserted camps where coyotes hunted in the streets, fatigues and dreams and voices of the night. And at the last it appeared there was a woman in it.

Curiously, long before I learned of her connection with the story, I had known and liked her for a certain effect she had of being warmed and nourished from within. There was about her a spark, a nuance that men mistook—never more than once, as the stage-driver told me confidently—a vitality that had nothing, absolutely nothing, but the blank occasionless life of the desert to sustain it. She was one of the very few people I had known able to keep a soul alive and glowing in the wilderness, and I was to find out that she kept it so against the heart of my story. Mine! I called it so by that time; but hers was the right, though she had no more pertinence to the plot than most women have to desert affairs.

She was the Woman of the Eighteen-Mile House. She had the desert mark upon her—lean figure, wasted bosom, the sharp, upright furrow between the eyes, the burned, tawny skin, with the pallid streak of the dropped eyelids, and of course I suppose she knew her husband from among the lean, sidling, vacuous-looking Borderers; but I couldn't have identified him, so like he was to the other feckless men whom the desert sucks dry and keeps dangling like gourds on a string. Twenty-five years they had drifted from up Bodie way, around Panimint, toward Mojave, worse housed and fed than they might have been in the ploughed lands, and without having hit upon the fortune which is primarily the object of every desert adventure. And when people have been as long as that among the Lost Borders there is not the slightest possibility of their coming to anything else. And still the Woman's soul was palpitant and enkindled. At the last, Mayer—that was the husband's name—had settled at the Eighteen-Mile House to care for the stage relays, and I had met the Woman, halting there with the stage or camping nights on some slower passage.

At the time I learned of her connection with the Whitmark affair, the story still wanted some items of motive and understanding, a knowledge of the man himself, some account of his three months' *pasear* into the hills beyond Mesquite, which certainly had to do with the affair of the mine, but of which he would never be persuaded to speak. And I made perfectly sure of getting the rest of it from the Woman at the Eighteen-Mile.

It was full nine o'clock before the Woman's household was all settled and she had come out upon the stoop of the Eighteen-Mile to talk, the moon coming up out of Shoshone land, all the hollow of the desert falling away before us, filled with the glitter of that surpassing wonder, the moon-mirage. Never mind what went before to draw her to the point of talking; it could have come about as simply as my saying, "I mean to print this story as I find it," and she would have had to talk to save it. Consider how still it was. Off to the right the figures of my men under their blankets stretched along the ground. Not a leaf to rustle, not a bough to creak. No grass to whisper in the wind, only stiff, scant shrubs and the sandy hills like shoals at the bottom of a lake of light. I could see the Woman's profile, thin and fine against the moon, and when she put up her hand to drag down the thick, careless coil of her hair, I guessed we were close upon the heart of the story. And for her the heart of the story was the man, Whitmark.

She had been, at the time he came into the country seventeen years before, that which the world knows so little what to do with that it mostly throws away—a good woman with great power and possibilities of passion. Whitmark stood for the best she had known, I should have said from all I learned, just a clean-minded, acute, tolerably cultivated American business man with an obsession for accomplishing results.

He had been sent out to look after a mine to which the title was not clear, and there were counter-machinations to take it away from him. This much may be told without breach, for, as it turned out, I was not to write that story, after all; at least, not in the lifetime of the Woman at the Eighteen-Mile. And the crux of the story to her was one little, so little, moment, that owing to Whitmark's having been taken with pneumonia within a week afterward, was rendered fixed beyond change or tarnish of time.

When all this was going forward the Mayers kept a miner's boarding-house at Tio Juan, where Whitmark was in and out; and the Woman, who from the first had been attracted by the certain stamp of competency and power, began to help him with warnings, intimations of character and local prejudice, afterward with information which got him the reputation of almost supernatural penetration.

There were reasons why, during his darkest time, Whitmark could find nobody but the Indians and the Woman to trust. Well, he had been wise enough to trust her, and it was plain to see from her account of it that this was the one occasion in life when her soul had stretched itself, observed, judged, wrought, and felt to the full of its power.

She loved him; yes, perhaps—I do not know—if you call love that soul service of a good woman to a man she may not touch. Whitmark had children back East, and a wife whom he had married for all the traditions of niceness and denial and abnegation which men demand of the women they expect to marry, and find savorless so often when they are married to it. He had never known what it meant to have a woman that concerned in his work, running neck and neck with it, divining his need, supplementing it not with the merely feminine trick of making him more complacent with himself, but with vital remedies and aids. And once he had struck the note of the West, he kindled to the event and enlarged his spirit. The two must have had great moments at the heart of that tremendous coil of circumstance. All this the Woman conveyed to me by the simplest telling of the story as it happened: "I said . . . and he did . . . the Indian went . . ."

I sat within the shallow shadow of the eaves experiencing the full-throated satisfaction of old prospectors over the feel of pay dirt, rubbing it between the thumb and palm, swearing over it softly below the breath. It was as good as that. And I was never to have it! For one thing the Woman made plain to me in the telling was the guilt of Whitmark. Though there was no evidence by which the court could hold him, though she did not believe it, though the fullness of her conviction intrigued me into believing that it did not matter so much what he was—the only way to write that story successfully was to fix forever against Whitmark's name its damning circumstance. The affair had been a good deal noised about at that time, and through whatever illusion of altered name and detail, was bound to be recognized and made much of in the newspapers. The Woman of the Eighteen-Mile saw that. Suddenly she broke off the telling to show me her poor heart, shrivelling as I knew hearts to warp and shrink in the aching wilderness, this one occasion rendering it serviceable like a hearth-fire in an empty room.

"It was a night like this he went away," said the Woman, stirring to point to the solemn moonlight poured over all the world.

That was after twenty-two months of struggle had left Whitmark in possession of the property. He was on his way then to visit his family, whom he had seen but once in that time, and was to come again to put in operation the mine he had so hardly won. It was, it should have been, an hour ripe with satisfaction.

"He was to take the stage which passed through Bitter Wells at ten that night," said she, "and I rode out with him—he had asked me—from Tio Juan, to bring back the horses. We started at sunset and reached the Wells a quarter of an hour before the time.

"The moon was half high when the sun went down, and I was very happy, because it had all come out so well, and he was to come again in two months. We talked as we rode. I told you he was a cheerful man. All the time when it looked as if he might be tried for his life, the worse it looked the more his spirits rose. He would have laughed if he had heard he was to be hung. But that night there was a trouble upon him. It grew as we rode. His face drew, his breath came sighing. He seemed always on the point of speaking and did not. It was as if he had something to say that must be said, and at the moment of opening his lips it escaped him. In the moonlight I saw his mouth working, and nothing came from it. If I spoke the trouble went out of his face, and when I left off it came again, puzzled wonder and pain. I know now!" said the Woman, shaking forward her thick hair, "that it was a warning, a presentiment. I have heard of such things, and it seems as if I should have felt it too, hovering in the air like that. But I was glad because it had all come out so well and I had had a hand in it. Besides, it was not for me." She turned toward me then for the first time, her hair falling forward to encompass all her face but the eyes, wistful with the desire to have me understand how fine this man was in every worldly point, how far above her, and how honored she was to have been the witness of the intimation of his destiny. I said quickly the thing that was expected of me, which was not the thing I thought, and gave her courage for going on.

"Yet," she said, "I was not entirely out of it, because—because the thing he said at the last, *when* he said it, did not seem the least strange to me, though afterward, of course, when I thought of it, it was the strangest good-bye I had ever heard.

"We had got down and stood between the horses, and the stage was coming in. We heard the sand fret under it, and the moonlight was a cold weight laid upon the world. He took my hand and held it against his breast so—and said—Oh, I am perfectly sure of the words; he said, 'I have *missed* you so.' Just that, not good-bye, and not *shall* miss you, but 'I *have* missed you so.'

"Like that," she said, her hands still clasped above her wasted bosom, the quick spirit glowing through it like wine in a turgid glass— "like that," she said. But, no; whatever the phrase implied of the failure of the utterly safe and respectable life to satisfy the inmost hunger of the man, it could never have had in it the pain of her impassioned, lonely years. If it had been the one essential word the Desert strives to say it would have been pronounced like that.

"And it was not until the next day," she went on, "it occurred to me that was a strange thing to say to a woman he had seen two or three times a week for nearly two years. But somehow it seemed to me clearer when I heard a week later that he was dead. He had taken cold on the way home, and died after three days. His wife wrote me; it was a very nice letter; she said he told her I had been kind to him. Kind!" She broke off, and far out under the moon rose the thin howl of coyotes running together in the pack. "And that," said the Woman, "is why I made you promise at the beginning that if I told you all I knew about Whitmark and Lang you would not use it."

I jumped. She had done that, and I had promised light-heartedly. People nearly always exact that sort of an assurance in the beginning of confidences, like a woman wanting to be told she is of nobler courage at the moment of committing an indiscretion, a concession to the sacredness of personal experience which always seems so much less once it is delivered, they can be persuaded to forego the promise of inviolateness. I always promise and afterward persuade. But not the Woman of the Eighteen-Mile. If Whitmark had lived he would have come back and proved his worth, cleared himself by his life and works. As it stood, by the facts against him, he was most utterly given over to ill-repute. The singularity of the incident, the impossibility of its occurring in any place but Death Valley, conspired to fix the ineffaceable stain upon his wife and his children, for, by the story as I should write it, he ought to have been hung. No use to say modestly that the scratchings of my pen would never reach them. If it were not the biggest story of the desert ever written, I had no wish to write it. And there was the Woman. The story was all she had, absolutely all of heart-stretching, of enlargement and sustenance. What she thought about it was that that last elusive moment when she touched the forecast shadow of his destiny was to bind her to save his credit for his children's sake. One must needs be faithful to one's experiences when there are so few of them.

She said something like that, gathering up her hair in both hands, standing before me in the wan revealing light. The mark of the desert was on her. Heart of desolation! But I knew what pinchings of the spirit went to make that mark!

"It was a promise," she said.

"It is a promise."

But I caught myself in the reservation that it should not mean beyond the term of her life.

Every now and then arises some city-surfeited demand for a great primitive love-story: it is usually a Professor in the English Department or some young man on the Daily News at fifteen per who dreams of writing it. Only those who have learned it at firsthand understand that there is no such thing; that primitive love is the most complaisant, that is to say, the most serviceable to Life of all human passions.

But when we magnify it with bonds it chafes itself to dramatic proportions. Love is Life's own way of reducing the clash of human contacts in order that the pair may turn a more opposing front to the adversary, the Wilderness.

It springs up, oh, it springs up, as Life divinely meant it, wherever, in the press of existence, men and women come together; requires, when the conditions are of a simpleness called primitive, no other inducement. But Life did not invent Society, seems somehow never to be properly aware of it; though it justifies itself of Love, cannot yet square with Respectability, with the Church and Property. Threading through these, Love weaves the fascinating intricacy of story, but here in the Borders, where the warp runs loose and wide, the pattern has not that richness it should show in the close fabric of civilization. If it lived next door to you, you probably wouldn't have anything to do with it.

Frustrate

I know that I am a disappointed woman and that nobody cares at all about it, not even Henry; and if anybody thought of it, it would only be to think it ridiculous. It is ridiculous, too, with my waist, and not knowing how to do my hair or anything. I look at Henry sometimes of evenings, when he has his feet on the fender, and wonder if he has the least idea how disappointed I am. I even have days of wondering if Henry isn't disappointed, too. He might be disappointed in himself, which would be even more dreadful; but I don't suppose we shall ever find out about each other. It is part of my disappointment that Henry has never seemed to want to find out.

There are people who think it is somehow discreditable to be disappointed; and whatever comes, you must pretend to like it, and just keep on pretending. I don't know why. It must be that some things are right in life and some others are not, and unless somebody has the courage to speak up about it, I don't know how we are ever to find it out. I don't see, if nobody else is hurt by it, why we shouldn't have what we like out of life; and if there's a way of getting or not getting it, people have a right to know. Sometimes I think if I'd known a little more, just a very little . . . !

It all began, I suppose, in the kind of people I was brought up among. They'd none of them had the kind of things I wanted, so of course they couldn't tell me anything about the way to get them. There was my mother. She had to work hard, and had never been anywhere but to a Methodist conference and once to the capital when father was a delegate or something, and her black silk had been turned twice; but she didn't seem the least disappointed. I think it must have been the way things were between her and my father. Father died when I was sixteen, so I couldn't tell much about it, but I know mother never so much as thought of marrying again. She was like a person who has had a full meal, but I—I am just kind of hungry . . . *always*. My mother never talked to me about her relations to my father. Mothers didn't; it wasn't thought suitable. I think sometimes, if she had, it might have made a difference about my marrying Henry.

The trouble was in the beginning, that though I knew the world was all full of exciting, interesting things, I thought they came to you just by living. I had no idea there was a particular way you had to go to work to get them. I think my people weren't the kind to make very nice discriminations about experiences or anything. They wouldn't have thought one way of being in love, for instance, was much better or different from another. They had everything sort of ticketed off and done with: such as that all church-members were happier than unbelievers, and all men naturally more competent and intelligent than their women. They must have known, some of them, that things didn't always work out that way; but they never let on about it—anyway, not to us young people. And if married couples weren't happy together, it wasn't considered decent to speak of it.

I suppose that was what got me to thinking about all the deep and high and shining things that I had a kind of instinct went with being married, belonged to it naturally, and, when you had found a suitable man, came along in their proper place without much thinking. And that was about all I knew when Henry proposed to me at the Odd Fellows' Festival. We were both on the decoration committee, and drove out to the old Lawson place that afternoon for roses. I remember the feel of them against my cheek, hot and sweet, and the smell of the syringa, and a great gold-and-black butterfly that fled and flitted down the green country road, mottled black and gold with shadows. Things like that gave me a strange kind of excitement, and yet a kind of lonesomeness, too, so I didn't mind Henry holding my hand between us in the buggy. I thought he must be feeling something of the same sort, and it didn't seem friendly to take my hand away. But I did take it away a moment later when he proposed. It turned me kind of cold. Of course I meant to accept him after a while. I liked him, and he was what my folks called suitable; but I seemed to want a little time to think about it.

Henry didn't want me to think. He kept hinting, and that evening under the grape-arbor at the minister's, where we had gone to get the sewing society's ice-cream freezer, he kissed me. I'd heard about engaged kisses, but this wasn't anything but just a kiss—like when you have been playing drop the handkerchief. I'd always had a feeling that when you had an engaged kiss something beautiful happened. There were times afterward when it almost seemed about to, and I would want to be kissed again to see if the next time . . . Henry said he was glad I had turned out to have an affectionate disposition.

My family thought I was doing well to marry Henry. He had no bad habits, and his people were well-to-do; and then I wasn't particularly pretty or rich or anything. I had never been very popular with young men; I was too eager. Not for them, you understand; but just living and doing things seemed to me such a good game. I suppose it is difficult for some folks to understand how you can be excited by the way a shadow falls, or a bird singing on a wet bough; and somehow young men seemed to get the idea that the excitement had something to do with them. It made them feel as if something was expected of them; and you know how it is with young men: they sort of pull back from the thing that is expected of them just because it is expected. I always thought it rather small, but I suppose they can't help it. There was a woman I met at Fairshore who explained how that was; but I didn't know it then, and I was rather sensitive about it. Anyway, it came about that I hadn't many beaux, and my mother was a good deal relieved when I settled down to Henry. And we hadn't any more than got the furniture as he wanted it when I discovered that there hadn't anything happened at all! Instead of living with my mother, I was just living with Henry; I've never done anything else.

There are things nobody ever tells young girls about marriage. Sometimes I think it is because, if they knew how to estimate their experience in the beginning, there is such a lot they wouldn't go on with; and when I was married, nobody ever thought of anything but that you had to go on with it. There were times when it seemed as if all it needed was just going on: there was a dizzying point just about to be reached from which Henry and I should really set out for somewhere.

It took me fifteen years to realize that we hadn't set out for anything, and would never get anywhere in particular.

I know I tried. Times I would explain to Henry what I wanted until he seemed to want it as much as I did; and then we would begin whatever we had to do,—at least I would begin,—and then I would find out that Henry had forgotten what we were doing it for—like the time we saved to set out the south lot in apricots, and Henry bought water-shares with the money. He said it would be cheaper to own the water for the apricots; but then we hadn't anything left to pay for the planting, and the man who had sold Henry the shares turned out not to own them. After a while I gave up saving.

The trouble was, Henry said, I was too kind of simple. It always seemed to me, if you wanted things, you picked out the one nearest to you, and made a mark so you could keep tab on whether you were getting it or not; and then you picked out the next nearest, and went for that, and after a while you had all of them. But Henry said when it came to business it was a good deal more complicated, and you had to look on all sides of a thing. Henry was strong on looking on all sides; anybody that had any kind of reasonableness could always get over him, like that man with the water-shares. That was when I was trying to make myself believe that if we could get a little money together, we might be in things. I had been reading the magazines, and I knew that there were big, live things with feelers out all over creation, and if I could just get the least little tip of one. . . . But I knew it wasn't money. When I wasn't too sick and overworked and worn out trying to keep track of Henry's reasons, I knew that the thing I was aching for was close beside me . . . when I heard the wind walk on the roof at night, . . . or heard music playing . . . and I would be irritated with Henry because he couldn't help me lay hold of it. It is ridiculous, I know, but there were times when it seemed to me if Henry had been fatter, it would have helped some. I don't mean to say that I had wanted to marry a fat man, but Henry hadn't filled out any, not like it seems men ought to: he just got dry and thinner. It used to make me kind of exasperated. Henry was always patient with me; he thought it was because I hadn't any children. He would have liked children. So would I when I thought I was to have one, but I was doing my own housework, and I was never strong. I cried about it a good deal at the time; but I don't suppose I really wanted it very much or I would have adopted one. I will tell you—there are women that want children just for the sake of having them, but the most of them want them because there is a man—And the man they want gets to hear of it, and whenever a woman is any way unhappy, they think all she needs is a baby. But there's something else ought to happen first, and I never gave up thinking it was going to happen; all the time I kept looking out, like Sister Anne in the fairy-tale, and it seemed to me a great many times I saw dust moving. I never understood why we couldn't do things right here at home—big things. There were those people I'd read about in Germany—just plain carpenters and butchers and their wives—giving passion-plays. They didn't know anything about plays; they just felt grateful, and they did something like they felt. I spoke to the minister's wife about it once—not about a passion-play, of course, that wouldn't have done; but about our just taking hold of something as if we thought we were as good as those Germans,—but she didn't seem to think we could. She kind of pursed up her mouth and said, "Well, we must remember that they had the advantage of having lived abroad." It was always like that. You had to have lived somewhere or been taught or had things different; you couldn't just start right off from where you were. It was all of a piece with Henry's notion of business; there was always some kind of queer mixed-up-ness about it that I couldn't understand. But still I didn't give up thinking that somehow I was going to pull the right string at last, and then things would begin to happen. Not knowing what it was I wanted to happen, I couldn't be expected to realize that it couldn't happen now on account of my being married to Henry. It was at Fairshore that I found out.

It was when we had been married eighteen years that Aunt Lucy died and left me all her property. It wasn't very much, but it was more than Henry would ever have, and I just made up my mind that I was going to have the good of it. Henry didn't make any objection, and the first thing I did was to go down to Fairshore for the summer. I chose Fairshore because I had heard about all the authors and painters being there. You see, when you never have any real life except what you get from reading, you have a kind of feeling that writers are the only real *own* folks you've got. You even get to thinking sometimes that maybe, if you had known how to go about it, you could have written yourself, though perhaps you'd feel that way about bridge-building or soldier-ing, if it was the only real kind of work you saw much of. Not that I ever thought I could write; but I had so many ideas that were exactly like what I'd read that I thought if I could only just get somebody to write them for me— But you can't; they've all got things of their own. Still, you would think the way they get inside the people they write about that they would be able to see what is going on inside of you, and be a little kind.

You see, it had come over me that away deep inside of me there was a really beautiful kind of life, singing, and burning blue and red and gold as it sang, and there were days when I couldn't bear to think of it wasting there and nobody to know.

Not that Henry didn't take an interest in me,—his kind of interest,— if I was sick or hurt, or seeing that I had a comfortable chair. But if I should say to Henry to lean upon my heart and listen to the singing there, he would have sent for the doctor. Nobody talks like that here in Castroville: only in books I thought I had heard the people calling to one another quietly and apart over all the world, like birds waking in a wood. I've wondered since I came back from Fairshore if people put things in books because they would like to have them that way.

It is difficult to tell what happened to me at Fairshore. It didn't really happen—just the truth of things coming over me in a slow, acrid dribble. Sometimes in the night I can feel the recollection of it all awash at the bottom of my heart, cold and stale. But nothing happened. Nobody took any notice of me but one woman. She was about my age, plain-looking and rather sad. I'd be proud to mention her name; but I've talked about her a great deal, and, with all my being so disappointed, it isn't so bad but it might be worse if everybody got to find out about it. She was really a much greater writer than the rest of them; but, I am ashamed to say it, just at first, perhaps because she was so little different from me on the outside, and perhaps just because she was a woman, I didn't seem to care much about her. I don't know why I shouldn't say it, but I did want to have something to do with interesting men. People seem to think that when a woman is married she has got all that's coming to her; but we're not very different from men, and *they* have to have things. There are days sometimes when it seems to me that never to have known any kind of men but Henry and the minister and old man Truett, who does our milking, would be more than I could bear. I thought if I could get to know a man who was big enough so I couldn't walk all around him, so to speak,—somebody that I could reach and reach and not find the end of,—I shouldn't feel so—so frustrated. There was a man there who wrote things that made you feel like that,—as if you could take hands with him and go out and rescue shipwrecked men and head rebellions. And when I tried to talk to him,

I found him looking at me the way young men used to before I married Henry—as if he thought I wanted something, and it was rather clever of him not to give it to me. It was after that that I took to sitting with the writer woman. I'd noticed that though the men seemed to respect her, and you saw them in corners sometimes reading manuscripts to her, they never took her to walk, or to see the moon rise, or the boats come in. They spent all that on the pretty women, young and kind of empty-headed. I'd heard them talk when they thought I wasn't listening. And the writer woman sat about with the other women, and didn't seem to mind it.

I hoped when people saw me with her, they'd think it was because she was so famous, and not guess how terrible it was to find yourself all at once a middle-aged woman sitting on a bench, and all the world going by as if it was just what they expected. It came over me that here were all the things I had dreamed about,—the great sea roaring land-ward, music, quick and gay; looks, little incidents,—and I wasn't in it; I wasn't in it at all.

I suppose the writer woman must have seen how it was with me, but I thought at first she was talking of herself.

"It's all very wonderful out there, isn't it?" she said, looking toward the blue water and the beach shining like a shell, with the other writers and painters walking up and down and making it into world stuff. "Very wonderful—when you have the price to pay for it!"

"It *is* expensive." I was thinking of the hotel, but I saw in a minute she meant something else.

"The price you pay," she said, "it isn't being fit to be in the Great World or being able to appreciate it when you're in; it is what you contribute to keep other people in, I suppose."

I must have said something about not being able to see what the kind of women who were in contributed—just girls and flirty kind of married women.

"It's a kind of game, keeping other people in," said the writer woman. "They don't know much else, but they know the game. We are, most of us," she said, "like those matches that will not light unless they are struck upon the box: there is a particular sort of person that sets us off. It's a business, being that sort of person."

"If anybody could only learn it—" I tried to seem only polite.

"It is the whole art," she said, "of putting yourself into your appearance." She laughed. "I have too much waist for that sort of thing. I have my own game."

I seemed suddenly to want to get away to my room and think about it. I know it is absurd at my age, but I lay on the bed and cried as I hadn't since they told me my baby hadn't lived. For I knew now that all that beautiful life inside me couldn't be born either, for I was one who had to have help to be worth anything to myself, and I didn't know the game. I had never known it.

All the time I had been thinking that all I needed was to find the right person; and now I understood that, so far as anybody could guess, I wasn't the right person myself. I hadn't the art of putting myself into my appearance. I'm shy about talk, and my arms are too fat, and my skirts have a way of hanging short in front.

I've thought about it a great deal since. It doesn't seem fair. Nobody told me about it when I was a girl; I think nobody tells girls. They just have to sort of find it out; and if they don't, nobody cares. All they did tell me was about being good, and you will be happy; but it isn't so. There is a great deal more to it than that, and it seems as if people ought to know. I think we are mostly like that in Castroville: we've got powers and capacities way down in us, but we don't know anything about getting them out. We think it is living when we have got upholstered furniture and a top buggy. I know people who think it is worth while never to have lived in a house without a cupola. But all the time we are not in the game. We do not even know there is a game.

Sometimes I think, if it would do me any good, I could turn in and learn it now. I watched them at Fairshore, and it seemed to me it could be learned. I have wild thoughts sometimes,—such thoughts as men have when they go out and snatch things,—but it wouldn't do me any good. Henry's folks were always long-lived, and there are days when I am so down that I am glad to have even Henry. As long as people see us going about together they can't know— I'm rather looking forward to getting old now. I think perhaps I sha'n't ache so. But I *should* like to know how much Henry understands.

The Divorcing of Sina

Ordinarily when a Piute gentleman comes home to supper to find his wife sitting beside the hut completely wrapped in her blanket, he goes away quietly and pretends to be thinking about something else. But there were several reasons why Bill Bodry felt obliged to depart from this excellent custom. For one thing he was hungry, in the next place he was very fond of his wife, and last of all there was his mother peering out from her own wickiup with eyes keen and bright as a gopher's, ready to cry fool to him who could not manage his own household. Bill's mother had been all for his marrying Black Rock Maggie, who though she had followed the glint of a white man's eye to an extent which prejudiced her in the opinion of the young and romantic, had acquired merit in the eyes of Bill's mother by her superior powers of wheedling tinned salmon and potato culls out of the white housewives. And because there was always Maggie in the back of his mother's mind as a standard of comparison, it was not possible for Bill to admit the complete overthrow of all his domestic authority as implied in the circumstance that he had come home three successive evenings to find the hearth cold and Sina sitting with her head wrapped in her blanket. Not that some allowance must not be made for young wives, even in a campody; but even in a campody, for a man to go three nights supperless to bed points to something more serious than bridal vapors.

He was aware that it was already beginning to be whispered about the camp that Sina, his wife, had put a spell on her husband. He was aware of it while he raked up the sticks between the cold stones and when he brought up the wicker water bottle from the creek to make the coffee—and how indeed does a Piute gentleman come to be boiling his own coffee unless somebody has put a spell on him? To make matters worse, here was Black Rock Maggie coming up the trail to visit his mother. Completely at an end of his devices for having it appear that the household arrangements were going on as usual, Bill came and stood over the slender huddled figure. He stood with his back to his mother so that she could not see his face working. It was time when any husband would have been justified in coercive methods, but Bill was still very much in love with his wife. What he could see of her, the little moccasined foot sticking out, and the slim shape of her under the blanket, moved him strongly.

"Look, Sina, what I got for you." He spoke in English, for his mother did not understand English very well, and the use of the foreign tongue created the effect at least, of an excluding bond between him and Sina. He opened his shirt now to show his young wife the present he had brought for her, a bead necklace of blue and amber that had cost him the half of his week's wages as bronco buster. It clicked as it dropped from his hand to her lap, and in spite of herself the girl peeked curiously out of her blanket, her little hand moving instinctively, but stopped when she saw Black Rock Maggie.

Maggie was the sort distrusted by young wives immemorially. She was believed to have gone with a white man as far as Pharump valley, she wore corsets, and could read writing, and little moving yellow lights swam just under the surface of her beady eyes. Moreover, she had a way of making Bill's marriage appear a mere ripple on the surface of her own superior intimacy with him. Oh, no, these things are not the product of sophistication! They are as old as men and women, or perhaps older, and it was with a sense of utter inescapability that Bill, as he heard Maggie's voice greeting his mother behind him, begged desperately.

"Won't you tell me what it is you want, Sina?"

Sina was perfectly explicit. "I want to go home to my mother!"

Ordinarily there is no reason why, when a Piute lady finds marriage impossible, she cannot gather up her dowry in a perfectly amicable arrangement and go back to her father's house, supposing that he will have her. But the reasons why that could not be done in Sina's case are a considerable part of this story. Once before she had run away from her young bridegroom, and been brought back by Wind-in-the-face, her father, promptly and honorably. That this was exactly what would happen to her again Sina knew as well as anybody, and the unreasonableness of her request would have moved Bill to do what any Piute husband would have done much earlier, but at that moment he heard Maggie's voice purring behind him.

"Don't you want me to get you some supper, Bill?" and in the moment when he looked up at her and back at his young wife again he noted that the blue and amber necklace had disappeared.

"I guess I don't want any supper," he denied, manfully. "I guess I'll take Sina to her mother, she's sick."

"A good dose of the stick will cure her complaint," jeered the mother of Bill Bodry; but Maggie's cue was sympathy.

"I guess Bill don't want to beat her if she's sick." This brought Sina out of her blanket like a slim little snake.

"I guess Bill's got a right to beat me if he wants to," she flashed a cold, withering scorn on her lord and master. "You got a right to beat me just like a horse, Bill Bodry, you bought me!" Bill shifted miserably from foot to foot in the dust of the mesa.

"Aw, Sina—I—" not for worlds would he have laid the stick on those round young shoulders, not so round by half as when he had married her.

"You goin' to beat me, Bill Bodry?"

"I—I'm goin' to take you to visit your mother, Sina."

She couldn't have known with what desperation he clutched at this last remnant of his husbandly prerogative as he moved in the trail before her, thus to present to the scoffing eyes of his mother the spectacle of a wife following at her man's back in the ancient Piute custom. It might have answered, if, at the moment behind him, Black Rock Maggie had not suddenly and shortly laughed. He heard that and then he heard the hurrying steps of Sina breaking past him. He put out his arm, he knew in his heart it was merely to prevent her stumbling, for the girl was really sick with misery, but she must have mistaken the supporting clutch of his arm for violence, for with a cry she turned and struck him full in the face with something that rattled and stung as she tore free and fled from him; something that as he stooped to gather up and stuff into his bosom before he turned aside in the twilight to hide his discomfiture, the peering eyes of old Ebia recognized as a blue and amber necklace.

II The reasons why Sina could not be divorced from Bill Bodry in the infrequent but traditional way, had to do with her father's appetite for fresh-water clams in excess of his discretion. He had spent too much time kicking them out of the soft mud of the river bottom with his toes, but he thought he was being persecuted by the ghost of an enemy reincarnated in the form of a coyote. Either that, or else he had been going about on some inauspicious occasion with his mouth open, and a *Winuputs*—one of the million little devils who are responsible for the inside pains of Piutes—had jumped down his throat and worked from that to his knees. Catameneda, his wife, was inclined to the latter opinion, but by the time Jim had lost the fall rodeo and the piñon harvest on account of the swelling in his legs, she was ready to believe anything.

It was just as this juncture, while she was tending Jim's pains with relays of hot stones as he lay in his rabbit-skin blanket on the sunny side of the wickiup that Bill Bodry came by on the trail with a swing in his walk like the smooth play of the flanks of a cougar. The light cotton shirt parted carelessly over the arch of his chest, his thighs were knit with power, about his head thick locks of blackness lay like sculpture work banded by the shining crease where the sombrero rested. Besides being good to look at, Bill Bodry spoke Government School English as befitted a man with a whole white name who owned a dollar watch and could tell time by it.

He had come over the barranca to talk with Yavi, grandson and sole prop of the Basket Maker, about the next rabbit drive, and had stopped neighborly to inquire as to the progress of Jim's pains. "Hurt-like-Hell," had been Jim's rejoiner, in compliment to the English in which as a member of the younger generation, Bill had addressed him. And that might have been all there was of it if at that moment Bill Bodry had not had sight of Sina.

Sina was slim and brown with budding breasts, and her eyes were as brown as the brown shadow of the creek under the birches. She was painting her face by a fragment of mirror propped in the rabbit brush, cheeks and chin a plain vermilion, as a sign that her affections were disengaged. When she saw Bill Bodry watching her she laughed, and Sina's laugh was like the sound of running water in a rain-less land. Therefore Bill Bodry lingered to bargain with Sina's father for the making of a rabbit-skin blanket. Wind-in-the-face was the best blanket maker at Sagharawite. He cut the skins in thin strips around and around, and strung them on the wattles to dry. Evenings, when he sat with hot stones between his shins, he would take up the strips with his thumb and finger, twisting them between his palm and knee, ready for weaving. On one of these occasions he confided to the Basket Maker that Bill's blanket was to have a hundred skins.

"That's a large blanket for a man not married," said the Basket Maker.

"But he will not say what he means to do with it," Jim concluded his information.

"Ah," said the grandmother, "Bill Bodry was not fed on meadow larks' tongues," which is Piute for saying that Bill talked no more than necessary.

"And Black Rock Maggie talks enough for two," suggested a neighbor who had observed Maggie making eyes in Bill's direction, and she began to tell the story of Maggie and the white man, but Catameneda of the Round Arm nudged her. It was not the kind of story to be told before Sina, for there is no place in the world really where a nice young girl is kept more thoroughly nice than in a campody.

But as a matter of fact, Bill had not thought so far ahead of his blanket as that. He had said a hundred skins because it was a large number, and as he brought them as he found them, it afforded so many more occasions on which he could recommend himself to Sina by taking an interest in her father's rheumatism. But it was the whisper about Black Rock Maggie which kept Sina's mother from suggesting what he was thinking. Sometimes Bill would see the girl behind the slight screen of rabbit brush, busy about her toilet with the considered, slow movements of Indian women, unobtrusive as the preenings of quail. Other times she would be walking in the twilight with young girls of the campody. They would walk with their arms about one another, their cheeks bright with vermilion and their breasts bore up the folds of their red and purple calico gowns like apples. It was on such occasions that Bill would lend a neighborly ear to the complaint of Wind-in-the-face that there needed nothing to his recovery but the professional attendance of the Medicine Man from Fish Lake valley. When it was learned later that that distinguished practitioner had been brought over to cure Jim's legs at Bill Bodry's expense, there was probably no one in the campody besides Catameneda and her daughter who did not know what was in Bill's mind.

The therapeutic of the Medicine Man from Fish Lake valley belongs to that strip of country between the desert and the tolerable outposts of the Sierras, known as Lost Borders. It depends for its efficacy on being able to cross the border between sense and spirit by a method which ought to prove immensely popular in more sophisticated circles, since it consists largely of singing and dancing. The point in the case of Sina's father was that it succeeded; it drove the *Winuputs* out of his legs and set him back a matter of seventeen dollars or so with Bill Bodry.

It was about this time that Bill began to build him a house with a door like a white man's and Catameneda of the Round Arm began to be uneasily aware of the frequency of his visits to her wickiup. She egged on her husband to discharge his obligation.

"I gonna pay you, Bill, soon as I get workin' for Watterson," Jim assured him, speaking English as a way of putting himself quite on an equality with his creditor. "How in hell I gonna pay you when I got no money, thass what?"

"You don' never need to pay me," Bill earnestly reassured him. "What I needin' with money when I got me a new house, I got plenty blankets, I got a sack of pine nuts, I got a house, I got blankets—" avoiding the dangers of repetition, he dug the toe of his boot into the earth floor of the wickiup. "I guess I gonna get me a wife," he concluded.

"Who you gonna get?" Windy inquired sociably. Bill smoothed out the mark of his boot carefully. Said he at last:

"I gonna get Sina."

"Huh!" remarked Sina's father. He had moments of thinking, however, when he came to break it to Sina and her mother, that it would have been better to put up with the rheumatism. For Sina of the budding breasts did not in the least wish to get married. The burden of primitive housewifery lies heavy on maiden dreams in Sagharawite, and Sina had been thinking of Bill Bodry as a friend of her father's. Sina was a spoiled and only child, and even a maiden of the Stone Age may be forgiven for insisting on being courted for herself alone rather than being handed over from one man to another in discharge of an obligation. That was the mistake Bill made, and Ebia, his mother, who should have instructed him in the proper way to win a wife, was touting for Black Rock Maggie. If a man must marry, why not have a wife who can bring something in, rather than a half-grown girl who would waste his substance in the measures of inexperience? But Bill stuck to it that Sina he would have and no other, and once the subject of the debt had been broached what was Wind-in-the-face to do, as an honorable Piute gentleman, but hand his daughter over? If a girl is to be allowed to exercise her own choice in the face of her parents' necessities, what is to become of the institution of the family? It is one of the ways, indeed, in which the family becomes an institution, by the exercise of vicarious obligation. To do them justice, Sina and her mother never thought of resisting; the most they could do they did, which was to render their men folk thoroughly uncomfortable. No doubt Catameneda could have reconciled herself in time to a match so eminently desirable. For the House with the Door had worked the accustomed effect of prohibition and mystery. Probably there was nothing more behind it than the usual Piute furnishing, but an inch of pine planking, in place of the ordinary rag of blanket or buckskin, by preventing prying eyes, magnified the bridal setting forth of Bill Bodry to magnificence. What, demanded the interested and gossipy campody, did the girl want anyway? Sina wept and surrendered, but between the girl and her mother there was the secret, unendurable pang of violation. People who have forgotten that a favorite goddess of the ancients was a fleeing virgin, must needs be reminded that the age of chipped flint was before the complaisance of women had been forced by social exigencies. Sina's time for loving had not come, and even in a house with a door her uncaptive heart pined like a wild thing in captivity. She hated Black Rock Maggie always hanging about with her proffers of superior competency, and if she could have spared any energy from hating Bill, she would have hated that whining old fox, Bill's mother. All of which would have led in due time to a proper divorce except for the distinction at which I have hinted.

Piute society is, unlike our own, when you understand it, perfectly simple. Anything that is an Indian's can always be taken back, no matter how many times he gives it, since it remains always in some respect peculiarly his own. But what he receives is never his at all except upon sufferance. If Sina had given her heart away, she could have taken it back on any justifiable occasion. But Sina had given nothing; she had been taken on demand in payment of money given by Bill Bodry, and not even Bill could release her.

That was why, when Sina, after three weeks of married life had run away to her mother, Wind-in-the-face had girded up his affections as a father, and notwithstanding his wife, who called him offal, ditchwater and many other names fit to cause him the greatest possible embarrassment, had carried Sina back to her husband. It was after this that Sina took to sitting with her head in her blanket and Black Rock Maggie's visits to Ebia had been of almost daily occurrence. And now that Sina had run away again after publicly shaming all his tenderness, the young husband, simple savage that he was, whose hurts are sore and immediate, lay alone in his blanket of a hundred skins beside the House with a Door and nearly died of it.

III Tribal laws are to the highest degree exigent. That they present themselves as inexorable to our unaccustomed eye, is only because the human circumstances with which they deal have the quality of inexorable sameness. Sina couldn't divorce herself and Bill couldn't give her back, but on the other hand the tribe of Sagharawite couldn't afford to let a healthy young woman fret herself into a wasting fever. That's where they have the advantage of us, for with all our precaution against hookworm and typhus we suffer the social waste of heartache and humiliation with indifference, and permit our young to wound one another to the death with impunity.

In the case of Bill and Sina nothing was neglected which could have helped. Everybody took sides with the greatest heartiness. Bill's mother and Sina's outdid each other in the—sage hen, and flea-bitten whelp of a coyote—epithets heaped respectively on the other's offspring. Wind-in-the-face remonstrated with his child as he was duly bound, but she turned her back on him; then he beat her and she lay on the ground at his feet and whimpered like a hurt animal. Being thus at the end of his resources he painted his face, draped himself in his best blanket and asked for an Order in Council.

Infrequently as it occurs, there is no particular condemnation implied in a Piute taking his domestic affairs to the Council instead of settling them in the privacy of his wickiup, which is about as private as a bird cage. But it was unfortunate from Bill Bodry's point of view that Wind-in-the-face should have summoned the Council to sit on the case of his daughter Sina at the time of the spring shearing. That was when the shallow tide of prosperity ran at its highest in the campody. Sweet sap dripped from the canes, the earth was full of foodful roots, the clink of the shearing wage in every pocket. It was the moon of tender leaves and not far from the time of the dance of Marriageable Maidens. Those who remembered Sina as she had appeared in it for the first time the last season, saw in her drooping frame and bitten lip the figure of young pitiableness. The girl was plainly ill, ate nothing, slept little and moaned as she slept. There was not a woman in the camp who had not had the whole story from Catameneda, who was wild with fear lest her daughter should eat wild parsnip. In the open life of the campody, where there are no distractions and few concealments, death as a surcease from disaster is more often than we imagine resorted to. And though no woman may speak in Council, there was not an elder among them who did not know that he would have to answer at home for whatever was done to Sina; and it was against all considerations of tribal profit that the heart of women should be fretted. For one thing, who was to do the work if the women were discontented? "A grudging heart makes cold the hearth," says the proverb.

The Council met at the moth hour in a hollow under Togobah. New shorn sheep were white across the slope, shepherd fires winked out along the foot-hills, musk-scented gilias bloomed, burrowing owls whoo-whoed at their mating. The whole earth was full of comfortable twitterings; Sagharawite looked at Bill Bodry, handsome as he was but with the alien touch of a year of white-schooling, looked at Sina, wan and violated by a hateful marriage and decided against him. Bill, quite as sensitive as anybody to the intimidation of the mating season, whose every fibre ached with desire of her, ached indeed to the point of dumbness, made the mistake of saying nothing of his love and staking all on the ancient ruling. The girl had come to him on a debt, who could take her from him? Of course if the debt were paid—but seventeen dollars and a half! Yavi, grandson and sole support of the Basket Maker had an inspiration. They would take a leaf out of the white-man's book and take up a collection. Yavi was thought to have an eye for Sina herself before Bill Bodry came by, and there were none too many marriageable girls that year in the campody. The suggestion had the smack of romance to which in the spring even a Piute is susceptible. Dimes and dollars came out of the shearing wage and clinked in the ceremonial basket. Thus the divorcing of Sina was accomplished without any violation of the tribal custom. Sina went home to Wind-in-the-face, Bill Bodry boarded with his mother, the House with the Door was shut up, and Black Rock Maggie veiled the yellow lights in her eyes and waited.

IV Nothing much can happen in the campody in the summer-time when the snakes are about to run and tattle of it to the gods. Later, when the long grass is eaten short, when the heat haze has gone up from the bare bones of the mountain, and the qualities of the earth and sky are interchangeable, about the end of the piñon harvest when the old sit with their toes in the ashes, many summer-hidden things come to the surface.

So it was about the first of November that it began to be whispered around Sagharawite that Bill Bodry had put a spell on Sina who had been his wife. How else could it be when divorce didn't help her? To lose appetite and sleep and waste with no fever; that was the way when Bad Medicine had been made against you. That was what happened to the children of Bed Morning when Poco Bill had a quarrel with him; four of them one after another thinned like fat on the fire, and died in spite of all that could be done for them. And then there was a man in Fish Lake valley—instance multiplied instance to show that Sina had been coyoted.

Ebia, who knew perfectly what would happen to her son if the story gained credence, laid Sina's wasting to her general incompetence, as witnessed by her failure to rise to the honor which had been thrust upon her in becoming the wife of the one man in Sagharawite who had a house with a door like a white man's. In this she was seconded to her face by Black Rock Maggie, who had of late left off corsets and taken to wearing her blanket folded over her breast as becomes a Piute maiden who has not married nor walked in the trail of a white man. But away from the mother of Bill Bodry, Maggie was observed to listen to the tale of the man from Fish Lake valley with marked conviction. If she had doubts she used them to draw the talk in that direction.

It would have suited her very well to have Bill driven from the camp as a Coyote Doctor.

She managed her game so well that by the time the winter constellations had wheeled to their station midway over the narrow, knife-cut valley, there was open talk of bringing Bill Bodry to book for evil practices. Weevil had got into the pine nuts that year and there were many cases of pneumonia, evidence enough that Bad Medicine was working somewhere. And always there was Sina. For a month or so after the divorce she had brightened, but now she sat leaning her young head against the wickiup, her hands falling listlessly still over her basket plaiting, and nothing would induce her to paint her cheeks vermilion and put on the purple calico. It was plain enough what was the matter with her, but whenever anybody ventured to suggest it to Catameneda, she moved her closed fingers before her face, extending them suddenly outward in a gesture which is one of the oldest resources of nature against the evil suggestion, so old that it is no longer polite to explain its origin. In the privacy of their blanket, which is the only privacy possible in a wickiup, she confided to Wind-in-the-face that she had looked the girl all over for signs of ordinary sickness and found none. What she had been really looking for was the blue and amber necklace. Ebia had told of it as evidence of her son's unappreciated munificence, but not even Ebia knew what had become of it. All of Sina's dowry had come home with her, but the necklace as a present had surely been hers in some degree, and if the smallest thing of hers, say a string of beads or a ribbon, remained in the custody of Bill Bodry, might it not serve to make a spell upon Sina's undoing? So Catameneda of the Round Arm brooded over the business of the necklace, but dared not question her daughter lest by mentioning the evil thing she bring it to pass. Thus matters stood until within a week of the annual Council when, if there were any such thing as coyote doctoring going on in the camp, it would surely be looked into.

That all this could go on without Sina's knowing anything about it, was due as much to the girl's sick indifference to life as to the inviolable rule of the campody that one does not speak to another of that other's private business without invitation. It was a woman from Black Rock, visiting the Basket Maker the week before the Council, who inadvertently brought it to her attention.

Sina had moved to the further side of the wickiup to be free from her mother's solicitations, which brought her in range of Seyavi's hut and the voices of the two old crones as they sat gossiping on the kitchen-midden. As she lay there inert in her blanket, if they saw her at all, and sight goes early in the smoky huts, they must have thought her sleeping, and voices carry far in the clear afternoons of November. The woman from Black Rock was numbering the affairs of importance which should come before the Council, and along toward the end came this business of the coyote doctoring and Bill Bodry. Did Seyavi think there was anything in that story? Since Bill had got his money back, why should he put a spell on Sina, especially as he had so pointedly recovered from his brief infatuation for her. Or, certainly, hadn't Seyavi heard? The Black Rock woman had it from a friend of hers, who had it from the wife of Bed Morning, who had seen for herself, going up the creek to leash acorns of an early morning, Maggie and Bill folding up Bill's blankets—pity Bill was such a fool about women. First Sina and then this hot-eyed draggle-tail—he had only to come to Black Rock—*they* could tell him what Maggie was—

Slowly and unobtrusively as a snake changes its place in the sun, Sina crept out of sight behind the wickiup. She moved at first with the hurt creature's instinct for concealment, and as she moved two entirely distinct and contradictory impulses woke within her. She wanted to stand for Bill before the Council, to defend him from stones and obloquy, and she wanted quite as much to get him off to herself where she could kill him quietly. She remembered the affront Bill had put upon her in his House with the Door, when the moon was up and the door was shut, she remembered Black Rock Maggie and something alive and terrible stirred and turned in her. There ran a screen of black sage from the hut to the creek, and up along that were the thick, fringing willows. Past these Sina stole with a strange sick thing inside her; so at last to a close copse of willows and brown birches, within which she had often hid herself from the detested sight of Bill and the sharp tongue of Bill's mother. From here she could see the House with the Door, and a thin trail of smoke going up beside it. There was no one about, and she could not tell from this distance whether it were Bill's smoke or Ebia's. But she could not have seen very well in any case, for the sight of the smoke brought sudden tears and the strange, sick something that tore in her and strove to rend itself forth by bitter sobbing. Oh, there was no doubt about it at last, that somebody had put a spell on Sina!

She must have lain there a long time before her vision cleared, and quite empty of crying she looked back toward the House with the Door and saw Bill moving about with the awkward fumbling of a man whose hearth is deserted, and the divine instinct to mother her man awoke in Sina—but go to him? She who was bought with money? Let him get Black Rock Maggie. She saw Bill coming with the water bottle to the creek, and sure enough there over the barranca as though to an appointment came Maggie. All this was part of Maggie's game, which she played cleverly—to appear always just when a man feels himself most in need of a wife, and to answer the need in her person. That was how she had been seen by the wife of Bed Morning, folding up Bill's blankets for him on the morning after Bill, to ease his desperate ache, had set the door of his house ajar and lay in it all night calling his young wife from her father's hut and calling vainly. On this particular evening Ebia was gone with two other of the campody to dig tule roots where the water of Salt Creek comes down to the river. Maggie meant to pretend she had forgotten all this—and a man likes to have a warm meal of an evening no matter who cooks it for him. Besides she had heard that at Black Rock which warned her to move quickly. If it came to Council that Bill was a Coyote Doctor, bringing evil on the camp by reason of the evil thoughts that brewed in him, he would be stoned and driven out for it. She could follow him, of course—what man could refuse comfort in banishment? They could go out Paniment way and winter in Coso, and when summer had restored the equanimity of the camp they could come again—but Maggie was a sociable soul; what she wanted more than anything else was to pose proudly before the other women as mistress of the House with the Door. If she could persuade Bill to take her before the Council convened, who could accuse him, the happy bridegroom, of putting spells on other women? So as she came over the barranca to meet him at the creek, Maggie unloosed the yellow flame in her eyes, and her hot heart shook her. It might have been that, or the unwhispered protest of Sina watching from the willows that caused her to begin badly. She slipped the bottle from him as it sagged in the water.

"Are there no women left in Sagharawite that you wait on yourself like a white man?" she laughed.

To the man sore with the want of the only woman who mattered, it sounded like a taunt to be answered. "Loss of women like white men more better than Piutey."

Bill made a practice of sticking to English with Maggie, possibly because it was so much less explicit than the speech of his fathers. Maggie met it with a flash of her fine eyes.

"And if I have followed the white man's trail and heard what he thinks in his heart, I have come back, Bill Bodry—does any one ask why I came back—" The language of the Piute is ample and lends itself to passion as easily as mountain stream to the spring freshet. "I came back," she said, "because my heart was as dry under his hand as the earth in summer. Because the blood of the white man is pale like his face, Bill Bodry—" She swung herself across the stream to him, challenging, magnificent. "But I didn't expect to find that the men of my race had turned white also—you, Bill Bodry—wasting yourself on a girl whose breasts are scarcely grown—who weeps in the night—who shudders—"

She saw by the lift of his shoulders how the thrust had gone home to him. She swung the water bottle dripping from the creek to her shapely shoulder. "White man"—her eyes danced with veiled provocation— "come up to your house and I will cook a meal for you—" She should have gone then; past question he would have followed her, but the eternal feminine desire to be taken at more than her worth overcame her. She leaned the wicker bottle on a rock and came slowly back to him, all fire and softness. "I shall cook you a meal," she said, "and you shall teach me—all that you could not teach Sina."

You are to understand that there is nothing in Piute etiquette which prohibits love-making of this explicit character. Maggie came close and laid her hands on Bill's breast, which had tightened under her challenge, and as her hands came to rest there, they touched something hard and sound under the cotton shirt, like a woman's necklace. At the touch Bill stepped back and quivered as he would have done if the little horned snake of the desert had struck him.

"I guess you pretty fine cook, Maggie," he stuck obstinately to English, "but I ain't carin' much about anybody's cooking but Sina's."

Maggie for her part turned venomous. "Care!" she cried, "*you* care when it is known as far as Black Rock and Fish Lake valley that you have put a spell on Sina. You that bought a wife for money and couldn't keep her!" She pushed him from her. "You that turned Coyote Doctor so that she should eat parsnip root and you will be done with her. You that will be stoned in the Council—" Right here there was a sound of breaking branches and a sudden slim form flashed upon them from the opposite bank of willows. The dusk was falling and the girl with her wasted face and her once white doe skins looked unearthly.

"You snake of two tongues—" she addressed herself to Black Rock Maggie. "What right have you to say that I have a spell put on me, making trouble for Bill Bodry? For what should I eat wild parsnip when I am married to a good man and have a house with a door and plenty of blankets." She panted white with weakness, but with all the dignity of the proper matron. "You go to the Council with a story like that," said Sina, "and you'll see what you get, you—white man's leavings!" It was not for nothing that Sina had been daughter-in-law for three months to the sharpest tongued woman in the campody.

Maggie's game was up, but Maggie herself was undaunted. She struck her foot sidewise along the ground causing a little spurt of dust to fly up, an immemorial gesture of belittlement. "Prutt," she laughed, "seventeen dollars and a half's worth!" She gathered the ends of her blanket over her breast and as she ran up the trail they heard her laughing. The two young things stood still on opposite sides of the stream and looked at one another. Sudden inspiration unsealed the lips of Bill Bodry.

"Sina," he said, "I ain't never cared at all about that money. All the time I comin' to your father's house, it ain't the money I thinkin' about, Sina, it's you—Sina." He came across to her, all his young heart was in his eyes, but Sina had no word for him. She was staring at something that showed on Bill's breast where the shirt had parted under Maggie's vehement fingers, something that hung against his heart and rose and fell with its quick panting, a blue and amber necklace.

V Bitter anxiety came and camped that night by the wickiup of Wind-in-the-face and Catameneda. Dusk fell with the owl's calling, but no Sina. A hurried round of the neighboring huts yielded no trace of her. One by one the little fires winked out. Catameneda sat in the hut and moaned on the Basket Maker's shoulder while Wind-in-the-face and Yavi went down along the river marsh where the wild parsnip grows, groping and fearing. The campody slept and searched by turns and whispered apart things best not spoken openly among the covert dangers of the night. Opinion grew as the dark thinned to blueness; by dawn it was concentrated in one word: Bill Bodry. Who else had any interest in the girl's disappearance? Just about break of day Catameneda, wild of heart, had run out across the mesa crying and calling. Close by the wild olive tree she had come upon a night-hawk squatting under the bushes; it had not stirred nor flown, but looked up at her, its eyes bright and beady—she could have taken it in her hand—it looked as if it would have come to her hand. How if that had been her daughter? Well, look at all the things that had happened of late in the campody—three deaths since the new moon! weevil! And Red Morning's mare gone lame in the night without visible occasion! And now Sina—but for all that they waited until the light was well advanced before they called him up to answer for such evil practices.

The sun was not up from behind the desert ranges, but the vast arc of heaven was filled with the light of it and the earth with pulsating blueness as the little knot of neighbors went up the trail toward Bill Bodry's. Sticks and stones they gathered by the way, but they put Wind-in-the-face foremost; after all it was *his* daughter.

Bill was out building the fire as they crossed the creek, and had turned facing the sound of voices when the first stone struck him. "Coyote whelp! Sorcerer! Spell binder!" the cries assailed him. He stood rooted with astonishment; another stone sailed by and struck plump on the door of the wickiup, the door like a white man's; prompt as a hornet out came Sina. She was looking very well and very much the mistress of her house. Catameneda of the Round Arm wept distractedly.

"Sina, Sina, my girl, come away from him—come away home with me—" When one has expected to find one's only child turned into a night hawk or a wood rat, one may be forgiven for a touch of hysteria. "Sina, Sina, daughter of my heart, come away from the Worker of Evil!" Sina looked at her husband's cut lip which was beginning to bleed, and then at her parents, and the look took on a touch of severity.

"I don't know what you mean," she said, though she did perfectly, for she remembered what the Woman of Black Rock had said about bringing Bill to Council. "But I know one thing," said Sina in the lisping English which was the hall-mark of the younger generation, "I don't thank you for comin' here makin' trouble for me and my man so early in the morning."

The Coyote-Spirit and the Weaving Woman

The Weaving Woman lived under the bank of the stony wash that cut through the country of the mesquite dunes. The Coyote-Spirit, which, you understand, is an Indian whose form has been changed to fit with his evil behavior, ranged from the Black Rock where the wash began to the white sands beyond Pahranagat; and the Goat-Girl kept her flock among the mesquites, or along the windy stretch of sage below the campoodie; but as the Coyote-Spirit never came near the wickiups by day, and the Goat-Girl went home the moment the sun dropped behind Pahranagat, they never met. These three are all that have to do with the story.

The Weaving Woman, whose work was the making of fine baskets of split willow and roots of yucca and brown grass, lived alone, because there was nobody found who wished to live with her, and because it was whispered among the wickiups that she was different from other people. It was reported that she had an infirmity of the eyes which caused her to see everything with rainbow fringes, bigger and brighter and better than it was. All her days were fruitful, a handful of pine nuts as much to make merry over as a feast; every lad who went by a-hunting with his bow at his back looked to be a painted brave, and every old woman digging roots as fine as a medicine man in all his feathers. All the faces at the campoodie, dark as the mingled sand and lava of the Black Rock country, deep lined with work and weather, shone for this singular old woman with the glory of the late evening light on Pahranagat. The door of her wickiup opened toward the campoodie with the smoke going up from cheerful hearths, and from the shadow of the bank where she sat to make baskets she looked down the stony wash where all the trails converged that led every way among the dunes, and saw an enchanted mesa covered with misty bloom and gentle creatures moving on trails that seemed to lead to the places where one had always wished to be.

Since all this was so, it was not surprising that her baskets turned out to be such wonderful affairs, and the tribesmen, though they winked and wagged their heads, were very glad to buy them for a haunch of venison or a bagful of mesquite meal. Sometimes, as they stroked the perfect curves of the bowls or traced out the patterns, they were heard to sigh, thinking how fine life would be if it were so rich and bright as she made it seem, instead of the dull occasion they had found it. There were some who even said it was a pity, since she was so clever at the craft, that the weaver was not more like other people, and no one thought to suggest that in that case her weaving would be no better than theirs. For all this the basket-maker did not care, sitting always happily at her weaving or wandering far into the desert in search of withes and barks and dyes, where the wild things showed her many a wonder hid from those who have not rainbow fringes to their eyes; and because she was not afraid of anything, she went farther and farther into the silent places until in the course of time she met the Coyote-Spirit.

Now a Coyote-Spirit, from having been a man, is continually thinking about men and wishing to be with them, and, being a coyote and of
the wolf's breed, no sooner does he have his wish than he thinks of
devouring. So as soon as this one had met the Weaving Woman he
desired to eat her up, or to work her some evil according to the evil of his
nature. He did not see any opportunity to begin at the first meeting, for
on account of the infirmity of her eyes the woman did not see him as a
coyote, but as a man, and let down her wicker water bottle for him to
drink, so kindly that he was quite abashed. She did not seem in the least
afraid of him, which is disconcerting even to a real coyote; though if he
had been, she need not have been afraid of him in any case. Whatever
pestiferous beast the Indian may think the dog of the wilderness, he has
not reason to fear him except when by certain signs, as having a larger
and leaner body, a sharper muzzle, and more evilly pointed ears, he
knows him the soul of a bad-hearted man going about in that guise.
There are enough of these Coyote-Spirits ranging in Mesquite Valley
and over towards Funeral Mountains and about Pahranagat to give
certain learned folk surmise as to whether there may not be a strange
breed of wolves in that region; but the Indians know better.

When the Coyote-Spirit who had met the basket woman thought
about it afterward, he said to himself that she deserved all the mis-
chance that might come upon her for that meeting. "She knows," he
said, "that this is my range, and whoever walks in a Coyote-Spirit's
range must expect to take the consequences. She is not at all like the
Goat-Girl."

The Coyote-Spirit had often watched the Goat-Girl from the top of
Pahranagat, but because she was always in the open where no lurking-
places were, never far from the corn lands where the old men might be
working, he had made himself believe he would not like that kind of a
girl. Every morning he saw her come out of her leafy hut, loose the
goats from the corral, which was all of cactus stems and broad leaves of
prickly-pear, and lead them out among the wind-blown hillocks of sand
under which the trunks of the mesquite flourished for a hundred years,
and out of the tops of which the green twigs bore leaves and fruit; or
along the mesa to browse on bitterbrush and the tops of scrubby sage.
Sometimes she plaited willows for the coarser kinds of basketwork, or,
in hot noonings while the flock dozed, worked herself collars and neck-
laces of white and red and turquoise-colored beads, and other times sat
dreaming on the sand. But whatever she did, she kept far enough from
the place of the Coyote-Spirit, who, now that he had met the Weaving

Woman, could not keep his mind off her. Her hut was far enough from the campoodie so that every morning he went around by the Black Rock to see if she was still there, and there she sat weaving patterns in her baskets of all that she saw or thought. Now it would be the winding wash and the wattled huts beside it, now the mottled skin of the rattle-snake or the curled plumes of the quail.

At last the Coyote-Spirit grew so bold that when there was no one passing on the trail he would go and walk up and down in front of the wickiup. Then the Weaving Woman would look up from her work and give him the news of the season and the tribesmen in so friendly a fashion that he grew less and less troubled in his mind about working her mischief. He said in his evil heart that since the ways of such as he were known to the Indians,—as indeed they were, with many a charm and spell to keep them safe,—it could be no fault of his if they came to harm through too much familiarity. As for the Weaving Woman, he said, "She sees me as I am, and ought to know better," for he had not heard about the infirmity of her eyes.

Finally he made up his mind to ask her to go with him to dig for roots around the foot of Pahranagat, and if she consented,—and of course she did, for she was a friendly soul,—he knew in his heart what he would do. They went out by the mesa trail, and it was a soft and blossomy day of spring. Long wands of the creosote with shining fretted foliage were hung with creamy bells of bloom, and doves called softly from the Dripping Spring. They passed rows of owlets sitting by their burrows and saw young rabbits playing in their shallow forms. The Weaving Woman talked gayly as they went, as Indian women talk, with soft mellow voices and laughter breaking in between the words like smooth water flowing over stones. She talked of how the deer had shifted their feeding-grounds and of whether the quail had mated early that year as a sign of a good season, matters of which the Coyote-Spirit knew more than she, only he was not thinking of those things just then. Whenever her back was turned he licked his cruel jaws and whetted his appetite. They passed the level mesa, passed the tumbled fragments of the Black Rock and came to the sharp wall-sided cañons that showed the stars at noon from their deep wells of sombre shade, where no wild creature made its home and no birds ever sang. Then the Weaving Woman grew still at last because of the great stillness, and the Coyote-Spirit said in a hungry, whining voice,—

"Do you know why I brought you here?"

"To show me how still and beautiful the world is here," said the Weaving Woman, and even then she did not seem afraid.

"To eat you up," said the Coyote. With that he looked to see her fall quaking at his feet, and he had it in mind to tell her it was no fault but her own for coming so far astray with one of his kind, but the woman only looked at him and laughed. The sound of her laughter was like water in a bubbling spring.

"Why do you laugh?" said the Coyote, and he was so astonished that his jaws remained open when he had done speaking.

"How could you eat me?" said she. "Only wild beasts could do that."

"What am I, then?"

"Oh, you are only a man."

"I am a coyote," said he.

"Do you think I have no eyes?" said the woman. "Come!" For she did not understand that her eyes were different from other people's, what she really thought was that other people's were different from hers, which is quite another matter, so she pulled the Coyote-Spirit over to a rain-fed pool. In that country the rains collect in basins of the solid rock that grow polished with a thousand years of storm and give back from their shining side a reflection like a mirror. One such lay in the bottom of the black cañon, and the Weaving Woman stood beside it.

Now it is true of Coyote-Spirits that they are so only because of their behavior; not only have they power to turn themselves to men if they wish—but they do not wish, or they would not have become coyotes in the first place—but other people in their company, according as they think man-thoughts or beast-thoughts, can throw over them such a change that they have only to choose which they will be. So the basket-weaver contrived to throw the veil of her mind over the Coyote-Spirit, so that when he looked at himself in the pool he could not tell for the life of him whether he was most coyote or most man, which so frightened him that he ran away and left the Weaving Woman to hunt for roots alone. He ran for three days and nights, being afraid of himself, which is the worst possible fear, and then ran back to see if the basket-maker had not changed her mind. He put his head in at the door of her wickiup.

"Tell me, now, am I a coyote or a man?"

"Oh, a man," said she, and he went off to Pahranagat to think it over. In a day or two he came back.

"And what now?" he said.

"Oh, a man, and I think you grow handsomer every day."

That was really true, for what with her insisting upon it and his thinking about it, the beast began to go out of him and the man to come back. That night he went down to the campoodie to try and steal a kid from the corral, but it occurred to him just in time that a man would not do that, so he went back to Pahranagat and ate roots and berries instead, which was a true sign that he had grown into a man again. Then there came a day when the Weaving Woman asked him to stop at her hearth and eat. There was a savory smell going up from the cooking-pots, cakes of mesquite meal baking in the ashes, and sugary white buds of the yucca palm roasting on the coals. The man who had been a coyote lay on a blanket of rabbit skin and heard the cheerful snapping of the fire. It was all so comfortable and bright that somehow it made him think of the Goat-Girl.

"That is the right sort of a girl," he said to himself. "She has always stayed in the safe open places and gone home early. She should be able to tell me what I am," for he was not quite sure, and since he had begun to walk with men a little, he had heard about the Weaving Woman's eyes.

Next day he went out where the flock fed, not far from the corn lands, and the Goat-Girl did not seem in the least afraid of him. So he went again, and the third day he said,—

"Tell me what I seem to you."

"A very handsome man," said she.

"Then will you marry me?" said he; and when the Goat-Girl had taken time to think about it she said yes, she thought she would.

Now, when the man who had been a coyote lay on the blanket of the Weaving Woman's wickiup, he had taken notice how it was made of willows driven into the ground around a pit dug in the earth, and the poles drawn together at the top, and thatched with brush, and he had tried at the foot of Pahranagat until he had built another like it; so when he had married the Goat-Girl, after the fashion of her tribe, he took her there to live. He was not now afraid of anything except that his wife might get to know that he had once been a coyote. It was during the first month of their marriage that he said to her, "Do you know the basket-maker who lives under the bank of the stony wash? They call her the Weaving Woman."

"I have heard something of her and I have bought her baskets. Why do you ask?"

"It is nothing," said the man, "but I hear strange stories of her, that

she associates with Coyote-Spirits and such creatures," for he wanted
to see what his wife would say to that.

"If that is the case," said she, "the less we see of her the better. One
cannot be too careful in such matters."

After that, when the man who had been a coyote and his wife visited
the campoodie, they turned out of the stony wash before they reached
the wickiup, and came in to the camp by another trail. But I have not
heard whether the Weaving Woman noticed it.

Introduction to *One-Smoke Stories*

The corn-husk cigarettes, which for ceremonial purposes are still used
south of Green River and west of the Rio Grande, last only a little
while. Since they are filled with the biting native *tabac,* this is perhaps
not to be regretted. You select your husk from the heap and gather your
pinch of the weed from the dark bowl as it passes the ancient ceremonial road from east to north by west to south, and holding the dry
roll delicately between your lips endeavor to dispatch the salutatory
puffs to the six, or, if you happen to be among the Navajo, the four
world quarters. Try as you may, you will probably never master the
unobtrusive art, though I have seen white men whose standing in the
country is that of "old timers" allowing the smoke to escape from their
lips in the appointed directions, but in such a manner that they are able,
if you accuse one of them of it, to deny it successfully.

Thus after a day of preparation for the unending seasonal rituals
that keep the Indian snug in his environment, sib to it, in the old sense
of communicable, answering back again, around the embers sit the
meditative Elders. Now and again holding the crisp cylinder between
thumb and finger tip, unlit, one begins, always gravely, and holds on,
for the space of one smoke, tales each as deft, as finished in itself, as a
ceremonial cigarette. Or if not a tale, then a clean round out of the
speaker's experience, such as in our kind of society, might turn up a
sonnet or an etching. And between them, the ingoing and outgoing
sense of the universe pulses and spirals with the ascending smoke.

The essence of all such stories is that they should be located somewhere in the inner sense of the audience, unencumbered by what in our
more discursive method is known as background.

Your true desert dweller travels light. He makes even of his experience a handy package, with the finished neatness that distinguishes his artifacts. How else could they be passed intact from tribe to tribe, from generation to generation? Just before the end, like the rattle which warns that the story is about to strike, comes the fang of the experience, most often in the shape of a wise saying. Then the speaker resumes the soul consoling smoke, while another takes up the dropped stitch of narrative and weaves it into the pattern of the talk.

Folk experience admits many tellable items which, in a world of pretentious sophistication like ours, are inhibited. It admits the friendly dead, the talking animal whose wisdom is profounder than ours because his mysteriousness is nearer to the Great Mystery. It admits the Surpassing Beings whom we blunderingly designate as Gods—the Sacred Trues who are themselves the instigators of experience. Some of the tales most esteemed by the audiences that originally heard them are unintelligible to our so much more objective minds. They dip too deeply, pass beyond our ken into the region mastery over which man resigned as the purchase price of intelligence. Others, and these are often the wittiest, are inhibited by our proprieties. Not that I was ever told anything unsuitable for a woman to hear, but between their suitabilities and ours is all the distance we have travelled to know that the joke the Trues placed upon man when they tied procreation to responsibility is not a joke to women.

As for the manner of telling, I hope I shall be found adhering closely to the original method, but if occasionally I am discovered adding to the austere relation such further perception of the scene as is necessary to have the fang of the story strike home, I shall hope it is not too much. In the words of the sacred formula: I give you to smoke.

The Medicine of Bow-Returning

There was a man of the Plains whose mother named him Taku-Wakin, which means Something Wonderful. She felt in her heart that he would do some great thing, and to that end she reared him.

When the time came, according to custom, she sent him into the hills to fast and find his Medicine. This is the way it happens when a youth is of age to become a tribesman; he walks apart, keeping holy silence, seeking. During his search he eats nothing, drinks a little water, sees no one, visits the holy places. After two or three days the One-who-Walks-in-the-Sky is revealed to him in the form of a bird or an animal, or it may be as the small grass, or the rainbow. Whatever thing appears, that becomes his Medicine. Through it he reaches up to the Allness and receives much *wokonda,* that is to say, strength of Spirit. According to the strength of his Spirit a man prospers.

So Taku-Wakin, who was afterward called Bow-Returning, went towards the mountain called Going-to-the-Sun for his fast, and as he went he felt the thoughts of his mother push him. He went far, climbed the high mountains, and bathed in the sacred lakes, keeping holy silence. On the mountain, when by fasting he was removed from himself, his eyes were opened. He saw all the earth and the sky as One Thing, even as the bow is one thing and the cord of the bow which draws it. Even so he saw the thoughts of men pulling at the corners of the world as the cord pulls at the bow, and the bow bending and returning. In the silence he heard in his heart the One-who-Walks-in-the-Sky talking.

"This is true Medicine, Taku-Wakin. All things are one: man and the mire, the small grass and the mountain, the deer and the hunter pursuing, the thing that is made and the maker, even as the bow and the cord are one thing. As the bow bends to the cord, so all things bend and return, and are opposed and together. The meaning of the Medicine is that man can hurt nothing without also hurting himself." Thus said the One-who-Walks-in-the-Sky to Taku-Wakin.

Taku-Wakin ate and drank and went down the mountain, walking carefully that he might hurt nothing. To his mother he said, "It is my Medicine to know that man can hurt nothing without hurting himself also," and to the tribesmen he said that from this time forth he should be called Bow-Returning. From that time also he was much respected because of his strong Medicine. Meat he ate according to the law of food taking, but there was no man who could say he had hurt of any sort at the hands of Bow-Returning.

In the counsel of time it came into the heart of Bow-Returning that he ought to go about among his tribes teaching the Medicine of Bow-Returning. Then he said there will be no man hurting another. This he said to his wife, for by this time he had a wife, and though she was sad to think of his leaving her, she began at once to make him moccasins. From tribe to tribe, strong in his Medicine, went Bow-Returning with a great following. But as he went, his *wokonda* began to go from him. When his Medicine would no longer work, then men refused to believe him, and one by one his following fell away from him. Troubled in heart, as Taku-Wakin he returned to his home camp. But his tent was not among the others; for his wife had died of grieving, and his son had been given to another. Bow-Returning purged himself in the sweat lodges; with smoke of sweet grass he sanctified himself, and went again on the mountain, keeping holy silence.

After long seeking, he heard the voice of the Sky-Walker. Then said Bow-Returning: "This is my Medicine, that everything is One Thing, and in this fashion I have kept it. Meat I have taken for my needs according to the law of food taking, but I have hurt no man. Neither the flower in the field have I crushed, nor trodden on the ant in my pathway. How is it, then, that my wife is dead, my son given to another, and my Medicine is gone from me?"

Then said the One-in-the-Sky to Bow-Returning, "Did I not also make woman?"

The Spirit of the Bear Walking

Hear now a Telling,

Whenever Hotándanai of the *campody* of Sagharawíte went hunting on the mountain, he took care to think as little as possible of Paháwitz-na'an, the Spirit of the Bear that-Fathered-Him. For it is well known that whoever can see Paháwitz-na'an without being seen by him will become the mightiest hunter of his generation, but he can never be seen by anybody who is thinking about him.

On the other hand, if a tribesman should himself be seen by the Spirit of the Bear Walking, there is no knowing what might happen. Hunters who have gone up on Toorape and never come back are supposed to have met with him. So between hope of seeing and fear of being seen, it is nearly impossible to hunt on the mountain without thinking of Paháwitz-na'an.

Hotándanai alone hoped to accomplish the impossible. He might have managed it at the time his thoughts were all taken up with wondering whether the daughter of Tinnemahá, the Medicine Man, could be persuaded to marry him, but at that time he did not hunt at all. He spent his time waiting at the spring where the maidens came with their mothers to fill their water bottles, making a little flute of four notes and playing on it. But after he was married, he tried again to dispossess his mind of the thought of Paháwitz-na'an. "For," he said, "when my son is born he will have pride in me, and keep a soft place in the hut for the man who was the mightiest hunter of his generation." Thus it was that he never went out to hunt on Toorape without thinking both of his son and the Bear Walking.

In due time the son was born, and though Hotándanai had not yet become the mightiest hunter, he was very happy. Always when he went to the mountain of Toorape he remembered his wish, and so missed it.

In the course of years the tribe fell into war with the people of the North, and the son of Hotándanai went out to his first battle. But, as it turned out, the battle went against Sagharawite, and the son of Hotándanai was brought home shot full of arrows. Then the heart of Hotándanai broke when he buried him. He said, "Let me go, I will build a fire on the mountain to light the feet of my son's spirit, and there I will lament him."

Clad in all his war gear, he went up to Toorape, and all the way he thought only of his son and how he should miss him. So when he had lighted the spirit fire, he said, "Oh, my son, what profit shall I have of my life now you are departed!" And as he wept he saw something moving on the slope before him. He looked, for his eyes were by no means as keen as they had been, and behold, it was the Spirit of the Bear Walking.

Wolf People

Said Antelope-over-the-Hill to the teacher of the Indian School: Mamaita, I have come to tell you that this is not true what you are telling my children in the school, how the dog is a Wolf cub tamed by a woman and bred up to be another with the children. I have come to let you know what has been known to Our Ancients, that the Wolves are a people. They have their own speech, their own chiefs and hunt leaders. They have been long friendly to the man pack, and go with them to the hunt, although somewhat far off, for the smell of any people is good only to itself. They go on the trail of the Deer and the Buffalo peoples, and the Wolves and the Indian people are helpful to each other in the hunt. They see one another and signal, and as they travel they sing their hunting songs. But the hunting song of the Wolves is more powerful than that of men; therefore men learn it for times of need. The Wolves, when they hear men singing, will arise and drive the game towards the man pack; for men are more skilful at the kill, and Wolves on the trail. Therefore they wait until the men have killed, and what the men leave the Wolves take, and there is enough for all. This is how it is that lone Wolves left their kind, and followed, and came to live with the man pack. So the children of men came to know the Wolf children and give names to them. This is how it is that the Wolf becomes a dog, of its own free willing; because man is the better killer. I have come to let you know.

The Shade of the Arrows

You have heard, *compadres*, that we Paiutes have a saying that whoever goes on an untried venture must sleep in the shade of his arrows. Concerning this there is a telling.

It was told by our fathers that Pamaquash, the elder of those Twain that were like unto the right hand and the left hand of Power, wearied at last of the pranks of the younger, and banished him to the unrained on land beyond the Borders. This was after they Twain had been through the land of the Utes and the Paiutes—who are the Utes of the running streams, whereas the Utes are in the Great Basin—doing after their kind; Hinuno, the younger, destroying, Pamaquash, the elder, upbuilding. After Hinuno had broken the baskets and lost the *taboose* of the maidens of Sagharawite, and killed the children of the Bear by bending down the tops of tall trees for their playing, after all these things, his brother banished him.

With his bow and his quiver and his Medicine pouch only, according to the law of banishing—for the bow is as the thought of man, and the arrows are his purposes which he launches therefrom, and his Medicine no man can take from him. For four days after the banishing, the land was full of the sound of his fury, hills rending, and the sky yellow from the dust stirred up in the Dance of the Younger Brother. Then a day of silence.

Said Pamaquash, "By this time my brother is dead, and it becomes me to bury him."

Smoke he made, with his Medicine pipe, cloud smoke ascending, and on the cloud, Pamaquash, hurrying over the land, looking for his younger brother to bury him. Everywhere was the desolation of that unrained-on country and the wreckage of the wrath of the younger brother: hills powdered to sand, knife-cut cañons, even the great cañon of the Colorado; never a spring of sweet water nor a tree to lie under. Then as Pamaquash floated over the land on the smoke cloud, he heard someone calling, "Hi, Brother, I am here in the shade of my arrows!" Thus he had placed them, half-circlewise about his head, and their featherings were between his head and the sun. So a man sits under his purposes when all else fails him. Therefore Pamaquash forgave Hinuno, seeing how he had saved himself. And to this day it is a saying among the Paiutes, when the young men would do that which the elders, being cautious, deny them. "But," say the young men, "we shall sleep in the shade of our arrows."

6

Articles and Essays

Mary Austin depended considerably on the earnings for the articles she wrote, of which she published more than two hundred in periodicals such as the *Century,* the *Nation,* the *Bookman,* the *Forum,* and the *Saturday Review.* Austin's subject matter ranged from opinion pieces (frequently on American cultural questions) to American Indian tribal customs, American literature, important current topics like "Making the Most of Your Genius," and literary people she admired. She was a lecturer of some note, and she often used material she had gathered in England for her talks—many to women's clubs throughout the country—as well as for her writing. The articles included here are all somewhat autobiographical.

Austin held decided ideas on fiction, and included here are excerpts from one representative article, "Sex in American Literature," which the *Bookman* published in June 1923. While to today's reader, the article may appear conservative and intolerant, and perhaps bigoted in its insistence on Anglo-European cultural superiority, Austin anticipates major arguments of our time about the representation of sexuality in a literature wrought by writers from diverse ethnic and cultural backgrounds. Her discussion of contemporary writers is especially illuminating: criticism for the naturalism in Dreiser's writing, a negative reaction to the unrealized woman characters in Sinclair Lewis's novels, and unqualified admiration for Willa Cather's understanding of gender in her texts.

In 1927 Austin was asked by the *Nation* to contribute to a series called "These Modern Women." She agreed to do so on condition that her contribution be anonymous. In her article, "Woman Alone," she rehearsed the details of unhappy family life that she would include in her autobiography. Her essay goes on to capsulize the central problem at the core of a patriarchal society in autobiographical terms: "As for not being under the necessity of being liked, which began as a defense, it has become part of my life philosophy. I see now that too many of the impositions of society upon women have come of their fear of not being liked."[1] Austin risked not being liked by many; she particularly singled out New York for criticism. "Don't you be disturbed by anything you read about me in the New York Magazines," she wrote from the National Arts Club in New York to a friend in 1923, the year *The Land of Journeys' Ending* was published. "They don't know me. They think I have no humour because my humour is directed against them, and egotistical because I am not afraid of anything, not even New York."[2]

Austin maintained throughout her career that she wrote without thinking of style. In an article originally entitled "My First Publication," which Gelett Burgess had solicited for his anthology *My Maiden Effort* (1921), Austin stated that after she wrote her first book, *The Land of Little Rain*, reviewers praised it for its style. "Nothing was further from my mind when I was writing it," she wrote. "I had never exchanged a dozen words with anybody on the question of style, nor thought of it as being a writer's problem. What I did think was that the kind of people who could have enjoyed my country as I had enjoyed it probably had a different medium of communication from that employed at Lone Pine." She imagined this different form to be "the way I supposed highly cultivated people talked to one another."[3] Austin's statement appears disingenuous in light of the fact that she was known to have read all the "classics" in her girlhood, and that she read the major newspapers all her life. She had no doubt a rather clear idea in mind of literary prose versus "the way my neighbors talked."[4] However, another reading of what she says here might suggest that she was a natural writer with an effortless grasp on matters of style.

To the modern taste, Austin's journalistic prose occasionally seems needlessly convoluted and formal—not her best writing. Yet in her journalism and other published essays, Austin gives us essential ideas about culture that she thematically infused into her fiction and plays. She was very interested, for example, in the notion of "genius," which she believed herself to possess, and which she had attributed to the mythic *chisera* figure of her 1911 American Indian play, *The Arrow Maker*. Austin often spoke about genius and its cultivation in her lectures, and in 1923 and 1924 she wrote a series of articles for the *Bookman*, "Making the Most of Your Genius." In 1925 she published the book *Everyman's Genius*. The novel *A Woman of Genius* (1912) contains an early version of her interpretation of the female artist or genius who must overcome the obstacles that society places in her path to greatness.[5]

Austin frequently complained to her friends and publishers that her journalism interfered with her more creative projects; the truth is that as well as supporting her, the writing that she did for the magazines informed her book-length projects and helped to establish her reputation as an intellectual commentator on the American scene during the first third of the twentieth century.

How I Learned to Read and Write

I have just one recollection of the process by which I learned to read and write, which, according to family tradition, occurred when I was between four and five years of age, without any other aid than might have been furnished by a brother two years older. I can recall having trouble with my reading, and asking to have passages which I had imperfectly apprehended read aloud to me, but of the process of learning to write not a scrap remains. That I could do both, for my own pleasure, by the time I was admitted to school at the age of six, is pricked upon my mind by an event that illuminates the educational methods of that day.

It had never occurred to me to tell, nor the teacher to ask, if I could read, so I was entered in the "chart class" and for weeks stood up with the others and recited a-b, ab, b-o, bo.

To relieve the boredom of the hours between recitations I smuggled a book under my desk and read. But, being one day absorbed to the point of missing my class, I was obliged to admit that I had been reading, and was made to stand on the floor for having told a lie, since it was obvious that being only in the chart class I could not read. I bore this very well so long as there were only my fellow pupils present, but when the principal entered on his daily round, I was provoked to protest in my own defence. He must have been a good principal for that time, for he promptly put the matter to a test and discovered that I could read very well. He promoted me on the spot to the next room.

I have a very definite impression of myself, a small, gawky girl, burdened with my school belongings, my hood and cloak and my tin lunch bucket, under the hostile eyes of half a hundred children two or three years older than myself, who felt their dignity as second and third graders assailed by my intrusion among them. I mention it here because the partial isolation which resulted from their attitude drove me rather earlier than might otherwise have happened to the solace of writing.

At first it was only sentences, possibly incomplete phrases, always written separately on little slips of paper which I kept rolled up like cigarettes and used to secrete in various places about the house. They were immensely precious and important to me, but they must also have been childishly absurd, because it was the delight of my family to rout them out of their hiding places and read them aloud to one another and especially to company. I can recall the rage of violated privacy into which these occasions always threw me as the most poignant emotion of my childhood. I have often suspected that this early experience has something to do with my still active and not always successful resistance to editorial interference with my later work.

My first organized piece of writing was in verse and called by me "A Play To Be Sung." That was because, being brought up on the outskirts of a mid-Western town, and a Methodist to boot, I had never heard that plays to be sung were usually called operas. Up to my sixteenth year I had never seen any kind of stage performance except a Sunday School entertainment, so I have no idea where this libretto of mine came from. My memory of it is distinctly of a thing seen, people in a closed in space, moving about and singing to one another, where they might be expected to talk.

The only way in which I can account for it is as something I had heard read aloud. My father had several years of invalidism, during which it was my mother's custom to read him to sleep. Though I was often caught and punished for it, I could seldom resist creeping out of my own bed and huddling just outside the door to listen, dropping asleep myself occasionally and being spanked awake as I was put back to bed.

I wrote High School notes for the local paper, of course, and nearly all my seat-mate's compositions as well as my own and some of my brother's. I wrote for my College paper and, when I was twenty, I wrote two short stories.

I recall that after having paid to have them typewritten my husband mislaid one of the manuscripts, the original copy of which had been destroyed. The other I sent to *The Overland Monthly,* the editor of which wrote me that he would like to publish my story but that he could not pay for it as Eastern magazines paid. I replied that he could pay me whatever he was accustomed to pay, which turned out to be nothing at all. Two years later, while moving and settling in another house, the lost manuscript came to light among some papers of my husband's. *The Overland* was having a short-story prize contest then, so mine was submitted. I never heard from it officially, but after a year or so I ran across it in the pages of *The Overland.*

These experiences discouraged me from sending out manuscripts and indeed I finished almost nothing during the next six or seven years while I was occupied with my house and my baby. One story was sent to *The Black Cat* by my husband, who thought it would please me to see it

Mary Austin in the late 1920s. (Courtesy of the California State Library, Sacramento, California)

in print, which it did. But when about 1900 I began seriously to devote myself to a writing career, I made a list of the magazines for which I meant to write in the order of their literary excellence, with *The Atlantic Monthly* at the top.

Accordingly, I sent them my first story, which was accepted and paid for magnificently, as I thought, with a check for thirty-five dollars. There were two or three other short stories, if I remember rightly, variously placed, and then all at once, in the period of convalescence after an illness, I wrote "The Land of Little Rain."

To understand what the writing of this, my maiden book, meant to me, you must realize that up to that time, and for many years afterwards, I was living in a California town of about three hundred inhabitants, and, with the exception of the middle Western college town of about six thousand, it was the only kind of town I had ever known. I had seen but two plays, both of them without the knowledge of my parents. I had never seen an opera, nor a good picture, nor heard any good music. There was no library in the town, not many books of any sort. Happily, I did not know enough to know that this was not the atmosphere out of which books were supposed to be written. I confidently expected to produce books. For twelve years I had lived deeply and absorbedly in the life of the desert.

I was languid with convalescence, I was lonely; and quite suddenly I began to write. I began at the beginning, and, with an interval of months for another illness, wrote straight to the end, practically without erasures or revisions. I remember the day very well—one of those thin days when the stark energies of the land threaten just under its surfaces, the mountains march nakedly, the hills confer. The air was so still that one could feel, almost hear, the steady pulse of the stamp-mill away East under the Inyo. There was a weeping willow whose long branches moved back and forth across my window like blowing hair, like my memory of my mother's long and beautiful hair. I think it was this which gave the reminiscent touch to my mood. For though I was there in the midst of it, I began to write of the land of little rain as of something very much loved, now removed. As I wrote, two tall, invisible presences came and stood on either side.

I don't know now what these presences were . . . are. For two or three years, until I moved away from that country, in fact, they were present when I wrote. Sometimes, I felt them call me to my desk—sometimes I summoned them. I suppose they were projections out of my loneliness, reabsorbed into the subconsciousness when the need of them was past. Though I could never quite see them, almost but not quite, and it is years since they have been present to the outward sense, I am still occasionally aware of them inside of me.

"The Land of Little Rain" was promptly accepted by Houghton Mifflin Company and published serially in *The Atlantic* before appearing in book form. It had an instant success of esteem and is still selling creditably, enough to warrant, even in this year of high cost production, a popular edition.

And now it is time to make a confession concerning my first book, which might have been made earlier if I had been able to make up my mind whether the joke about it is on me or on the public.

The book had been much praised for its style. Nothing was further from my mind when I was writing it. I had never exchanged a dozen words with anybody on the question of style, nor thought of it as being a writer's problem. What I did think was that the kind of people who could have enjoyed my country as I enjoyed it probably had a different medium of communication from that employed at Lone Pine. When I wrote I tried always to write the way I supposed highly cultivated people talked to one another. I knew it was not the way my neighbors talked because everybody, even the young woman who did my typewriting, corrected my diction and my phraseology. "It sounded so queer," she would cheerfully explain her alterations of my text. Even my husband would offer to correct my proof so as to bring it within the local range, and the village school-teacher would tactfully send me copies of the magazines containing my articles, with penciled suggestions of her own. But I stuck to my original conception of the proper form to be employed between me and the sort of people I hoped to reach.

So that's all there is to the question of my maiden style. I simply didn't know any better. I was astounded to the point of consternation when the reviews began to come in and I discovered that I was supposedly to have "style." Since I did not know in the least how it had been achieved, I was always afraid of losing it. And now I am afraid I never shall. I know now that even members of the Poetry Society and the Authors' League do not talk to one another in that fashion, that they do not, in fact, talk very differently from the people in Lone Pine. But the final effect of my maiden experience as a writer has been to wish it onto me for life.

Sex in American Literature

Anyone who accepts an invitation to write on the subject of sex in American literature is sure, at least, of a definite limitation of the field of comment. He would not be expected, supposing we had an American equivalent for those immortal works, to discuss "Aucassin et Nicolette" or the "Paradiso" of Dante. He would be able to omit all mention of an American "Romeo and Juliet" and need not even think of an "Antony and Cleopatra," though one of these be the supreme drama of young love, and the other the outstanding instance of a world well lost for an infatuation. For sex in the United States is never taken to mean the whole complex of the individual love life. It is quite definitely restricted to a physiological crisis and its immediate reactions, occurring under circumstances sufficiently incriminating to remain reasonably outside the parlor consciousness of the average citizen.

In no way does the American public evince the unsophistication of its sex perceptions so readily as in this general acceptance of the parlor as the determinant of aspects of sex that may, or may not, be treated in fiction. There is practically no limit to the detail with which the eternal encounter of male and female may be discussed, so long as it happens in the parlor or some of its accepted substitutes. It is only when the threshold of the bedroom is crossed that the hackles of American propriety begin to rise.

This idea that there are aspects of the love life which cannot profitably be discussed in public, or at all except under well defined limitations of occasion and participation, is the distinctive characteristic of the Anglo-European culture out of which our American culture took its rise. The further you get away from the narrow strip of modern civilization which incorporated into its social inheritance the best traditions of Greek and Roman life, which projected itself into the great experiments of Christian celibacy and Christian mysticism, which gave rise to chivalry and to the scientific approach, the further you are from its prevailing separation of sex experiences into those that enlarge the field of spiritual perceptivity, and those which are believed to be limiting and disintegrating. I am doubtful if there is any people on earth among whom no distinctions are made as to the quality of sex relations, but it is quite certain that the distinctions I have just noted are to be found generally among the peoples who maintain the highest intellectual and constructive cultures of today. For this reason it is impossible to treat the American disposition to designate the acceptable types of personal adventure as "love stories" and the unacceptable as "sex" stories, as the evidence of hypocrisy, or moral bigotry. I may be vastly entertained by our literary distinction between sex and love, but I am bound to bring to its discussion some better founded attitude than the supercilious contempt with which it is too often approached. . . .

This must be kept in mind always, as one of the supreme achievements of the Anglo-European civilization, that it learned early how to make the love life a means of enlarging the borders of its understanding of man and his place in society. This is what Hawthorne managed to do with "The Scarlet Letter," which, though it treats plainly of adultery, fixes the attention of the reader not on the act but on the consequent spiritual adventure of the participants. Mr. Galsworthy in his "Forsyte Saga," though he shows his fellow English as failing of this ideal, sometimes cheaply failing, sometimes tragically, never implicates his readers in the failure. Rather, he puts the reader in the position of electing that ideal for himself. . . .

We cannot quite get to the bottom of this state of things by referring it to the young desire to startle by defying the conventions of sex propriety. Nor can it be dismissed as an effort to trade upon the public appetite for salaciousness. For many of the transgressors are not young, and books of this character do not sell at anything like the rate of the commercially "pure" love story. Nor does the complete capitulation of our half baked American intellectualism to the Freudian premise, account for the pre-occupation of writers like Sherwood Anderson and Edgar Lee Masters with phases of our national love life so generally unpleasant and uninforming that they go by the name of "sex" stories.

It is much more likely that the prevailing American obsession with psychoanalysis—so much more obsessing than it has been in any other English speaking country—is itself attributable to the schism which appears to exist between the traditional American ideal of love life and the present literary expression of it. Psychoanalyzing the psychoanalyst, one is inclined to say that the easy substitution of the Freudian libido for the personal devil of our forebears is merely the younger generation's way, by putting their responsibility on the Puritans, of excusing itself for finding sex a tormenting and unmanageable business.

The real question is, why does the newer group of writers find sex so tormenting and unmanageable that it is driven to the point of denying that love life ever was or ever could be anything else? . . .

All Theodore Dreiser's people love like the peasants in a novel by Bojer or Knut Hamsun. His women have a cowlike complaisance such as can be found only in peoples who have lived for generations close to the soil; his men in their amours resemble those savages who can count five only, on the fingers of one hand. Having used up one set of digits they begin all over on the other hand and count five again. So "the Genius" and "the Financier" pass from Susan to Jane and from Jane to

Maria, and so to Edith and Emily, by nearly identical progressions, learning nothing at all and teaching their author very little.

If occasionally one of Dreiser's characters exhibited a more informed approach to the highest type of American love life, one might then suppose that he had chosen to write stories like "Jenny Gerhardt" and "Sister Carrie" for some one of the reprehensible reasons that his critics sometimes credit to him. But the exceedingly narrow range of the multifarious love affairs of Dreiser's people, as well as the restricted outlook of the author's own confessions, admit of no other conclusion than that here is a man of talent, outside the stream of traditional Anglo-American experience, honestly engaged in expressing not only all that he knows, but the limitations of his capacity to know. So far as the evidence of his writing goes, Mr. Dreiser knows no more of the power of the love life to inform and vitalize the whole nature and outlook of man, than the finger counting savage knows of trigonometry. And what is true of Dreiser is also true of a very large contingent of the newer American writers, so that one is continually being surprised among the younger generation not, as they themselves fondly suppose, by the "advanced" nature of their views on sex, but at the quaint, village folk lore antiquity of them.

I do not mean to deny that there are thousands of people in the United States whose love life is the sordidly restricted episode it is descried as being in books like "Winesburg, Ohio" and "Spoon River Anthology." Or that there are millions whose experience is limited to the turgid, tormenting bounderism suffered in the novels of Waldo Frank and Ben Hecht. There are quite certainly any number of people who, while sedulously cherishing the earlier ideal, fail as completely as do the inhabitants of Zenith City and Gopher Prairie in registering its high mark. But one does not need to accuse any of these authors of anything less than entire honesty in order to prove that there may be more beauty and aspiration in American love life than gets into their books. What one does suspect them of, with the sole exception of Sinclair Lewis, is the nursing of their limitations in this direction under the illusion that it is the advertisement of a superior attitude toward life and society.

Mr. Lewis writes with a photographic fidelity which appears at times not wholly conscious of what it reflects. One wonders if he was fully aware of how much of Carol Kennicott's failure to find herself in Gopher Prairie was owing to the lack of sex potency, a lack which he records without relating it to any other of her insufficiencies. Insufficiency in every one of the centres of personal power, in sex and art and religion, is the note of George Babbitt. Here also Mr. Lewis seems disposed to charge the shortcomings of his hero, as of his heroine, to the social environment, rather than to any incapacity, either native or acquired, to experience art or love or religion with intensity. Mr. Lewis does not seem to know anything about the relationship of sex potency to the thin muddiness of social perception which he so ruthlessly exposes, but we must be grateful to him for leaving his Americans empty as he found them. He at least never stuffs them with the findings of the neuropathic clinic.

Probably Sinclair Lewis is more nearly right than any of our young men writers about the love life of the average middle class American. It is thin rather than vicious. I am as skeptical of the turgid nastiness which the psychoanalytic writers find below the level of American consciousness, as I am doubtful that the monumental repressions of the Puritans are responsible for it. Why assume that they had so much to repress? Long before they came to New England they ceased to need or to find pleasure in ritual and symbol or any representative art; their religious mysticism was reduced to a pale phosphorescence of renunciation. The latter progression of their stock has been toward sterility, intellectual as well as physical. What one suspects is that the average Puritan under his skin was not unlike George Babbitt, with this advantage over George that he was still able to get some warmth out of denouncing the things that no longer warmed him in any other fashion. Poor George didn't even have anything heartily to hate.

One cannot escape the suggestion that much of the present insistence on Puritanism as the prevailing influence in American love life comes from the Slavonic and Semitic elements in our intellectual life. Neither the Russian nor the Jew has ever been able to understand that puritanism may have been a way of escape; or that not to have had any seriously upsetting sex adventures may be the end of an intelligently achieved life standard. The avidity with which the Jew is intellectual in particular has seized upon psychoanalysis emphasizes a need of proving that everybody is as full of secret troubling as himself, a need which could easily arise out of a lack of that intensity of experience it undertakes to demonstrate. . . .

But the present literature of sex which most offends the Anglo-American strain falls readily into two categories: the intricate, tormented type of which D. H. Lawrence is an outstanding example, and the type of earthbound intensity of Sherwood Anderson's blond-white middle westerners. Partaking of both these strains, but definitely disengaging itself from the limitations of both, there is a progressive adventure which has been variously treated by the best English novelists but has, for the moment, no recognized prophet in the United States. The Negroes have not yet begun to write love stories, nor our recently incorporated oriental factors. That which they may yet bring to light of the interior processes of the love life may prove as astonishing as it will be valuable. . . .

Of the women novelists Willa Cather gives the best evidence of comprehending the range of sex experience which our varied American makeup offers to the novelist's hand. Though her extraordinary intuition penetrates to the slow, ashen heat of the peasant heart, it also takes in, on the other side, extensions of the love adventure into regions untrodden by most of our men novelists.

It is worth noting that every one of the eight or ten women novelists in America who might be quickly named is of the earlier Anglo-European stock. Which may account for their preference for the more intellectualized and highly elucidated love adventure, pushed occasionally into regions of spiritual clarity that constitute a real "advance" in the love life of the race. I have in mind that cool touch by which the traditionally happy marriage of "The Brimming Cup" is saved from a suspicion of overripeness, the ability of the husband to remain detached from his wife's projected excursion into infidelity and to refrain from many of the traditional male compulsions of her affections. One has hopes of yet seeing a story in which a wife, refusing to "hold" her husband, successfully enforces her demand that he hold himself. And now, here is Gertrude Atherton with a novel in which is shown a mature woman who, with sufficient beauty to "hold" a much younger man, frankly rejects him in favor of the community of achievement offered her by an older and less romantically stimulative man. Mrs. Atherton makes her point with far too much precision not to know what she refrains from saying: that the whole institution of marriage is built up out of this subconscious conviction of women that the common life of husband and wife, what they may achieve by way of offspring, by conquest of the maternal environment, or on the plane of perceptive consciousness, is more important than what they feel for one another. Two years ago I tried a novel myself in which the woman of the story undertook to persuade a man that he ought to bring his love life into line with his own demand for equity in the fields of economics and politics, but the result proved that there is still a great deal of work to be done among the critics of literature in persuading them that uncovering concealed nastiness is not the only way of being "advanced" in writing about sex.

In nearly everything that gets printed in the United States there is a marked absence of a certain kind of knowledge which is the sum of woman's age long preoccupation with the practice of loving. One observes our young men essayists trying to ensnare this personal lore in nets woven clumsily of quotations from Frazer, Jung, and Havelock Ellis, with all their conclusions falling into the interstices.

Curiously, although we are exceedingly frank talkers in the United States on what might be called the static aspects of sex life—physiology, hygiene, and economics—all its experiential lore is hedged about with conversational inhibitions, the most daunting of which is the convention that bars informing intimacies between young men and older women. In more primitive societies it is the social function of mature women to mediate between the young men and the older, as it is the business of young women to bear children until, by virtue of their experience as mothers of men, they join the ranks of mediators and advisers. Something of this function the mature woman still retains in European and Asiatic society. The French or Italian mother not only advises her son in the selection of a wife, but she is not infrequently his confidante in matters which it is the dutiful business of the American son to prevent his mother from suspecting. The effect on the resulting literatures of the personal life is outstanding. Balzac is full of this experiential lore, Meredith has more than a little, Hardy brings up double handfuls of it from the hearts of English country women; but we have no man novelist in America who dares to concern himself very intimately with the love life of any but extremely young women. Our young men are, as a matter of fact, a little inclined to be shocked at the notion that a woman who has reached the years in which she is definitely recognized as "older" has any love life which should intimately concern them, or, in view of the general refusal of the mature American woman to use her knowledge for the purpose of creating sex "situations," that she has any knowledge that needs to be taken into consideration. Well, where do you suppose it went, all the lore of Aphrodite and Proserpine, all the intricate, heart piercing illumination of the cloisters, all that was thought and suffered by the queens of love and beauty and the fair ladies pining in bowers while their husbands and lovers were proving the quality of those same ladies' charms by sticking pay-nims and restoring ravished virgins to their homes?

What do you suppose the wives of American pioneers were thinking about as they trekked across the continent behind their husbands? Where do you suppose the unmarried English and American woman novelists—who are the only novelists ranking close to the greatest men novelists of the world—inform themselves, except out of the inexhaustible storehouse of women lore, lore chiefly about men's ways with women, which, in America, social use has rendered incommunicable? . . .

Making the Most of Your Genius

Even the people who have it do not always know what genius is. Nor has science so much as an inkling how we came by it. In studies such as Galton's "Hereditary Genius" the subject is obscured by making genius synonymous with exceptional ability. Common usage, taking its cue from science, classes all individuals of unusual capacity as geniuses, without any reference to varieties or processes. But all working artists, and such critics as are able to distinguish between a work of art and a method of artistry, know that by calling a particular book or picture or musical composition a work of genius, they have merely described the process by which it was produced. Since any work of genius, as opposed to works of invention or of intellect, tends to be superior, we have fallen into the careless habit of using the term only in reference to works of standard excellence. But since it is our business in these articles to discuss the genius process, I wish to establish from the outset the use of the word to indicate the process, apart from comparative merits of the thing produced.

Genius as a personal endowment seems to strike as haphazardly as lightning. Either you are born with it, or you are not. Probably I am the only person to be found who will insist that it can be acquired, and very likely I shall not be able to make you agree with me. The earliest intimation the possessor of genius has of its operation is the sudden appearance of ideas or concepts, often of the greatest complexity, in his mind, seeming to come not by way of observation or intelligence but from somewhere above or beyond him, with sourceless connotations of authority. It is this unexpectedness and authoritativeness which led the Greeks to name the experience genius, conceiving its initial impulse to be the whisper of a spirit at the ear of the inner mind. Modern science admits the whisper, but names the source of it as the deep-self, the sum of accumulated emotional and conceptual experience called the race mind, expressing itself through the immediate-self, called the individual. . . .

It is true that genius operates *sub-consciously*. The more exceptional the type of genius the more successfully it conceals its operations from its host. But not every subconscious operation of the mind is a work of genius. Items introduced into the immediate mind in childhood can easily slip into the outer fringes of consciousness and, returning under emotional stress or in connection with some sort of hocus-pocus, such as the ouija board, or spirit communication, get credit with the uniniti-ated as coming from the deep-self. There is also a pseudo-genius ap-pearing frequently among children, especially those who have lived rather exclusively among grown ups, which can almost always be traced to submerged memories of things they have heard discussed or read aloud among their elders. Sometimes the profound wish of the parent to have the child prove among the gifted, even when not directly ex-pressed, produces in a suggestible child superficial traits of the genius process; many of our infant prodigies are undoubtedly of this type. . . .

What the young genius feels behind him is the urge of this impulse to growth; deep-life demanding of him more life, experience aching to add experience to itself. Genius, therefore, is the most natural thing in the world. . . .

Biology, as far as it goes in this direction, tends to rank genius with the disposition of caged canary birds to build nests, and captive beavers to attempt to stop leaks in the water bucket with a dam. This view of genius accounts rationally and wholly for the authority the genius impulse has with its host, for the joy and the sense of at-one-ment with the universe which its unrestricted operation affords its possessor, for the terrific struggles of genius to realize itself in a given medium, and for the agony of frustration. But this view also obliges us to treat with equal respect the operations of genius in any and every field of human activity. There can be genius for chess playing and for chemistry and for sex provocation. I have a friend who has a genius for cooking. She has had no training, and does not know the difference between calories and calomel, but shut her up in an ordinarily equipped kitchen with an utterly unfamiliar article of food, and in the course of the morning she will have discovered the one perfect method of preparing it. This is the way genius, in the presence of its predestined material, works.

Although what I shall say in these papers will be in reference to literary genius, it is probable that most of it is equally applicable to painting, picking pockets, music, or engineering. . . .

My own studies lead me to the conclusion that almost everybody has a little genius of some kind or other, but that most of it is lost to the world, through our stupid handling of it, by the time the subject has reached adolescence. Most of the vagaries of that difficult period, generally ascribed to sex adjustments, could probably be more successfully handled as the struggle of the deep-self to come into working partnership with the immediate-self. It is natural that this conflict would occur at the period when the capacity for handing on the racial inheritance is ripened. Probably the one factor that is most inhibitory to the freeing of genius in the adolescent youth is the rooted fear of being different, the instinctive herd aversion to any sort of "queerness." It is more than likely that as many tendencies toward fortunate variation are strangled at this period, as unfortunate tendencies are checked. At any rate, it is not until this period is passed that the individual can seriously take stock of his equipment for living the genius life.

The young person thus taking stock of himself must first consider the nature of his deep-self. From what the biologists tell us of the nature of inheritance it seems certain that no two deep-selves are exactly alike. Nor do we all have access to the whole sum of human inheritance; we possess only the experiences acquired by the races that have contributed to our blood stream. Thus a genius whose inheritance is wholly Latin does not have access to experiences acquired exclusively by the Scandinavian peoples.

The question of the limitation of genius by the racial type is of the utmost importance in the United States. Nobody has done definitive work in this field, but my own studies, which are by no means final, indicate that genius *never crosses the blood stream.* It does not appear possible for individuals of one race to have anything but intellectual access to the deep-life of another race, although there is some reason to conclude that such access may become instinctive after long association of one people with another, even without intermarriage.

Let me illustrate by a concrete example:

What we know as harmony in music is comparatively new in our racial experience, less than a thousand years old. It seems to have been acquired by the various present European races at about the same time. As a result, in all of them there are now born a large proportion of children who not only play instruments of harmony by ear—that is, from deep-self—but have been known to compose harmony as early as the age of five.

The American Indian, however, has not yet arrived at appreciation of harmony. Consequently, though he is exceedingly musical in his own medium—almost any Indian you meet being capable of composing musical themes and melodies in the aboriginal scale—I have never found one of undoubted pure blood who can play an instrument of harmony by ear. Indians have been taught to play and sing in harmony, but if you watch any Indian school band, you will discover that each performer is playing his part alone, and a shallow effect of harmony is produced by the aboriginal faculty for rhythmic coordination which enables all the players to come out at the same place. Half a dozen times in my search, which has extended over twenty years, cases of ear playing Indians have been reported to me, but in every case not apparent at once to the eye, a little inquiry has shown the blood to be mixed.

On the other hand the Negro, who had already acquired rudimentary harmony before leaving Africa, has while living in a social environment where harmony is the accepted musical mode developed an almost universal genius for it. All this is important to writers in America, since it seems to indicate that genius of pure blooded stock, but outside the Anglo-Saxon blood stream, especially if outside the Anglo-Saxon social inheritance, will not be able to draw on any racial experience but its own, and will tend to produce art forms distinct from those developed within the Anglo-Saxon stream. I say tend, because there is always the unifying effect of a common environment. There is also the possibility of the newcomer's picking up within the Anglo-Saxon stream traits that came into it from his own blood stream. Thus an Italian or a French youth, growing up in an older American group, may assimilate himself to the Roman and Norman inheritance, which is certainly a part of our English ancestry. But a Jew or a Serb or a Slav, however much Americanism his immediate-self may take on, when he begins to draw upon his deep-self will find himself able to reach only the experience of his racial past. If he has a very acute and critical intelligence, as the genius product begins to pass through that intelligence into a book or a play he will be able so to modify his expression as to bring it within the understanding of other racial minds he wishes to reach. But if this hypothetical foreignly derived genius prove to have crossbred ancestry, such as is already in the American stream, he may attain a characteristic American expression of it. These are things that you can verify by an examination of the fiction written in America by geniuses of many strains. It does not seem possible for one of them to treat love, marriage, destiny, or any vital issue in the light of anything but his own racial experience.

I am aware that this does not cover quite all the instances of interracial genius; how for example Joseph Conrad, a Pole, became an English country gentleman and a master stylist in the English language. What I am trying to do here is not exhaust the subject, but to make some suggestions by which the foreignly derived young American genius may handle himself most successfully.

We are probably safe in asserting that to be a genius means to have the use of racial material without the trouble of acquiring it by conscious effort on your own account. But we must not think of that material as lying wholly in the past. There is a racial life of the present, and a racial trend prophetic of its future achievement, both of which are, in the nature of things, part of the resources of genius. . . .

Among the other resources of genius must be reckoned the subtle influence of natural environment. There may also be something from the social environment that passes over into the deep-self and is worked up by it into the stuff of life, quite without our knowledge. I am certain, for instance, that I get much of my knowledge of Indians not from anything I read or consciously observe, but just by being in their vicinity. Processes like this probably go on in all of us and, since they are beyond our control, must be reckoned as part of the sum of the material to which the possession of genius gives us access in the degree of our possession.

The degree and kind of genius possessed by the individual is difficult to determine. It appears to be strictly conditioned by the kind of intelligence through which it reaches us, as the shape of the fountain is conditioned by the nozzle. It can never be exactly alike in any two people—no two of us have exactly the same deep-self from which to draw, neither do we have identical immediate-selves through which we draw it. Every attribute of the immediate-self, commonly called a talent, plays its part in determining the final expression of genius in a work of literature. . . .

There have been cases in which genius has dispensed with all but a minimum of intelligence, as in Blind Tom, who had great musical ability along with the mentality of a seven year old child. In other cases, such as Dante Gabriel Rossetti, genius of a high order played back and forth between two nearly equal talents for writing and painting. Now we have Thomas Hardy who began as an architect, became a novelist, ends as a poet; whose lasting fame will probably rest on a single dramatic work, "The Dynasts," combining the best of all three talents for construction, relation, and interpretation. Sometimes we have genius accompanied by high intellectual capacity and rather limited talent, as in George Meredith; or a genuine talent for story telling and a moderate intelligence with not a spark of genius, as in Harold Bell Wright. Also in the United States we have many examples of pyrotechnic talent, divorced from the deep-self, on negligible terms with its intelligence, operating "on its own," as a survey of any season's output of popular fiction will show. Occasionally we have also examples of genius imperfectly stabilized, either through uncoordinated intelligence, or through the lack of adequate talent for displaying it, so that it becomes tormented and agonizing, a perpetual gadfly to its possessor. One suspects some such constitutional incapacity for fulfillment in men like Poe and Frank Harris. Perhaps Whitman too was a genius inadequately equipped, though he seems never to have suffered any realization of the meagreness of his poetic gifts in relation to the immensity of his inspiration.

The happiest fortune is, of course, to be born with a first rate intelligence, and one or two talents, exactly proportioned to the scope of our allotment of genius. The next best thing is to be able to administer our gifts so that the most is made of them with the minimum of effort. Such comfortable coordination seldom is achieved once [and] for all. Every time a new piece of work is undertaken there must be a new alignment of the various faculties of the self that produces it. So at the beginning of every piece of literature there is almost always a time of struggle and torment for the producer. It is with the hope that by informing ourselves fully of the processes and their relation to one another we may establish a habit of rapid and successful coordination, that these studies have been undertaken.

Woman Alone

The founder of my mother's family came across with Lafayette and married a Massachusetts farmer's daughter with a tradition of Indian blood. By successive removals the family pioneered into Pennsylvania, the Ohio Valley, and the prairies of Illinois. There, in 1861, my mother married a young Englishman who had just won his captaincy in the first three months of the Civil War. A few years after the close of the war I was born as the third of six children. My mother's people were mostly farming folk, though my father was admitted to the bar; he died when I was about ten, of a long-drawn-out war disability. None of the family attained any distinction beyond that of being—the men, good fighters, and the women, notable housewives, rather more forceful and inventive than the men. To account for myself, who turned out to be that blackest of black sheep to a Middle Western family, a radical-minded literary artist, I can record only that my grandfather played the flute and that a member of the French collateral branch was distinguished as a physicist and chemist.

I scarcely know why my being a radical should have proved such a cross to the rest of the family, since they were themselves shouting Methodist, black Abolitionists—my grandfather was known to have entertained Negroes at his table—and my mother a suffragist and an ardent member of the W.C.T.U., which at that time represented the most advanced social thinking among women, saving itself from ostracism only by remaining well within the orthodox religions and confining its activities to moral crusades. There were also "purity leagues" for achieving a single standard of sex behavior, and in connection with the temperance movement what would now be called "eugenic" propaganda, though the word had not then come into use. My mother saw to it that I read the pamphlets and heard the lectures pertaining to all these matters, without in the least realizing that she was thus preparing me for a radical career. I personally "sat under" Susan B. Anthony, Frances Willard, and Anna Shaw.

With this background it was inevitable that I should become a fighting feminist. But I cannot make clear my approach and method in regard to this problem of my generation without describing my own position in the family as an unwanted, a personally resented child. Probably few families in that age of enforced maternity were without some such member; but in fewer still did the intrusion take on such proportions of offense. Not that I ever blamed my mother, when I came to know them, for not wanting a child under the circumstances to which I was born. Nor do I, sorely as it hurt at the time, any longer resent that I should so early and so sharply have had my status as alien and intruder forced upon me. As you will see, it was my poor mother who lost the most of the conflict of irreconcilable temperaments never modulated by personal sympathy. Could she possibly have anticipated that I should end by being included in a list of prominent feminists, nothing would have pleased her so much; the trouble was that with that terrible pre-natal bias between us, she could never by any whipping-up of a sense of duty grow to like me, and the rest of the family took its tone from her. Long before I came to an intellectual understanding of the situation I had accepted as fact that I was not liked and could not expect the normal concessions of affection. By that adaptive instinct which still intolerably wrings my heart when I see it operating in young children, I had learned that it was only by pushing aside all considerations of liking and insisting on whatever fundamental rightness inhered in a particular situation, that I could secure a kind of factual substitute for family feeling and fair play. This began so early that though I can recall many occasions of mystified hurt at being rebuffed in the instinctive child's appeal, I can recall no time in which I did not have to conceal that hurt in order to bring all a child's wit and intelligence to bear on making good my right to be treated, factually at least, as a lawful member of the family. Out of this I developed very early an uncanny penetration into the fundamental ethics of personal situations which my mother was too just to refuse and not always clever enough to evade. By the time I was old enough to discuss our relationships with my mother the disposition to seek for logical rather than emotional elements had become so fixed that I had even made myself believe that being liked was not important. I had, at least, learned to do without it.

All this must be told in order that the bias and the method of my feminism may be understood. For life played an ironic trick on my mother. The pretty and darling daughters were taken away, and only the unwished-for ugly duckling left, between the oldest and the youngest sons. As if this were not enough, by the time the elder son was ripe for college there began to be signs that the daughter and not the son was the clever one. After my father's death mother's affectional interests, as is often the case with widows, gathered and intensified around my older brother, who proved a good son and a good citizen, but without any distinguishing gifts. When in college he had, chiefly I suspect in response to my mother's passionate wish, displayed literary and forensic tastes which he was unable to support without liberal contributions from mother and sister. These he accepted at first gingerly, and finally with such freedom that many a theme, many a quip and paragraph which appeared in the college journal over his name had been wrung out of me by such concessions as sisters do to this day obtain from older brothers by ministering to masculine complacency. Although my mother was often a party to our traffic and occasional squabbles over it, she was always able, when the things appeared, to accept them as evidence of what she so much wished. After her death I found a scrapbook in which they were all carefully arranged with my brother's name in her handwriting underneath. And lest any of the generation for whom the woman's right to the product of her own talent is completely established should think this is an unusual situation, I recommend the reading of the current if out-moded novels of that period, such, for example, as the novels of Madame Sarah Grand or May Sinclair's "Mary Olivier." For the greater part of the nineteenth century, in fact, it was not only usual but proper for parents openly to deplore that the sons had not inherited talents inconveniently bestowed upon the daughters.

I seem always to have known that I would write. Probably there was evidence of my having the necessary endowment, had there been anybody able to recognize literary talent, or tell me what to do about it. The attitude of the family was crushing. "What makes you think *you* can write?" In truth, I did not know. Looking back on the idea of a literary career which prevailed in the Middle West of that period, it was probably as well for me that nobody knew. I won a college degree by dint of insisting on it, and by crowding its four years into two and a half. My brother had the full four years. That I got so much was partly a concession to the necessity of my earning a living. With a college education I could teach, and teaching was regarded then as a liberal profession, eminently suited to women. Being plain and a little "queer," it was hoped rather than expected that I would marry. My queerness consisted, at that time, in entertaining some of the ideas that have got me elected to this list, in stoutly maintaining against all contrary opinion that I would some day write, and in the—to my family—wholly inexplicable habit of resting my case on its inherent rightness rather than upon the emotional reactions it gave rise to.

The summer I was out of college my mother decided to go West with my brother, so that he might "take up land" and grow with the country, taking me with her as being still too young for self-support. No use inquiring now whether this was a good move for me. Before the Pacific Coast filled up with Middle Westerners it was a gorgeous, an exciting place to be. Probably it proved a retardation of my literary career and a stimulus to radicalism. The immediate result was that I married. My mother had sunk all her capital in giving my brother his start; there was no place in the home for me, and no money to prepare me for any happy way of supporting myself. I taught a couple of years, not very successfully. And, anyway, I wished to be married. Contrary to the popular conception about literary women, I like domestic life and have a genuine flair for cooking. And I wanted children profoundly.

I still intended to write, but never in my life having met a professional literary person there was no one to tell me that the two things were incompatible. Under ordinary circumstances they are not. What I did not in the least realize was that the circumstances were not ordinary. I married a man with social and educational background not unlike my own; a man I could thoroughly respect for his personal quality, quite apart from any achievement. There seemed no reason why, had I been what I appeared to my family, and to my husband no doubt, the marriage should not have proved successful in every particular. What I appeared was an average young person, clever and a little odd, but not so odd that a house to keep and a baby every two years wouldn't restore me to entire normality. True, my health was not good. All my mother's babies had been sickly; I as the sickliest had always been the first to "catch" every childish ailment, and as it was not the custom of those days to send for the doctor until you knew what was the matter with the patient I seldom received medical attention. But no one had ever suggested that this need interfere with marriage and having children. It was a superstition left over from my mother's generation that ill health in women was cured by having children. Nor did I realize how compelling the creative urge would become in me. Had I even suspected it I would not have supposed it a bar to marriage. I thought that two intelligent young people could do about as they liked with life. But, like myself, my young husband was without preparation for maintaining a household. At the end of twelve years we were still living in a town of about 300 inhabitants on an income inadequate to reasonable comfort, with an invalid child.

My first baby came in the second year and left me a tortured wreck. I know now that I did not have proper medical treatment, but at the time nothing much was thought of such things. My memory of the first seven or eight years of marriage is like some poor martyr's memory of the wheel and the rack, all the best things of marriage obscured by a fog of drudgery impossible to be met and by recurrent physical anguish. For before I had discovered the worst that had happened to me I had tried a second time to have a child, unsuccessfully. Brought up as I was, in possession of what passed for eugenic knowledge, it had never occurred to me that the man I married would be less frank about his own inheritance than I had been about mine—much to his embarrassment, for nice girls were seldom frank at that time. I who had entered mother-hood with the highest hopes and intentions had to learn too late that I had borne a child with tainted blood. I had to find it all out by myself. My husband's family exchanged glances, and remained silent. My mother said: "I don't know what you have done, daughter, to have such a judgment upon you." But I, brutally and indelicately, as I was given to understand, insisted upon uncovering family history until I found out. I said to my husband: "Why did you never tell me?" He said: "Because it never occurred to me." At home, he told me, they were all brought up never to refer to the obvious handicap. That was the well-bred Chris-tian way of the 1890's. As for my own family, from beginning to end they never ceased to treat me as under a deserved chastisement.

In a way this tragic end of my most feminine adventure brought the fulfillment of my creative desire, which had begun to be an added torment by repression. Caring for a hopelessly invalid child is an ex-pensive business. I had to write to make money. In the end I was compelled to put my child in a private institution where she was hap-pier and better cared for than I could otherwise manage. My husband's family were good sports. They never forgot the birthdays and Christ-mases, and the probability that there might be normal human reactions. To my own family who demanded somewhat accusingly what they should say I said: "You can say I have lost her." Which was true and a great relief to them. My mother died shortly after, but was never quite reconciled to my refusal to accept my trouble as a clear sign of God's displeasure. So for sixteen years.

Released thus to the larger life which opened to me with literary suc-cess, I found plenty of reasons for being a feminist in the injustices and impositions endured by women under the general idea of their intellec-tual inferiority to men. What I have just related are the facts that gave color and direction to my feminist activities. But I must go back a little to explain the kind of thing that got me called a radical, which was not what is called a radical today. I was neither a Bolshevik nor a Commu-nist, not even a Socialist or free lover. I thought much that was said at that time about Home and Mother, sentimental tosh; I thought it penalized married love too much to constitute the man she loved the woman's whole horizon, intellectual, moral, and economic. I thought women should be free to make their contribution to society by any talent with which they found themselves endowed, and be paid for it at rates equal to the pay of men. I thought everything worth experiencing was worth talking about; I inquired freely into all sorts of subjects. I got myself read out of the Methodist church by organizing, along in the nineties, the first self-conscious enterprise of what has been called the Little Theater movement and acting in its plays. Worst of all, I talked freely of art as though it had a vital connection with living. One example of the sort of reactions an unbridled radical such as I was had to face must suffice. That was the beginning of various movements for applying the social wisdom of the more fortunate classes to the problems of the underprivileged—juvenile courts, probation officers, big brother and sister associations, and in particular, the activity finally objectified as the court of domestic relations, in which I was particularly interested. I had spoken freely and publicly about the necessity of bringing those unlearned in life into more or less compulsory compliance with our best experience. Just why this should figure as an offense to anybody I am still at a loss to know; but the next time I went to my mother's house, I discovered that there had been a family council, and it was put to me that, while the family did not attempt to dictate what I should say away from the neighborhood of the family, I must understand that in the neighborhood, and especially under the family roof I must refrain from all mention of so objectionable a subject as public remedies for private relations, or find my mother's door forever closed to me. Not a word, you see, about the incredible private tragedy which had come to me for lack of a public remedy! . . . Oh, yes, I took it, standing, for the same reason that I took it the day my pretty young sister was buried and my mother flung away from me and cried aloud on God for taking Jenny and leaving me. It wasn't until I caught the family—what was left of it—trying to put over on the younger generation the same repressions and limitations they had practiced upon me that I blew up. Suddenly I found the younger generation on my side.

As for not being under the necessity of being liked, which began as a defense, it has become part of my life philosophy. I see now that too many of the impositions of society upon women have come of their fear of not being liked. Under disguising names of womanliness, of tact, of religion even, this humiliating necessity, this compulsive fear goes through all our social use like mould, corrupting the bread of life. It is this weakness of women displayed toward their sons which has fostered the demanding attitude of men toward them. It puts women as a class forever at the mercy of an infantile expectation grown into an adult convention. So I have made a practice of standing out against male assumption of every sort, especially their assumption of the importance of masculine disapproval—more than anything else against their assumption that they have a right to be "managed." But it is the women I am aiming at, women and their need for detachment from the personal issue. At present the price for refusing to "manage" men is high, but not too high for a self-respecting woman to pay.

7 *Cactus Thorn*

actus Thorn, a recently discovered novella manuscript, is vintage Austin. It contains some of the character types used in Austin's New York social novel, *No. 26 Jayne Street* (1920), in which Austin unflatteringly portrays her Progressive friend Lincoln Steffens as the hypocritical protagonist Adam Frear.[1] Adam Frear makes a return appearance as Grant Arliss, this time in a southwestern setting. Arliss, a politician and double-dealing free lover, underestimates Dulcie Adelaid, with whom he had an affair. Grant ends the affair with Dulcie when he jilts her for an heiress who has the connections to further his political career. He had taken his free enjoyment of Dulcie, in short, for granted, without counting on her expectations of him or her ability to derive justice for herself, and by extension, for all women similarly exploited by free-wheeling men like Grant Arliss. In this fiction, the central male does not merely fall from grace; ultimately, Dulcie Adelaid murders Arliss, stabbing him with the beautiful dagger she had shown him at the beginning of the novel, when she used its bright edge to display the sensual bloom of a cactus after he had carelessly pricked his finger on its thorn. Impressed by the dagger on their first meeting, "he wondered where she carried it and what provocation would have brought it leaping against himself" (9). Austin could not have been insensitive to the import of this sentence; here she empowers her female character to wield the blade.

The manuscript of the novella *Cactus Thorn* probably was written before 1927, if a letter declining the manuscript from Austin's editor at Houghton Mifflin, Ferris Greenslet, can be relied upon to approximately date the manuscript. "Three or four of us have read *Cactus Thorn* with the greatest of interest," Greenslet wrote in June 1927. "We have all admired it but have been unanimous in doubting whether it could be made a successful piece of book merchandise. It is the most awkward possible length and, to one or two of us at least, the hero's defection and his subsequent murder by the lady are not made absolutely convincing."[2] Reading the novella some seventy years later, the modern reader might find the plot more plausible than did Houghton Mifflin. To my mind and to Melody Graulich's, the scholar who discovered the manuscript, *Cactus Thorn* "ranks with Austin's best writing and treats recurring themes which illuminate her career."[3]

Speculating upon Austin's motive to write these characters and this plot into being, several of Mary Austin's concerns surface, the rebuffed woman being only one. Read in another way, this is the narrative of the eastern man of power who comes to the Southwest merely to exploit it, as several male characters did in her earlier short fictions. A paramount concern of *Cactus Thorn* might have been Austin's own experience of self-important public personages who, however well intentioned, relegated women to subordinate positions. Dulcie Adelaid thinks Grant wants a helpmate, but she finds instead he wants an inferior to ensure his domestic tranquility. "And between political conferences he [Grant Arliss] discovered in himself new appreciation and responses to the accomplished domesticity of Alida [Alida Rittenhouse, the woman Arliss chooses over Dulcie Adelaid], the cozy fire, the shaded light, the choice but simple meals. Such things as these, he told himself, were the norm, the touchstone of reality" (82).

While Arliss plans his wedding in New York and conveniently relegates Dulcie Adelaid to the shadows of a former life with no connection to his present one, Dulcie begins to understand the vacuity and calculation of his noble protestations to her in the desert and that she had been merely a convenience for him, one that he would now brush aside for his marriage to the politically acceptable Miss Rittenhouse, daughter of a senator. Yet Dulcie refuses to accept her fate and meekly creep back to the Southwest in order to prevent upsetting his career. She resists the idea that the man alone decides when *he* can begin or terminate a love affair.

In this regard, Austin brilliantly allows us to see Grant's egocentrism by permitting us access into his consciousness. "So far as he could make out her point of view, she wanted to be treated as if her interest in the situation was equal to his, as if in fact, she was still in the situation, as if, in spite of his having distinctly abandoned the situation himself, she still had some power over it" (96). When Arliss becomes surly at her suggestion of interfering with his marital, and hence, his political plans, she takes the final measure of the man she once loved.[4] Without jealousy or anger, Dulcie manages the perfect murder, for "there was nothing known of Arliss or his life which could connect the weapon, a 'thorn-shaped dagger of foreign workmanship, the ivory handle mended with bone,' with the figure of a young woman [Dulcie Adelaid] who at the moment . . . was staring blindly at the fleeting of the Western landscape past the windows of the Overland Flier, her face slowly setting into the torpor of relief after great shock and pain" (99).

Although Austin makes no mention of *Cactus Thorn* in her autobiography, she does refer to the "financial failure" of *No. 26 Jayne*

Street (1920), perhaps a reason that she decided not to pursue the publication of the *Cactus Thorn* manuscript.[5]

Final Chapter

All that night and during the two intervening days before he saw her again, Arliss told himself steadily with a dogged persistency that he had been wrong. He was wrong to have initiated the affair without an explicit understanding, wrong not to have forced a note of finality into his parting with Dulcie Adelaid by the stopped spring. It was one of the things he had drilled into himself as part of his preparation for a political career, that if he didn't get on with people, it was his fault. Politics was the business of persuading other people; and the whole art of persuasion lay in sympathy with the other fellow's point of view. That was the way he got on so well with labor; he was always sympathetic to it; where other politicians made promises, Grant Arliss sympathized, and labor made promises to him. So in the midst of intolerable anger and alarm and a conviction of being badly dealt with by fate, Arliss steadily dinged into himself that he was wrong about Dulcie Adelaid. It was his business to sympathize with her point of view—which he told himself was outrageous—and conduct his own part of the affair accordingly.

So far as he could make out her point of view, she wanted to be treated as if her interest in the situation was equal to his, as if in fact, she was still in the situation, as if, in spite of his having distinctly abandoned the situation himself, she still had some power over it. Well, he would humor her to that extent, he would listen to her, draw out the poison of her wound in talk—he would do whatever she wanted except allow her to go to Alida Rittenhouse. He would prevent that if he had to take the senator into his confidence himself. He wasn't so sure old Henry hadn't a fund of experience to draw upon. On the point of Dulcie Adelaid disturbing Alida Rittenhouse he would be firm; kind, but inexorably firm. He wished to be kind. Until now his whole life had conspired to keep him in the position of being kind. The picture of himself as the source of suffering in others filled him with a sincere misery almost as acute as the thought of his own suffering at someone else's hands. By dint of keeping it up, amid his excited imaginings of what Dulcie Adelaid might do to his career should she prove impervious to kindness, Arliss managed by the afternoon of the next day to dispatch to her a note in which he took, humbly, the tack of having blundered in an effort to be kind according to his lights, and offering himself for any time in which she felt calm enough to talk with him. To this the only answer had been that there was no answer, and as that day and another went by, he grew steadily easier in his mind. The recollection of Dulcie's poise and docility grew upon him reassuringly; it worked, with his reiterated suggestion of sympathy and kindness, like a charm.

So when he discovered her waiting for him in the street a block or two from his rooms, on the evening of the third day, he was so far recovered in equanimity that he was able to speak very kindly to her.

He was sincerely stricken in his susceptibilities, when as they passed under the flare of the street lamp, he saw what had gone on in her; the wreck and damage of illimitable despair. If he had seen her face first and not her firm young figure and her free walk, he would not have known her. To his credit, he was incredibly touched by her appearance even before he was relieved by her first word.

"I came to say good-bye," she told him tonelessly, "I'm going back to Sweetwater tonight. . . . I'd like to go up to your room for a little while." There was a great weariness in her voice, and the appeal of finished sorrow in her face. Arliss put out his hand to hers and drew it through his arm. The street was very quiet; the purples of winter twilight contended in the shadows with the yellows of the electric lamps. The pavement echoed frostily to the feet of infrequent passersby. They walked the length of the block before Arliss spoke. "I've been wondering what had become of you." He meant her to know that he meant to be kind.

"Oh, I've been thinking—and talking to your friends. Oh, not telling them things—" as his instant uneasiness communicated itself along his arm, "asking things. Things about your work the newspapers couldn't tell me. I have been trying to find out if your ideas are something meant to be lived, or just . . . talk."

"I am afraid you always had too high an opinion of me, Dulcie." Poor girl, he must allow her a little bitterness.

"Yes," she admitted drearily, "I guess I was just—innocent. I thought they were things to be lived by, the things you said. They were—they are—the sort of things I live by myself. You understand that, don't you?"

"As far as I can understand how social principles *can* be personal— I'm sure you never did anything but what you thought was right, my dear."

"Yes," she said, again. "But you see, I thought it was just the point you made that there wasn't to be any difference between what was social and what was personal, not any difference in rightness." She turned her fine eyes upon him, dark now with despair. "I don't think so now," she said.

"My dear, my dear," he murmured. What other answer could he make? This at any rate seemed to serve, for she fell silent beside him.

The hall had not been lit when he let her in with his latchkey, and by the light from the street he let in with her, she passed on ahead of him up the dark turn of the stair. Arliss halted a moment as his habit was, to turn over the letters laid on the newel; his landlady, hearing him, came out to hold a wax lighter to the gas. She had the greatest respect for Mr. Arliss as a prompt-paying lodger and a pleasant-spoken gentleman, and that was how it was she was able to testify when it was required of her, that he had gone to his rooms a little past six, alone, and that no one after that had gone up to him.

"Don't make a light," Dulcie had said to him, as he let her into his room, faintly illuminated from the street, "I shall only be a moment." She moved over to the window as Arliss removed his hat and coat, turning as she heard him come toward her.

She put her hands up to his shoulders the old way; he felt her tremble, and he put his arm about her reassuringly, meaning to be kind.

"I wanted to see you," she began, "I wanted to make sure. To make sure . . . if it was ever real . . . if there was ever *anything* real at all."

"Dulcie, I'm sorry this has turned out badly for you. I never meant—"

"No you never meant—*anything*. You just—*felt*." He moved uneasily and she quieted. "So I wasn't real to you, ever," she spoke despairingly, almost to herself. "I was just used—exploited—in the eternal war—the war between men and women."

"I hoped, Dulcie, we could part in kindness."

"Yes. I don't come to quarrel. My train leaves in an hour. If it is to be good-bye—"

"Good-bye—" He felt her arms go about him and a sudden surprising pain in his side like a thorn. "Dulcie!" He had time to say her name again, in a great terror of blackness, before she eased him quietly to the floor.

Dying thus, at the flood tide of his career, Grant Arliss had the public advantage of being remembered as martyr to the cause of justice and true democracy to which he had dedicated the life so lost. For when the weapon which had been found thrust deep into his heart had been passed upon by the savants of the police, it was shown to have been a sort that could only have been used by the professional gangster who had made himself the tool of the political ring, whose peace and profits Arliss had so successfully disturbed, and from whom he was known to be the recipient of anonymous threats. There was nothing known of Arliss or his life which could connect the weapon, "a thorn-shaped dagger of foreign workmanship, the ivory handle mended with bone," with the figure of a young woman who at the moment this decision was being arrived at was staring blindly at the fleeting of the Western landscape past the windows of the Overland Flier, her face slowly setting into the torpor of relief after great shock and pain.

8

Starry
Adventure

In her autobiography *Earth Horizon* Austin speaks briefly of *Starry Adventure,* published in 1931. It was, she said, the novel "in which I gathered up the knowledge I had gained of the various levels of native life in New Mexico" (357). Austin wrote *Starry Adventure* during the period of her most extensive involvement in the revival of Spanish colonial arts in New Mexico, a project on which she worked closely with her Santa Fe neighbor and friend Frank Applegate, himself an artist involved extensively with Spanish arts and crafts. Certainly the presence of New Mexican folkways insinuates itself throughout the book; yet the magnificent descriptions of the Sangre de Cristo Mountains and the eloquent and, at times, poetic descriptions of New Mexican flora give the book its acute sense of place. The novel, which concerns a family who has come to New Mexico on account of the father's illness, contains many moments of Austin's personal history, as readers of her autobiography, published only a year later, will see.

Most interestingly, the writer chose to tell the story in the second person much of the time: "All at once it was coming winter again and Father wasn't well. It was a thing you didn't talk about; you heard it in asides and whispers" (308). This enabled the protagonist (you), Gardiner Sitwell, to enter into an intimacy with the reader that was not possible in first- or third-person narrations.

Austin's idealization of the invalid father almost certainly recalls her own much-beloved, tubercular father, and she endows young Gard, the idealistic son of his family, with many of her own experiences. Gard's bewilderment through much of the book suggests that Austin wished to write a coming-of-age story, how things might have turned out had she herself been born male and grown up in New Mexico rather than in Illinois, how things might have been had she been unencumbered by femaleness and able to set out on a "starry adventure" instead of being prematurely cut off in youth by the constraints placed upon girls and women of her era.

Gard's idealism is almost shattered by the immensely monied Eudora Ballantine, beautiful and shallow. Austin's description of this important character masterfully satirizes her wealthy friend Mabel Dodge Luhan and her circle, who came to New Mexico in the 1910s because of its exoticism.[1] In the course of working on Eudora's home—a Hispanic restoration—Gard compromises his ideals by having an affair with her, and also by coming into contact with her friends, celebrity figures like D. H. Lawrence, who drink champagne and chatter about Freud in the beautiful Hispanic home he has helped to restore. Austin might have missed the mark on the Indians in the book, as several critics of her time asserted, but she takes deadly aim at the horde of invading Anglos who came with their money and power to New Mexico to "go primitive." By pursuing his dalliance with Eudora, Gard comes perilously close to missing a life with Jane Heatherington, the feminist foil to Eudora Ballantine and the quintessentially "true woman" of the novel.

In 1930 the writer shot off a fiery letter to Ferris Greenslet of Houghton Mifflin about what she perceived as their misunderstanding of her novel. Pressured to cut excessive dialogue from the novel, she responded, "This is a novel of New Mexico, where it is a great singularity of the more serious citizens, that we not only talk, but we have something to talk about." Taking up an ongoing argument with the eastern literary establishment, which she had begun almost thirty years earlier, Austin added, "I suppose it is difficult to realize, east of the Hudson that this is chiefly what draws intellectual people here from all over the world. The number of new aspects of life and society which are presented here and the high quality of the talk about them."[2] Her novel, she said, was meant for readers "who are really interested and curious about what is going on here," not those obsessed with Freud. Austin believed that the novel would do what Willa Cather's novel *The Professor's House* (1925) failed to do, that is "to graft her story on the living tree of life in New Mexico."[3]

By the conclusion of *Starry Adventure*, Gard has ended his false "adventure" with Eudora and has come to the epiphanic realization that marriage and life together with his friend Jane in New Mexico comprises the authentic experience for which he has been searching. Sentimentally perhaps, Austin leaves Gard and Jane as they set off for a "deferred exploration. . . . You were going to see all that was left of the indigenous architecture of the United States. You might go all the way to the Mimbres and Casa Grande. You would certainly go to Las Lunas, near which there was a Pit village site and the possible ancestor of the three-cornered fireplace. You were going with Jane on the trail of the House [*Huertas Cardena*, Eudora's recuperated house]. It wasn't an important adventure, like finding the South Pole, but it was your size. You liked it tremendously" (418). In so concluding the novel, Austin manages to rivet our gaze on the Southwest as a site of significance and true quest in American culture.

EXCERPTS FROM BOOK I
The Book of New Mexico

I The children had carried their supper out to the banco that ran along the west wall, to watch the sun set behind the Valles ranges. There had been thundery showers that day all along the Sangre de Cristo. Far off, the westward banks stood up, sunlit and towering, but the nearer ragged cloud-films kept the dark color of the rain. This was an arrangement that promised well for the Sitwell children's favorite evening game of seeing things in the clouds, strange shapes and portents by which they often set the next day's entertainment.

Laura, who had, as usual, finished first, had clipped off along the stone-paved portál⁴ to carry her dishes to Aloysia Liberadita in the kitchen, to be beforehand at the game of pretending. But Gard had dawdled, neglecting his half of the bread and butter while he played with the lovely color of his red raspberries and cream in a blue willow bowl. This was the first picking of berries such as comes on in New Mexico gardens after the September rains, but to Gard, whose consecutive memories did not run far back of the present, they were a novelty which must be savored deliciously, crushing each one in turn and seeing the luscious red juice trickle into the cream after a fashion which Laura, who was "going on" eight, considered babyish. Gard was always stopping the real performance of life to do things like that, just as he now neglected his berries to listen to the clippity-clip of his sister's feet along the pale raspberry-colored stones, and neglected that, to be utterly absorbed in the depth and aërial mystery of the cloud-bank below the crest of Jémez. It ran the whole length of the range in unbroken, transparent impenetrability, of a blue that had no other name than the name of the mountain, so that Gard was never quite able to think of one without the other, and was vaguely of the opinion that Jémez-blue was the name of a color which gave its title to that sector of his horizon. The contemplation of it had, as always, a curious, hushing effect upon him, so that the last few bites of his supper remained uneaten in the interval before the evening wonder began, while Laura lingered in one of her perpetual arguments with Aloysia Liberadita Montóya y Montóya in the kitchen. Suddenly, the wonder was all about him. The edges of the banked clouds were brightly gilt, the torn films flushed crimson, the gleaming cumuli behind them came hurrying; heaping and wheeling. Great sword-like beams of light slashed between them . . . the sword of the Lord and of Gideon . . . the chariots and the horsemen thereof . . .

Gard had no more idea that the half-remembered phraseology that flashed in his mind was from the Old Testament readings of his grandfather, to the sound of which he so often went to sleep, than that the pictures which shaped for him along the upper cloud-line were suggested by the illustrations from a book called "Classic Myths" which lay on his father's table. For him there was no reality more real than this array of bright swords and shining helmets and wheels dark with thunder.

Swiftly the rain rallied and blotted out the splendor; all but a thin slit through which a golden wing of light flew toward him. Gard saw it come, grow invisible with nearness, and take shape again in the tops of the yellowing aspens in the ciénaga[5] below the house, almost on a level with his round-eyed staring; a golden glowing brightness like hot brass, like molten ends of rainbows, and in the midst . . . in the midst. . .

Laura came running, sharp with disappointment, "Oh, Gard . . ." as if he could have put off the wished-for moment until her arrival. "Is it over. . . What did you see?"

Gard came to out of his hushed wonder.

"I saw God," he announced, with finality.

"Gard! You never!"

"Right there." He pointed solemnly. "He came out of the cloud and stood in the tops of the aspens."

"Gard! You storied!" Laura never allowed herself to be outdone, especially by anybody of Gard's age. "Nobody can see God. It says so in the Bible."

"Well, I did!" Gard was still pale with wonder.

"You didn't! You just made it up! You're only five and a half." This with Laura was the crushing retort. "If you keep on saying you did, it's a story."

"I saw Him in the aspens."

"Well, I'm going to tell Mother, so there!" She flew off, always prompt in decision and swift to action.

Gard, following more slowly into the unlit room, still blinking from the brightness, made her out, against his mother's knee, stiff and accusing.

"Well, I just did," Gard began, valiant, never troubled about making himself understood by his mother. "I was just looking, and He came out of the cloud like a bird—"

"Like a bird!" scoffed Laura. "That shows it's a story."

The mother put out her hand and drew the boy by the shoulders. "Tell me?" she questioned gently.

"It stood in the tops of the aspen trees. It was like fire, only there was no burning. And there was God."

"I have often thought," said his mother, "that if one could see God anywhere, it would be in the alpenglow." She kissed them both, smiling.

Laura was silenced but still skeptical, not feeling sure whether she had been snubbed, or if this were the sort of talk with which older people put off the serious convictions of mere babies of five and a half. She had so often been cautioned that her brother was too young to understand her own brusque affirmations of reality. "Bed, now," the mother reminded them. Laura sniffed a little as she set off to find her father. "Better tell that to Grampa," she threw back over her shoulder.

Gard lingered for the few moments of extra petting to which his status as the youngest entitled him, his body pressed close to his mother's warm softness, his head tucked sleepily into the hollow of her shoulder. "I am going down to the aspens tomorrow and *look*!" he confided, and by her confirming pats along his arm felt himself completely justified.

But when Aloysia Liberadita came in with the lights, he too went along toward the room that was known as "Father's Study." It was a small room, on a slightly higher level than the living-room, and Aloysia Liberadita had showed him the inequalities in the wall that had been broken out to make one room open into the other, and the built-up place that was once the wide door opening onto a portál of its own when the room was a tiny private chapel of the Montóya family. There was nothing else of the room's sacred character left but a pink-and-yellow scroll painted about the *nicho*, where once a blessed image had stood, now shelved in for his father's books. There was an old, carved, and painted table pushed against the wall below the *nicho*, where his father sometimes wrote, and a couch close to the little corner fireplace, where, oftener, he lay propped up by pillows and read and took notes interminably. For the rest there was only a chair or two, and a fire to be found in the study more frequently than in any room in the house. It crackled smartly now and the flames ran up the cedar logs as the children dutifully stopped for a good-night caress above the book which was laid face downward across the reader's lap for that ceremony.

This good-night kiss was always a trifle ceremonious. Father for some mysterious reason was never to be kissed as other people are. You stood by his couch or chair and felt his arm around you, turning your face away from him, inhaling a faint breath of pine balm as Father kissed you in the back of the neck. Sometimes, if you found it convenient, you kissed Father on his neck, but never, never on the face. And if Father seemed disposed to romp with you gently, you made believe to romp, too, but never really, truly. If you forgot and tussled with all your might, you brought on one of Father's spells of coughing, which you could hear guiltily thereafter as far into the night as you were able to keep awake. As if to see that you never did forget, Mother stood at Father's door with a candle, and two minutes later you were being tucked under your covers at the farthest possible remove from Father's bed on the sleeping-porch.

Gard's cot was next to the partition that shut off an end of the porch for Laura, but not so completely that they could not, if there was a pressing need, and nobody heard and stopped them, plan for the next day's play, or finish some unresolved argument of this. Mother and Grampa kept to inside bedrooms, which had a special sense of privacy and security, so that it became a privilege to be taken in by one or the other of them when the nights were snowy or the wind blew in with rain. Other nights there was always a cool stream of mountain air flowing over the cot beds, and beyond the straight edge of the roof the companionable stars. Always, after they were tucked in, there was Grampa coming to hear them say their prayers, and from within the door of his own room, Grampa's voice reading aloud out of the Old Testament.

It was not until his own God Bless Everybody had been capped by Grampa's deep Amen, that Gard remembered his sister's challenge about God in the aspen tree; he struggled with it drowsily. " 'N I did see God, Grampa . . . 'n the bush was not burned. . ." Far over him he could hear the husky whisper, "No man hath seen the Father . . . whereas . . . darkly . . . we shall see face to face . . ." but he knew by the sudden tremble in the hand that stroked the covers into place that he had not been disbelieved.

II It was about ten of the next morning when Gard remembered to go down to the ciénaga where he had seen God among the aspens. The creek, which had taken a wide turn about the ranch buildings and the orchard, spread out in a little meadow a hundred feet or more below the house level, and the aspens had sprung up there among the runnels. With their pale stems and their fragile, lace-leaved boughs, they were like ladies dancing in the path of the little wind that always follows the water-courses. The ciénaga was a favorite straying-place of the children; open, as it was, with a clear view of the house and the road leading up to it. Nothing frightening could happen there, and the grass was full of buttercups, white violets, and in midsummer the flower that is called red rain. The two milk cows were pastured there, Betsy and Trujillo. Trujillo was not properly a cow's name, but Grampa Gardiner had a way of referring to the black-and-white by the name of the man he had bought her from, as "that Trujillo critter," so that it had never occurred to the children that Trujillo was not her name any more than that "critter" was a survival of Grampa's boyhood on a farm "Back East." If it had, they would have treasured it as they did all reminders of that fairy region. Gard loved hearing of it, especially when it turned up as recollection of his parents or his grandfather. When it came from Laura, such reminiscences had the effect of making him feel just such an outsider as on this Saturday morning, which, *being* Saturday was a time of especial activity among the older members of the household: Laura hurrying importantly about to lay out her mother's gloves and clean handkerchief for the drive to town with a truck-load of farm produce; Aloysia Liberadita wrapping honeycombs and butter; Grampa packing peach-boxes. Usually Gard had to content himself walking about with his father, giving directions; but this morning after the rains his mother seemed to think the ground too damp for father. Gard suddenly remembered the aspens in the ciénaga.

As soon as he had set off, he began to think it odd that he could not recall very clearly what he had seen there. All that he could recall was the way he had felt about it; a deep, full feeling of wanting it to go on and on; a feeling of his vision still going on somewhere, even after he had ceased to see it. He had been quite certain that it was God he had seen. But when Laura, in the manner of one to whom further evidence would be welcome, had asked him, across the half wall that divided their beds on the sleeping-porch, what God had looked like, Gard had been glad that his mother coming in then with an extra blanket apiece had saved him from answering. Until then he thought he knew what God looked like; something like Grampa Gardiner when he was all clean-shaved as to upper lip, his white beard brushed out over his black coat, his limp-cover Bible clasped to his chest as he set out Sunday afternoons for the Mission. But Gard could not recall that he had seen any likeness to *anything* in the aspens. There was that feeling in his heart, and a burning . . . when Grampa bent over him, he had recalled the burning bush that was not consumed . . . something about a lamp and a furnace. . . Nor did he know what he expected to find this morning among the aspens.

The current of fresh air that began to move down the mountains toward the end of every morning, stirred the tops of the aspen softly. There was nothing on the grass nor along the streamside. But when Gard stood directly under them, looking up at the gracile leaves all in a twitter of airy movement, something of the feeling of the night rose in his heart as he observed their serrate edges touched lightly with yellow, as if from the burning. They seemed far above him, in the clear hollow of the morning blueness, bowing and recovering. Suddenly, far up on Pueblo Mountain, above the dark green of the pines, his eye was caught by long slanting patches of clear yellow; there, where the yellow light, that he had seen winging toward him last night in the alpenglow, had rested. The happy sense of fullness began to well up in him again and flowed over all the scene, which he took in now with a sense of wholeness that was new and yet not strange. There was the dark curve of the Sangre de Cristo behind him, crowned with the green-and-gold of aspens, and below that the dark wood of pines out of which issued the creek that ran all around Rancho Arríba and watered the ciénaga. Below the pines was the orchard which followed the sweep of the hills and came down toward the north in a steep barranca.[6] Against the orchard lay the long low house with a wide portál nearly the whole length of it, on which he could just make out the bright cocoon of Navajo blanket which he knew as his father taking the sun. The front of the house stood sharply against the trees, like a house cut out of pasteboard, pale pasteboard color, with doors and windows of bright blue. Where the portál left off, tall hollyhocks carried on a mysterious intercourse with their own shadows. Today all these things came together suddenly in a pattern, like the click of colors in a kaleidoscope, and the name of the pattern was New Mexico.

A long time ago, when he supposed he had just come from the vaguely remembered "Back East," Gard had been afraid of the mountains. Sometimes still, when he had been walking near them alone, he had a frightening sense of their imminence. They had ways suddenly of swelling and threatening, of moving noiselessly about and jutting boldly out from the woods where you least expected them. But now as he took them in, inseparable from the pattern of his home, he saw that they were just earth and rocks, warm in color, with a warmth that came sensibly toward him, along with moving air that was fresh and pleasant-smelling. The slight stir of the air flicked the leaves of the aspens in bright patters of sound and set up a sudden trepidation in the straight scarlet slashes of the flowers called red rain. Quite naturally Gard found himself skipping to the same motion, as he ran toward them across the ciénaga. "New Mexico! New Mexico!" he chanted happily, and, as he came down in the wet places between the grassy hummocks with a pleasant splash, "God!" he shouted, "God and New Mexico!"

As the children climbed back from the ciénaga after seeing Mother off, they discovered Grampa moving about the peach orchard with extraordinary steady business. With one of his sudden sharp accessions of impatience at the leisurely motions of the Trujillo boy who had come up to help with the peach-picking, Grampa swept the pile of crates out of Ramon's arms and, adding them to his own, walked off with them. The young Sitwells stopped short for one of those wordless exchanges common to children who play much together.

"Have you told?" Gard wanted to know. He knew she hadn't, but it was always exciting when Laura drew down her lip exactly like Grampa when he caught you pretending you'd studied the Sunday lesson when you hadn't.

"No, I haven't. And I'm not going to. And you're not going to, neither!" Laura was firm.

What they were both referring to was what they had over-heard young Trujillo say to Pablo, the first time he came to work at Rancho Arríba. "That old man," Ramon had said while he judiciously rolled a cigarette, "that old man, he sure work like hell."

"It's not anything that I want anybody should say about my Grampa." Laura put the subject behind them. "Beat you to the orchard!" she proposed.

Although she always did beat him, or else let him see that she hadn't out of respect to his being only five and a half, Gard could never resist the challenge. Presently, as he leaned panting against the orchard bars, he was aware of Grampa going back and forth from the packing-tables to the workshed, with his steady slightly worried haste. Gard had sensed somehow that, as though Trujillo said it, working-like-hell had not meant, as Laura seemed to think it did, anything uncomplimentary. Just now he was touched with the saying's menacing quality. He squeezed through the orchard bars and, picking up a couple of stray crate covers, trotted helpfully after the tall hurrying figure.

VII All at once it was coming winter again and Father wasn't well. It was a thing you didn't talk about; you heard it in asides and whispers. Mother told it to Mr. Phipps on the portál the time he came up to paint the aspens, bright against the dark pines on Monte Piedra. Mr. Phipps said you never can tell. "When I first came to this country . . ." said Mr. Phipps ". . . and now look at me." He seemed to the children to have said all that a great many times, but Mother seemed always ready to hear it again. Gard, whenever there was anything whispered about Father, had a queer guilty feeling inside. For a while he remembered how that happened. It was when the rains began to come on, and Mother was flying about trying to get all the fruit in, that Gard had been called in to listen to Father's translation from the Latin. Both the children knew now that it was the Latin that Father was translating. If they met other children, they would manage somehow to mention carelessly that Father was translating something from the Latin, although not all the children who heard it seemed equally impressed. What happened on this particular afternoon was that, while Father read first from the Latin and then from the English, Gard's mind kept slipping away, walking in trails on its own.

Father caught him at it. "Well, Son, don't you get it?"

Gard came hurrying back. "Oh, yes, Father, only—"

"Well?"

"It doesn't gallop."

"Oh, by George—"

Gard was quite cheerful about it; really interested. "In the Latin," he explained, "it goes like this"—beating it out with his hands—"and in English, like this."

"Oh, so you think it goes like that, do you?" Father laughed, but he hadn't liked it.

When she was tucking him in that night, Mother told Gard he must be careful about not discouraging Father.

When she was gone, Laura rapped on the partition and wanted to know what about. "I should think you'd know better," she said. Gard understood only that he shouldn't have told Father about the translation not galloping.

It was after this that Father began to talk about going to Santa Fé to the San—sanit—something.

"The truth is, I'm getting stale; I need a change. Even the children notice it. . . ."

"Oh, Hubert . . . that child. . .!"

"Cooped up here . . . and that back number of a doctor . . . Phipps says it's the best Sanitarium in the country . . . He was there for six months. And now look at him!"

"I know, dear. . . I wish it could be managed."

"If I could get my mind limbered up, I could write something. Probably I could sell enough to pay. . . I'm told all sorts of interesting people go there."

Mother sighed and smiled. "We won't be needing Pablo during the really bad weather . . . perhaps. . ."

For a long time talk of this kind gave Gard that guilty feeling, even after he had forgotten what began it. It was arranged finally that, when the wood was all in and Pablo went away, Father was to go down to Santa Fé for two or three months. And immediately everything brightened sensibly.

That would be soon after Christmas. It was odd how, once it was decided, everything concerned with Father's going seemed to strike up a tune. It was a way Mother had, when she had made up her mind, to make a procession. You went marching toward the event. All New Mexico marched. Aspen gold ran down through the arroyos into pools of rabbit brush. Gold piled up about the house walls, and on the tops of portáls in nuggets of calabásas and pumpkins ripening. Strings of scarlet chile came out everywhere like still, triangular flames. The feet of goats went round and round at the threshing-floors. You must do what you could to arrange things so that Father could go to Santa Fé. Everything must be gathered, saved, counted. Every handful of beans picked over, every scarlet pod of chile threaded meant something toward that urgent end. Now you knew what ranching was for, what people got out of it; stores; full bags and barrels and heaped bins; a fine sense of achievement. You ran and gathered all day and went to sleep like a shot; and in the morning you were up and at it. Mother said she didn't know what she would have done without you. Fun, too! The day that Alfredo Tenorio came up with horses to trample the great heap of dried bean vines, the day that Pablo showed them how to rob the pack-rat's nest of nearly three quarts of piñones![7] Pablo insisted that the rats were really grateful; they would have all the fun of filling up again before cold weather. The children found four nests that one afternoon, and piñones were twenty cents a quart. And always the procession of work and of New Mexico moved toward Nóchebuéna.

Nóchebuéna was what you called Christmas Eve, the Good Night. Somehow it had worked out that the children's Christmas was to be a trip down to Todos Santos for Nóchebuéna. No presents; presents cost money. Only, of course, the box that always came from Gramma Sitwell and Aunt Harriet. *Hoo!* what were presents! All the kids had them. But Todos Santos at night, Los Pastores,[8] the Kiss of Niño Dios, supper at Mr. Phipps's studio, midnight Mass! The young Sitwells hugged themselves when they thought of it, going out night after night on the portál to count the herders' fires as they moved with their flocks from the high pastures in a converging ring on Todos Santos. Pablo would come out from the kitchen where he had just had his supper, and call the herders' names as they appeared from point to point; Manual Romero down Moras Cañon toward the Hondo; Feliciano García from Monte Piedra; he had summered at Big Meadow; Beningo Gutierrez with the two flocks of Huertas Cardenas. It was rumored that Beningo had suffered much from bears that season. So the procession moved.

It was Aloysia Liberadita who had told them about the kiss of Niño Dios, the little figure in the pie-plate hat who lived in the tin *nicho* in Aloysia Liberadita's room, and yet somehow was to be found in the church of Todos Santos on Nóchebuéna between the candles. Whoever with a clean heart went forward on his knees to kiss the Niño, might whisper a wish in its ear, and *that* wish would be granted. Aloysia was always furnished with convincing examples.

And some children thought that all Christmas amounted to was presents!

Even Aloysia Liberadita went with them to Nóchebuéna. It was too bad that, when they came to the road branching off to the Prado, Grampa got down and went walking briskly off toward the Mission, where they were to have something in the nature of "Exercises," whatever that might be. Whatever it was that the Cath'lics had done to Grampa, they made it so that he never wanted to be with them. As Grampa left, the sun went down behind Jémez, the square sail of Pedernál stood up, and over the bulk of Monte Piedra flowed the crimson purple stain of Sangre de Cristo. Todos Santos was like a thin-blown bubble down at the bottom of a wine-glass.

The church was like a hill hollowed out. Huge ribs of adobe buttressed it from behind, the very tower might have been shaped by a spade. The bells that hung in it had a muddied sound that kept on long after their slow, sweet pealing. Through the open door candles glimmered at the far end like the herders' fires on Monte Piedra. The stained-glass windows in the deep walls were many-colored embers at the backs of ancient fireplaces. In front of every house, as they drove along, there were neat square piles of cut wood; in front of Mr. Phipps's house too; suddenly, in the dark, fires began to break, through the town and up along the lomas; *lumináres*, watch fires. Mr. Phipps said it was an old custom, and allowed the children to light his own. It gave you a lump in your throat somehow; the church bells jangled; you wouldn't have been surprised to hear the angels singing.

After supper, which was exciting and informal, with Mr. Phipps's friends coming and going, and nobody noticing how many helpings you had, there was Los Pastores. Aloysia said it would begin in front of the priest's house, so the children were allowed to go out with her, hand in hand into the strange crooked little streets, where the *lumináres* had died down to winking red eyes along the ground, or to heaps of hot ashes which you strangely felt as you passed them in the clear, cold dark, like the warm breath of crouching, unseen beasts. The town was full of people; tall men in sombreros and spurs that clanked a little as they walked, women in black shawls with swinging fringes. In the plaza and in front of the priest's house there were huge bonfires. Pablo was there with his nine children and his wife all in black, the shawl tucked under her chin so that as the fire flared and died she was like a floating face; all the women wrapped in their dark rebózas were faces that showed and went out strangely as they turned and shifted. The plaza was full of children running from fire to fire and calling to each other and blowing horns and shaking *métracas*⁹ that made a chirping sound like gigantic crickets.

While all this was still going on, there arose in another part of town the sound of singing, but it wasn't until Aloysia pulled at them that they realized that there was a movement, especially among the black-shawled faces, away from the plaza toward the church. You heard one sound die behind you and the other increase, and presently you discovered that you were following a group of sheep-herders, carrying lanterns and the long crooks by which a straying sheep is jerked back into its place in the flock, singing as they walked.

De la reál Jerusalém
salió una estrélla brillándo
que á los pastores va guiándo
para el portál de Belén.

Aloysia had taught them that Belén was Bethlehem; they fell into the procession and walked almost tiptoe with expectation to the portál of Bethlehem, which was the church door. . . They saw the innkeeper come out and the herders go in.

The Rancho Arríba party managed to squeeze into the church in time to see the shepherds kneeling at the left of the high altar, where the tree was, and a glitter of candlelight. It must have been a quarter of an hour before the church cleared sufficiently for the young Sitwells to discover what it was that drew a steady stream of movement to that corner; time to take in the church as a whole, and to recover a little from that queer half-fear that, for the first ten minutes or so, kept the children from nudging each other in mutual recognition of what was explicitly Cath'lic, and therefore marked for talking over when the occasion permitted. There was definitely a churchly feeling; you breathed it in and tingled with it; a new exciting smell. Bright along the walls were pictures that came out and receded in the candle flicker, and everywhere santos and *bultos,* a whole company of Blessed Personages, like in Aloysia Liberadita's room, but larger, more resplendent. The place was full of a feeling of suppressed aliveness. You could imagine that when the people were all gone, the santos came out of their niches and talked things over, or made processions around the church as the singing shepherds were doing, kneeling and rising and going on quite independently of whatever else was happening. The rows and rows of candles about the high altar had a marching look; as if they knew themselves and knew that they were at church. Gard had to be nudged every time it was open to them to move up closer to the Nacimiento.

The Nacimiento stood, as Aloysia had told them it would, at the left side of the altar, a miniature manger with the child, Mary and Joseph, the ox and the burros and the angels on the roof, and shepherds kneeling with their sheep. The animals were as large as the other figures, and the infant Jesus larger than the ox, but you never thought of that until afterward. The children sat a long time before it while Aloysia prayed, and Gard tried to make up his mind what he would ask from Niño Dios. Not a toy, as he had several times thought of doing; that could be left to Aunt Harriet or to Santa Claus, supposing there was still a Santa Claus, as Laura seemed to think doubtful.

Niño Dios lay in a straw-filled manger, close to the chancel rail, almost life-size, pink and smiling. Rows of dark-eyed children stair-stepping up and down from their black-shawled mothers, slid along the chancel steps on their knees, stooping to kiss the outstretched hand. Gard could see their lips moving in the whispered wish. Behind them music sounded from the tiny organ loft, secretly, practicing for the midnight Mass, the solemn hour of the Borning. Over the Nacimiento, high up, hung a star that glowed red and yellow as the candles went up and down in the gusts of singing. Now it was just a star, and then it was the red heart of Scorpio, or the flaming lamp of Betelgeuse, white Rigel, any one of the bright orbs from which nightly Gard's starry adventure began. He would have liked to pluck it down and carry it away with him under his coat, hidden but warm and shining. It you went about touching people with it, you could do things to them, make them well, or rich and splendid. Presently Aloysia nudged him; it was time to go forward for the wishing kiss. Gard was conscious of the cold chancel steps under his knees and the waxen fingers, warmed by much kissing. Aloysia was nudging him from behind. *El deséo!*[10] *El deséo!* But Gard had forgotten what it was he had meant to wish, and Laura was crowding him. "I wish I had a star." The wish barely formed upon his lips; for the moment that seemed to cover all that was in his mind.

The Sitwells did not stay for the midnight Mass; that was for truly Cath'lics. Driving home, over every door they counted lanterns burning; so that anybody looking for a place to be born in need not seek in a stable. That was what Mr. Phipps had told Father, along with other things which they heard him reciting to Mother on the front seat. Too sleepy to listen, the children snuggled down between the seats, deep in blankets.

Suddenly Gard remembered. "What did you wish, Laura?"

"I wished that my father would get well."

Gard felt convicted of childishness, which he wasn't going to be by Laura, even if she *was* going on 'leven.

"I wish that, too." He hoped she wouldn't notice that he had said *wish* and not *wished*. It wasn't a lie, really. If he had the star he would touch Father with it, and he would be well instantly. He looked back in his mind at the glowing wonder over Niño Dios, and at the planets swinging white and low as the road began to climb to Rancho Arríba. After all, his wish covered everything.

EXCERPTS FROM PART 2, BOOK I
The Book of Eudora

XII ... In August there was a Thunder Dance at San Ildefonso. The summer rains hadn't come on as expected, and the signs were that they would be delayed beyond the possibility of the corn filling out in the ear. You could trust Indians to know what weather signs meant. And the pueblos themselves were in the throes of what promised to be their final struggle with the white invasion of their scant and indispensable water supply. All the better sort of people were immensely stirred by it; and when the word went out that an old dance of the Thunder, long discontinued, was to be revived at San Ildefonso, it was impossible that Gard shouldn't have heard of it and felt it obligatory to lend his presence to a last appeal to the Powers. He wasn't sure, as he told Marvin, that he didn't have as much faith in it as in the political appeal to Washington that was being worked up among the friends of the Indian. Mother said she would like to go, and Marvin drove her down to Española the night before, that Gard might drive her to the pueblo, and then on to Santa Fe on business of the architects.

It was one of those bright menacing days that come with rains delayed, brassy skies and bitter powdery puffs of dust from the earth, sullen with resentment. Indians know when there is need of meditation between the implacable forces. The drums began early; they beat up in you latent powers, hereditary blind impulses. That was what made it impossible that the earth and sky shouldn't obey them. Gard was, as most New Mexicans, susceptible to the Indian mode of investing all things with a personal aspect and a mystical apprehension of unseen powers at work beyond the veil of Things. Huge white thunderheads skulked behind the Valley ranges, they peeped surreptitiously from time to time as if calculating how long it would be safe to resist the summoning drums and the compulsion of the Earth Medicine. The steady pulse of the drums raised up in him urges, images. The image of Eudora which lurked ready at any rising tide to be floated into the field of his emotional prepossessions. It was the least happy of the restraints you had to put upon yourselves that you couldn't go about together to the colorful and unprecedented spectacle of New Mexico. Gard hadn't known of this dance the last time he saw her; still, she might have heard of it. His gaze swept the gathering ring of spectators that fringed the pueblo plaza. There were cars from Santa Fe, from Taos and San Gabriel. From clear across the dancing space he marked two strangers getting out of a superb Chrysler; and some one he knew: Eugenio Elfego. The strangers went off with their camera to find the Governor of the San Ildefonso. Young Cardenas leaned at the car window talking to some one within; a woman. Gard knew the poses that went with a focus of attention on feminine attraction. It wasn't until the second round of the dance began again that the suspicion of its being Eudora turned into a sore certainty. He told himself that there could be no offense in his discovery of her among the audience; completely to ignore the possibility was to emphasize the avoidance of recognition. As the audience milled, he thought he might come around naturally within her field of vision. But there were a number of people who hadn't known yet that his mother had come back; people who were glad to see her. By the time he had half-circled the plaza, the Chrysler was pulling out; Gard stared steadily at the dancers going back to the kiva. Because otherwise he might have to admit that Eudora refused to see him.

He rehearsed, in the added hour that he was driving Mother to Santa Fe, a number of ways of carrying off the possibility that he hadn't really seen her. And then, quite unexpectedly, in the lobby of the hotel where he was waiting for Marvin, he did see her. It had been sudden on his part, so that he didn't know how long before she might have seen him coming, and prepared for that quick excluding intimacy of meeting. "I've just got in from an interesting dance at San Ildefonso," she said, "you should have seen it."

"Oh, I did. I saw you there and tried to get around to you."

There was no abatement of that bright softness; it neither flushed nor wavered, perhaps after all she hadn't seen you. "My friends," she said, "had just this one day here. I'm waiting for them now." You sat down together.

"I had my mother with me; I wanted you to meet her."

"Oh," said Eudora, "is that necessary?"

"Not necessary, perhaps, important. At least my mother thinks everything that is interesting to me is important."

"She's a widow isn't she? Has she a fixation on you?" So she *had* seen you and knew that you had seen Eugenio. It was too bright; too excluding, the way her eyes held you.

"My father—Yes. I don't know what you mean."

"There's an awfully good book just come out. I must lend it to you. It's like the Oedipus complex, only it's the mother for the son. Have you read D. H. Lawrence?"

"I haven't been thinking of my mother—" Your tongue moved thickly.

"You should read Lawrence. There's my friends. I'm taking them to the Cathedral. So nice to have seen you."

She did know that you had seen her with Cardenas. She'd put that Freudian stuff over on you, to keep you from remembering it. Or else— How did you know whether a woman was lying, or simply obtuse. The way Eudora's self took flight in innocence! She must have taken what you said about Eugenio to heart or she wouldn't have been at so much pains to keep you from throwing him up to her. She wanted you not to be displeased with her. She'd probably been showing young Cardenas off as a fascinating Native. People—your friends from outside—always expected you to make New Mexico jump through the hoop for them. And she was a little jealous of your mother. She always did use that Freudian stuff for cover. . .

It was a satisfaction to feel that you'd already decided that Mother must be kept out of it. A whole generation's difference, *and* the vocabulary. Mother couldn't be expected to know what it was all about. Jane would get it. Jane had been too young to marry; he shouldn't have allowed it. But Jane was young enough to understand. It was a relief to know how completely Jane would understand, and not understand too much. In Jane's world, there were no betraying morasses of complexes and fixations. You knew where you were with Jane. And Jane would know that you had to marry Eudora because you didn't know where you were. You owed it to yourself and the felt rightness of your passion for her, to give to it a standing and a name. It wasn't decent not to marry a woman who had made you suffer so much. You'd come to that. Anguish had its own intimacies, its proprieties. It demanded for itself a certain dignity.

As Eudora's husband you would have a kind of propriety right in suffering. You weren't expecting happiness; that was too tame a word. There would be bliss and torment. What you knew about yourself now was that in the midst of these flaming uncertainties your soul had a kind of life that was not to be purchased out of trust and quietude. You had moments of realizing that in the cessation of bliss you welcomed the torment as a sort of guarantee that, in Eudora's own time, the bliss would recur again. Eudora was the sort of woman who made it a privilege that you should be jealous on her account.

In the relief of having settled all these things for yourself and in the relaxation of passing the peak of your building activities, you missed your step. It had been in your mind all the time that marriage with Eudora was to come as a homing flight from the highest point of one of those mounting spirals of ecstasy in which your male ascendancy was confirmed. You would snatch her off into marriage by a kind of sleight of passion, marriage by capture, in the hunt of your souls each for the other in the midst of flame. You measured yourself for that flight as a trapeze performer for his fling outward into space. You said: When I get this schoolhouse off my hands—

It wasn't off your hands entirely; you had still, under your easing tension, the finishers and decorators. And nothing else arising in the immediate eye of your partnership, Marvin was proposing a projected survey of Colonial Architecture in New Mexico which might later be shaped into a book. You'd take in all the villages and haciendas from El Paso to Taos; you'd trace the development of the native house from Pit-House to Small-House, to Community House and pueblo, and then on to shining examples such as Huertas Cardenas. And you were telling Eudora about that.

"From the middle of September on for six weeks," you said, "the Rio is a river of aspen and cottonwood gold. There'll be chile drying on the house walls and calabásas heaped on the roofs, like lumps of gold. If I could only have you with me!"

You'd been having tea with her in the torreón, and there was a fire lip-lapping on the hearth because already the afternoons had a tiny chill, like the unsheathed point of a sword. You looked across at her, flushed and velvety like a late-blooming rose.

"Darling," you said, "couldn't we manage it somehow?"

Eudora gathered her brows, quizzically, a little amused.

"After all you've said to me of the Native notions of propriety? What would they think of that?"

"The thing for us to do," you said, blundering into folly, "is to get married as soon as possible so they needn't think."

"Married!" said Eudora. "You and I!" The dove's look was there, the look you knew, and the soft trailing voice like a smooth snake. And between the two phrases there had been a flash of the owl's eyes, a lightning stroke. She managed, at the end, the pose of innocent curiosity, but she hadn't managed it soon enough.

"You mean," you said, "that you haven't thought of marrying me?"

Eudora laughed, delicately. "You mean to say *you* have?"

"You can't have imagined I would have thought of anything else." And in saying it you knew you had dropped yourself into the pit you had never dared to look into, and Eudora was not with you.

"I suppose I shall marry again sometime. Marriage," said Eudora, with complete negligence, "is a gesture one always expects to make, but one must make it in one's own key. And for me that would be the grand manner, don't you think?"

"You mean . . ." you heard your voice without recognizing it. "You mean . . . that there hasn't been anything . . . you haven't. . ."

"Oh," said Eudora, "really! But I supposed you *were* married. Very suitably, I should think. . ." The words dropped to you from considerate maternal heights. "I never imagined you could misunderstand. You are very young, aren't you?" She pushed you gently with her foot where you sat on the end of the chaise longue there was the invitation of extenuation in her voice. You shrank from it, not in loathing, but in the involuntary physical reaction from your stroke. The same unconscious motion carried you to your feet.

"I'm young enough," you said, "not to have imagined anything else."

Eudora yawned a little. She flung herself out of her chair on the opposite side.

"You're young," she said, "and you're also very bourgeois. These scenes fatigue me. I suggest we bring this one to a close."

You fumbled your going out of sheer shock. She got back in the interval a little of her dove's look. "These things should end beautifully," she said, "and be beautifully forgotten."

"I don't know about forgetting." You meant at least to be faithful to your experience. "You see, it's been real to me. I've meant everything. I—I wrote to Jane." What you thought you were saying was, This is how I've respected you. I haven't made you a light of love. . . You thought you were reassuring her against the time when she might suffer in having been lightly held. . . And you saw at once that wasn't at all what you had done.

"You wrote. . . You mean, you've *told*. . ." Horror and hate flared up in her, wide-open fear, too wide for anything the occasion afforded.

"Nothing you need be afraid of. I didn't mention your name. Even the bourgeois don't tell," you said. Long after, when you needed support, in recollection, against the intolerable injury of her, you thought that rather a good ending, even though it had been made in utter simplicity. It was true that, though you couldn't recall exactly what you had written Jane, you were certain that you had not mentioned Eudora's name.

The Land of Journeys' Ending

9

The well-received *Land of Journeys' Ending* (1924), Austin's exhaustive treatment of a journey with her friends through Arizona, was dedicated to her friend and frequent correspondent Dr. Daniel Trembly MacDougal, director of the Carnegie Botanical Laboratory in Tucson, Arizona. In a letter from New York, planning their journey for the spring of 1923, she tells him that *The Land of Journeys' Ending* "must be in a sense, a monument to our common delight in the Southwest."[1] Her dedication credits his botanical knowledge, on which Austin depended during the trip as she took voluminous notes, and later as she was writing. The enormous amount of information she tried to assimilate in the book prompted her to write to MacDougal from Santa Fe, "This is an SOS of an author in difficulties!" She was writing her saguaro cactus chapter and required specific information. "I should like the private diary of a sahuaro for a year, and for twenty-four hours, all its rhythms of times and seasons," she wrote somewhat humorously to her friend. She wanted each sentence of the book to be factually accurate without "shooting over the heads of my readers."[2]

In *The Land of Journeys' Ending*, Austin writes of the "singular charm of the sahuaro forest, a charm of elegance, as the wind, moving like royalty across the well-spaced intervals, receives the courtesies of ironwood and ocotilla and palo verde" (125). As she had endeavored to do in the earlier naturist books, *The Land of Little Rain* (1903) and *The Flock* (1906), Austin contextualizes the land, writing a history of its people and conquests juxtaposed against detailed description. Of the Spanish expedition of the 1560s, Austin gives us this account in the book's first chapter, "Journeys' Beginning": "It is likely that the splendor of the company was considerably abated by the time the advance party . . . arrived at the region known, from the clusters of small springs there, as Arizonac. This was in May, when the sahuaro was in bloom, the sand already hot underfoot, and the only gold they had seen, the honey-scented bloom of the palo-verde" (17).

Many times Austin mentioned that her two "land" books should receive a special edition, in a sense demarcating her California period from her later years in the Southwest. Although this never happened, readers will see how the books fit together and bespeak the writer's commitment to nature writing throughout her career.

Journeys' Beginning

Between the Rio Colorado and the upper course of the Rio Grande lies the Land of Journeys' Ending.

No such natural boundaries, but the limits of habitableness, define it north and south. About the sources of its inclosing rivers the ranges of the continental axis draw to a head in the Colorado Rockies. Southward they scatter, like travelers who have lost their heads in terror of desertness, among the vast unwatered plateaus of Old Mexico. But all the country east of the Grand Cañon, west and north of the Jornada del Muerto, is like the middle life of a strong man, splendidly ordered. This is the first sense of the land striking home to the traveler who gives himself up to it. Go far enough on any of its trails, and you begin to see how the world was made. In such a manner mountains are thrust up; there stands the cone from which this river of black rock was cast out; around this moon-colored *playa*, rises the rim of its ancient lake; by this earthquake rent, the torrent was led that drained it. What man in some measure understands, he is no longer afraid of; the next step is mastery.

That this is the first and the lasting effect of the country comprised in the western half of New Mexico and the whole of Arizona, may be discovered, if from no other source, from the faces of the men who first made it habitable. In any collection of pioneer portraits you will find one type of physiognomy predominating—full-browed, wide between the eyes, and in spite of the fierce mustachios and long curls of the period, with a look of mildness. Superior to the immediate fear of great space, of the lack of water or the raiding savage, there was a subtle content at work. Seeing ever so short a way into the method of the land's making, men became reconciled to its nature.

There can be no adequate discussion of a country, any more than there can be of a woman, which leaves out this inexplicable effect produced by it on the people who live there. To say that the southwest has had a significant past, and will have a magnificent future, because it is a superb wealth-breeder, is to miss the fact that several generations of men wasted themselves upon it happily, without taking any measure of its vast material resources. The nineteenth-century assault which found California a lady of comparatively easy virtue, quailed before the austere virginity of Arizona; but the better men among them served her without recompense. If the Southwest is becoming known as an unrivaled food-producer, still, food-producing is one of the things man has taught the land to do since he has lived in it. There was nothing that betrayed its crop capacity to the untutored sense of the Amerind savage and the unlettered American pioneer. Both of these married the land because they loved it, and afterward made it bear. If more lines of natural development converged here, between the bracketing rivers, more streams of human energy came to rest than anywhere else within what is now the United States, it was because men felt here the nameless content of the creative spirit in the presence of its proper instrument.

Such a country as this, calls its own from the four world quarters. It had called many known and some forgotten peoples before any European, just to hear of it, had been afoot, in that neighborhood, and that not of his own wish, for seven years.

In April of 1536, when San Miguel de Culiacan in Sinaloa was the northernmost outpost of Spanish settlement in the New World, and Diego de Alcaráz with twenty soldiers had pushed as far as he dared toward the frontiers of Sonora, on a slave-hunting foray, he met with a most deplorable spectacle. A man clad, so far as he was clad at all, in the feathers and amulets of an Indian shaman, twirling a painted gourd and followed by a negro and a handful of the natives of that region, burst, running, toward him, crying thanks to the mercy of God, in the Spanish tongue.

It was not until Maldonado and Dorantes, plainly Europeans, came up with them, that Alcaráz was convinced that the four were survivors of the party of Pánfilo de Narvaez, who, seven years earlier, had touched Florida and been forced to sea with all his company in open boats, hoping to drift along the gulf coast to ports of Mexico, all perishing except this Cabeza de Vaca, treasurer of the expedition, and his three companions. Now, whether, in their long walk from the coast of Texas, where their boat struck, to Sonora, the party of Cabeza de Vaca had heard anything of the terraced-house culture of the north, or learned that there was gold there, is a matter over which scholars to whom evidence, until it is printed in a book, scarcely exists, are still exercised. By Cabeza de Vaca's own published account, they came no nearer to what almost at once began to be known as the Seven Cities of Cibola, than the Sierra Madre, among whose somber pines he heard the green-plumed stitch scold. But there was also a private report whispered into the ear of the King of Spain, and why private if all was told in the *"Naufragios y Jornada"*? Gold, I am certain he did not hear of; for he was, after all, a Spanish gentleman, and if he had believed that there was gold in the north, he would hardly on his return have become the Adelantado of Paraguay as soon as the post was offered him.

But that he may have heard of large settled populations in the north, from speaking of which publicly he refrained, seems more than likely. There was, first of all, the trade in turquoises by which he had partly maintained himself in the latter half of his wanderings, to be accounted for; there were also the five emerald arrows which were given to Dorantes. If Cabeza de Vaca had inquired concerning the peoples from whom these things were purchased, and not heard of any other good reason for speaking of them, he would have found reason enough in what happened to himself and his companions on meeting with Alcaráz, who took them prisoners because they refused to betray their Indian companions to slavery. The wanderers themselves had been slaves to the wild tribes, and may have modified their account of the peoples of the north on the same principle that made them hold out against Alcaráz. But the negro, Estevan, whom the viceroy Mendoza bought from Dorantes, did not hold out.

Whatever was lacking from Cabeza de Vaca's account to make a good story of it, he seems to have added; and he was perfectly willing to return to the scene of his wanderings to search for the Seven Cities of Cibola, rumor of which sprang up too suddenly, in all the ports of New Spain, not to have received considerable augmentation from the survivors of Narvaez's expedition.

Of the stuff of which such rumors are made as presently set the whole tide of Spanish interest toward the territory that is now the United States, there was more than a little lying at hand in the popular report.

There was first of all, among the Spaniards, the story of the Bishop of Lisbon, who, fleeing before the Arabs, had founded seven settlements in the islands of Antilla, lying *ante insular* before some fabled *tierra* of the west. There was also a tradition current, among the Nahuatl tribes of Old Mexico, of seven caves in which their legendary Ancients had rested in their wanderings, easy to reduce to Seven Cities in a land where, as was afterward proved, whole cities may be built in caves and flourish there. It was said of the Aztecs, who appeared on the great central plateau of Mexico about the twelfth century of our era, that they came out of the north.

And in the north, among the pueblos of the Rio Grande, which even at that date had a trade in feathers and turquoise and cotton cloth south into Chihuahua, there was a tradition of Poseyemo or Poseueve, a

This Louis Betts painting of Mary Austin is said to have hung in the National Arts Club in New York, where the writer frequently stayed during her many trips to the city. (Reproduced, by permission, from a photograph in the collection of the Huntington Library, San Marino, California)

culture hero who, after being stoned out of the pueblos, in the manner of prophets had departed south, drawing after him the most revolutionary of their young men. Do they not dance yearly in the terraced-house country for his return? Whenever, as the Spanish conquistadores led them back and forth, there was mixing of the native tribes, and exchange of histories, it was inevitable that there should be surmises and identifications of their legendary great. Montezuma was Pose-yemo; and Poseyemo, Montezuma. Thus, the tradition of a many-citied culture to the north, capable of having produced the founder of the Nahuatl nation, grew apace.

That the legend of Poseyemo should have become identified with the local prayer rites for the return of the rainy season, as is indicated by the local names for him, He-that-Scattereth-Moisture, or Finely-Divided-Rain, does not disprove him as the prophet and leader of young rebellion. And since the revolt of youth against the despotic communism of the pueblos—more strangling to individual genius than the less happy tyrannies of kings—must be led, why not by Poseyemo, who was born at that ruined pueblo above Ojo Caliente, as you go toward Tierra Amarilla?

Is it any the less likely that New Mexico should have produced the founder of a veritable line of kings, than that the whole of that territory from which they sprang should have been rediscovered through the combined activities of a Spanish adventurer called Head-of-a-Cow, a negro slave, and a Frenchman—a Savoyard, to be exact—in the habit of a Franciscan? At any rate, the swift rise of a belief in Seven Cities having their doorways crowned with turquoise, and whole streets of gold- and silver-workers, must have had more confirmation than appears in documentary evidence, since it attracted the interest of the viceroy Don Antonio de Mendoza, one of the greatest administrative minds of the time. Pedro de Castañeda, who wrote an account of the expedition of Coronado, says that as early as 1530 Nuño de Guzman, at that time President of New Spain, had an Indian slave who told of trading with his father as far north as the streets of the silver-workers of Cibola, from which they had brought away good metal. But Guzman could hardly have believed it, or he would not have kept so long from the field. Even after the report of the Narvaez survivors, it was three years before anything happened.

There was, first of all, a tedious business of royal patents to make discoveries, and much politics. The wild tribes lying between New Spain and the Seven Cities were to be pacified by the revocation of the order reducing them to slavery; guides and interpreters must be found and trained. The choice of captains fell upon Francisco Vasquez de Coronado, who seems not to have had any particular qualifications for this business, except that of being a courageous gentleman with an expensive wife and a credulous disposition. But before Coronado's time there were exploratory sallies. Even Dorantes seems to have wished to have a try at the Seven Cities, which is another reason for thinking that his party knew more of the country north than appears in any report. Mendoza spent money in outfitting him, but nothing seems to have come of it. Finally the Franciscan Fray Marcos de Niza, the negro Estevánico, two Castilian greyhounds, and a handful of Indians set out for Cibola, arriving somewhere in the wilderness of Arizona about the time that Fernando de Soto sailed from Habana de Cuba to the conquest of Florida.

This was in March of the year 1539, and by the time the finely divided foliage of the mesquite began to gather like mist across the llanos, Fray Marcos and the slave had reached farthest north of the white man in New Spain. This would have been about the northern limit of the sahuaro in Arizona; but if our travelers made no mention of it, that was because they had seen cacti taller, in the place of their setting out. The *fraile,* while he paused to make the topographical observations required of every Spanish explorer, sent the negro on ahead, with instructions to send back crosses, beginning with a palm's span in size and increasing as the search for Cibola grew warm and warmer. In four days, came back a cross the size of a man. No doubt the confirmatory reports which the travelers began to hear on every side, of cities of stone houses four stories high, were magnified by contrast with the daub-and-wattle huts of the Pimas and Sobaipuris, which were all they had so far found.

What Fray Marcos could not guess was that the land had reached out and laid a hand on Estevánico. More a savage than the Indians who led him, the negro was the more sensitive to the concealed, pregnant powers of the land; like all lovers of the Southwest, he translated his subconscious impression of it into the certainty of success. From the first, in imitation of Cabeza de Vaca, he had adopted the rôle of the medicine-man. One sees him going north by trails the Indians showed him, his greyhounds well in leash; clad, you may be sure, in as much magnificence, Spanish and aboriginal, as the exigencies of the trail permitted, gathering goods and women at the villages that entertained him. Rumor ran before him that a god-man, one of Those Above, was passing. Such attention as this belief evoked, the Franciscan had borne with tact and modesty; but with every day's journey into the wilderness, Estevánico became less a slave and more a savage. He ended by disobeying the *fraile's* instructions to wait at the crossing of the Gila, and proceeded on his own account to the discovery of Cibola.

After him, through the country now known as White Mountain

Apache, Fray Marcos came hurrying, finding huts prepared for him, and lacking neither food nor water. Everywhere his inquiries were met with that pleasant disposition of the primitive to tell to those whom he would please, the thing they wish to hear. Great cities? Yes! Gold? Surely! Even the name Cibola, or Shivola, which appears to be a twice-corrupted version of Shiwina, by which name the Zuñi know themselves, was confirmed. It was with great surprise, therefore, that Fray Marcos met, on the last day of May, fugitives of the negro's band reporting the killing of Estevánico at the first of the Seven Cities.

It must be borne in mind that the negro is in most respects inferior to the Amerind, and the people of Zuñi are of particular astuteness. At Hawikuh, this side of Thunder Mountain, where Estevánico presented his trumpery claims to medicine power, the caciques were offended. They resented the boldness of his demands for women and turquoises; and when told of the numbers and might of his white brothers, they thought him a spy and a liar. For why should a white people have a black man to represent them? So that is the last we see of Estevánico, going into a city of Zuñi in his faked medicine trappings, with his greyhounds and his concubines, plumes on his arms and on his ankles; then confused rumor of flight and wounding.

Fray Marcos, to whom these things were told, was clear as to his duty. With two or three of the least timorous of his following he stole up to the heavily wooded southwestern rim of the valley of the Shiwina. Here he saw the red plain with the red river winding through it, and the flat roofs of Hawikuh crowning a brown, rocky promontory. He perceived that this was indeed a city, judging it larger than the City of Mexico. Having set up a wooden cross as a token of possession, he returned, according to his own account, with "more fright than food," to Mendoza. In this fashion was our Southwest made part of the known world.

Concerning the exploratory expedition of Francisco Vasquez de Coronado to the country so reported upon, which took place as speedily as possible after the return of Fray Marcos, there is this to say: it was undertaken at his own expense, and cost in the neighborhood of a quarter of a million dollars.

The charge that Fray Marcos magnified his report for the viceroy's ear, cannot be justified from documentary evidence. It has been naïvely recorded by a chronicler of that time that he produced the effect of having more to report than proved the case, by *not* talking about the

Seven Cities to anybody except in strictest confidence. The fact is that Mexico City had filled up with young Spanish bloods, sharp for adventure. Word had already reached them, about the time of Fray Marcos's return, that De Soto had landed in Florida, and might, for all they could guess of geography at that time, be making for the self-same gold- and silver-workers' streets of the Seven Cities. Men talked of little else; traded and gambled in Spanish ports of the New World for royal licenses to explore the country of Cibola.

Finally, in the latter part of February, in 1540, Francisco Vasquez de Coronado got off, with three hundred Spanish companions, most of whom were well horsed; about a thousand Indians, and four Franciscans in orders, including Fray Marcos. Besides food and goods for barter, they were provided with droves of sheep and swine, and half a dozen pieces of light artillery. The viceroy Mendoza saw them off from Compostela in four companies, in full military order. Fine-sounding names their captains had: Don Tristan de Arellano; Don Pedro de Guevara, nephew to the Count of Oñate; Don Garcia Lopez de Cárdenas; Don Rodrigo Maldonado, brother-in-law of the Duke of the Infantada, and, for ensign-general, young Don Pedro de Tovar, son of that Fernando de Tovar who was guardian and Lord High Steward to the Queen, Doña Juana. Noble gentlemen as ever were got together for the exploration of new continents. *Caballos* pranked in brilliant horse-cloths sweeping to the ground; lances and long swords; coats of mail scarcely less shining than the gilded armor of the viceroy; many-colored Spanish sleeves and hose; visored head-pieces of Spanish bull's-hide; crossbows for the footmen, and for the wild allies, who neglected nothing of paint and plumes for the occasion, war-clubs and bows and arrows.

Thus, amid an immense throng of onlookers and with great noise of flocks and herds, the expedition was set in motion. It is hinted by historians of that period that Mendoza found its departure good riddance, for many of that company were freebooters, trouble-makers in the provinces, and every ship from home brought new scions of noble houses that must somehow be accommodated in a country already looted to the uttermost. There was also at least one honest woman; for we find her husband, Juan de Paladinas, in 1560 petitioning his Majesty for some slight favor on the ground of what his wife did, in nursing the sick and mending the soldiers' clothes; he having undertaken this expedition with arms, horses, and servants "at his own expense like a good soldier."

It is likely that the splendor of the company was considerably abated by the time the advance party under Francisco Vasquez de Coronado arrived at the region known, from the clusters of small springs there, as Arizonac. This was in May, when the sahuaro was in bloom, the sand already hot underfoot, and the only gold they had seen, the honey-scented bloom of the palo-verde. North from the Salt River was unin-habited country, sparsely forested, leagues of red clay and needle-grass, gray marl, and menacing high cones of waterless mountains. About the fourth of July, lacking food and somewhat diminished in numbers, the expedition sighted the first of the Seven Cities.

This Cibola, Shivola, *Shiwina,* Zuñi, is a red-and-yellow plain reaching away to undulating hills in the west, blue with piñon, cloud-shadowed, dim with mirage and the whirling of dust-cones that on the stillest days rise unaccountably and go spiring skyward. The valley wall is banded red and white, and near its eastern end rises a vast rocky island, flat-topped, wind-carved along its streaked edges into towers and pinnacles, Toyoállanne, sacred Thunder Mountain. Where the mesa rises flat beyond Thunder Mountain is Uhanami, Mount of the Beloved Twins, guardians of *Shiwina.* Down the valley winds a glitter-ing red streak of river. Not too far from it at any point, rise brown hummocks, squaring into brown walls and flat roofs, bristling with ladder-poles and chimneys of bottomless brown pots stuck together with clay.

Out of the first brown mound the Spaniards saw the people issue like ants from an ant-hill, making, between them and the strangers, sa-cred meal roads by which it was vainly hoped danger would be averted.

Coronado demanded the submission of the town, in round Spanish fashion, promising amnesty. The Zuñi shut the town and defended it from the roofs, with arrows and throwing-stones by which the *coman-dante* himself was twice knocked from the saddle. Everywhere against the mud walls the crossbows were at a disadvantage, but superstition played on the side of the invaders. In the night, after the Spaniards had gained a few out-dwellings, the inhabitants fled to their stronghold on top of Toyoállanne. At Hawikuh, then, the advance party rested while the rest of the army could be brought up from the Valley of Hearts in Sonora.

Of how Coronado made terms with the inhabitants of Hawikuh; of Halona, and Matsaki, and other of the Seven Cities of the Zuñi; of how Don Pedro de Tovar subdued the cities of the Hopitu, chiefly through their fear of the horses which the natives believed to be man-eating; how Cárdenas was sent to discover the Great River of the West, which he did within the eighty days allotted, thus proving that California was not an island, must be left for another relation. What mattered most to the expedition was the rage of the young bloods over the way the land withheld its secret of the gold which they—rightly enough, as it proved in the long run—could not disbelieve in.

As for these Seven Cities of which the eager imagination of Fray Marcos had made marvels, they proved mere aggregations of mud huts, piled one upon the other, the whole aspect of them as pasteboard crumpled and thrown away. As for the turquoise over the doors; the Zuñi had no doors, but entered their dwellings through hatchways, by means of ladders, and though it was the custom to place blue stones there to put the dwellers under the protection of the Sky Powers, these were by no means so many nor so fine as had been reported. Silver there was none, gold not so much as heard of, and so loud were the cursings visited on Fray Marcos that Coronado found it expedient to send him south again with the detachment that brought up the rest of the army from the Valle de Corazones. While he waited, early in August, came the representatives from Cicuyé, most easterly of the Rio Grande pueblos, to make submission; and with them, rising as unaccountably as dust devils in the wind, new rumor of discoverable riches. Don Hernando Alvarado, being sent to reconnoiter, pushed as far beyond the last of the mud towns as the plains on which were first encountered the fabled humpbacked cows which had long figured in rumors of the north country. As a result of Alvarado's report, the winter quarters of the expedition were removed to Tiguex, near the site of what is now Bernalillo.

There they saw the quick snows of that region mantle and disappear, saw the poplars whiten before they broke into green flame, and the fragrant fire of the wild plums run in the underbrush. Here the gorge of the Rio Grande widens to a fertile intervale, and the basalt cliffs are modulated to low, breast-shaped hills. North and south on tributaries of the river, west about the skirts of Jemez, east on the Salinas between Sandia and Manzanos, and north on the upper Pecos, in high-piled, mud-walled towns, were gathered the sedentary tribes to the number of twenty thousand. But there was no gold at Tiguex, either. None, at least, that the expedition heard of; though whether or not its existence might, in time, have been brought to knowledge, was settled finally by the exorbitant demands of the *comandante* for food and blankets, and by the burning alive, though that was not directly chargeable to Coronado, of two hundred Indian hostages.

It seems certain that, as a thing of use and value, metal of any sort was unknown to the Pueblos until the Spaniards taught it to them. Of gold as a matter of secret superstitious reverence, it was impossible that, after the first three months of residence in the Pueblo country, the companions of Coronado should have heard anything. Only when the mud roofs are muffled in snow and the flames of cedar run up the walls of the three-cornered fireplaces, when the ceremonial cigarettes are lighted and the talk turns to the days of our Ancients, you may hear something of the Seed of the Sun which made sacred the places where it was found, known only to priests of the Sun and a few elders. At first it was not clearly understood that this gold for which the Spanish went everywhere peeking and prying, was the same sacred seed. But, say the old men, after the burning alive of the two hundred at Tiguex, out of every village one society was chosen, and of that society, two persons were made the keepers of the secret, no one knowing who they were, and each choosing his own successor.

Whether by this process the secret has altogether died out, or whether indeed the very Ancient who tells you this may himself be a keeper, there is no knowing; no knowing, in fact, if the legend of the Seed of the Sun may not be such a myth of the mystery of gold as all men who have once felt the power of gold love to make of it.

The conquistadores, if not myth-makers, proved most notable believers. There was at Pecos, then called Cicuyé, a slave taken in war, a high-nosed Pawnee nicknamed the Turk, who had probably acted as guide to Alvarado's excursion in search of buffalo, affording him ample opportunity to find out what the Spaniards wanted and what sort of stories they would believe about it. What he made them believe was that in his own country of Quivira, his people ate off golden plates, and their chief went to sleep to the sound of golden bells swung from the tree-tops over him. He confessed at the last, when the Spaniards were about to kill him, that the caciques of Pecos had persuaded him to this deception, in hopes that the Spaniards, drawn away from the pueblos, might perish utterly.

Perhaps he thought of it for himself, thinking only that as a slave he had little to lose, and if he died, at least it would be where a man most wishes to meet death, in his own country. Perhaps Coronado snatched at the story, finding no other way to restrain the disappointment of his men from breaking out against himself in default of other victim. At any rate, in April, when the willows redden and the land is full of the drip of snow-water, we find the whole expedition setting out, with the Turk chained to the *comandante's* saddle-bow, for Quivira, no one of them willing to be left behind, and all so full of this new fable that they could scarcely be persuaded to carry full horse-loads of food, for fear there would not be room for the gold they should bring returning.

North by west they went, across the short-grass country, where the moving horizon shut them in at the distance of a musket-shot, where the infrequent rivers hid themselves at the bottom of unsuspected ravines, and the treeless lakes, round as plates, gave back the color of the fleckless sky. Bison they saw, with Indians chasing them, white wolves following the bison, and gray deer pied with white, in great companies. It seems certain, from all accounts, that the Turk tried desperately to lose them, and that the difficulties of the way proved so insurmountable that the main part of the expedition returned to Tiguex, to await the outcome of the adventure. Somewhere en route they heard of the Father of Waters, which about this time—it was in July that the company parted—had been crossed by desperate De Soto.

The buffalo-grass bleached and withered, wild grapes ripened along the creeks, wild plums bent over with sweet purple fruit. But at Quivira, which seems to have been somewhere about Wichita, Kansas, even the rumor of gold ran out. Accordingly, having heard the confession of the Turk, they strangled him, Jaramillo says at night, so that he never woke up, but by another account, at early morning as a way of beginning the day well, which I prefer to think was the case. For, though you have only to look at the track of their wanderings on the map to see that the Pawnee purposely tried to mislead the expedition, I think there was much to be said on his side. And if he was what we suppose him, he would have wished to die at the hour when the Morning Star, guardian of all the Pawnees, consoled him.

Of the final draggletail withdrawal of the expedition from New Mexico, and its reception in New Spain, but one thing concerns us. This is the trap the land set, and the lure with which it was baited to draw to itself the sort of people to whom its treasures would finally be revealed. Not only did Coronado miss all the mineral wealth of the country visited, but there is not ever a mention, in Castañeda's account of the turquoise-mines which were at that time worked by the Indians, located within a day's ride of his permanent camp. The one thing, however, that the Franciscans would not let him miss, was that there were souls here to be saved. Fray Juan Padilla, with some acolytes he had trained and put into the Franciscan habit, asked leave, on the withdrawal of the expedition, to return to Quivira, on that business which he judged more propitious than the search for gold. There was also Fray Luis de Escalona, who with a few sheep, an adze and a chisel to make crosses with, and a great zeal for God in his heart, remained at Pecos. Of whom no more is known than a rumor that they died as became them. From that slender point of attachment was to be spun the thread that bound New Mexico to the known world.

After Coronado, the land had rest for forty years. The conquistadores turned their attention to Central and South America as offering the richest reward to their military and picaresque ability. The people of the pueblos worked the episode of the Spanish *entrada* into their dance-dramas, and named the pale-gold-colored papooses born to their women, "Children of the Moon." Of what finally became of Francisco Vasquez, nothing is known, but the Franciscans, who went everywhere in the New World, would not let that world forget the martyrdom of Fray Luis and Fray Juan de Padilla, news of which brought the brown skirts humming about the doors of the civil authorities, demanding as reparation the right and opportunity to convert the whole of that country to Christianity. We who are at the diminished outer ripple of the rings of missionary impulse, estimate it too feebly as one of the driving forces of the middle ages. Put it that Spain had swarmed, as a little later the English. Whatever the urge that compels great populations to sow themselves to all four quarters of the earth, the desire to spread the blessings of Christianity was, in the sixteenth century, a popular way of rationalizing it.

In forty years the colonization of New Spain had proceeded northward from Mexico City as far as Chihuahua, where it touched the extreme southern end of the immemorial trade trail that connected Mexico with the country of the Rio Grande. Across the wastes it traversed, trickled a sense of the true nodality of the land of the pueblos. It began to be thought of as the seat of a considerable culture, a center of human activity and interest, a *new* Mexico.

In 1581 there was a sally in that direction led by Fray Agustin Rodriguez to whom Don Lorenzo Suarez de Mendoza, Conde de Coruña, Viceroy of Mexico, had given permission, with two companions of his order and a handful of soldiers, to go missionarying among the Pueblos. There all three of the Franciscans met the supreme reward. The news of their killing aroused one Antonio de Espejo, a devout man of excellent repute and fortune, to undertake an expedition of inquiry and relief; for at the moment it was not certainly known that all three of the missionaries had perished.

The trail, which is one of the oldest traffic routes in America, emerged from Chihuahua, followed the Conchos River to its junction with the Rio Grande, up along the south bank, to a ford at about the present location of the city of El Paso. It also crossed the track of Cabeza de Vaca, as Espejo discovered from Indians he met, affording grounds, for those who like to believe it, that the survivor of Narvaez touched New Mexico and knew more of the terraced-house country than appears in his published account. North of this point the trail continues for a bitter interval along what came to be known as La Jornada del Muerto.

Espejo, being a man of tact, and the Indians by this time better instructed in the nature of white people, succeeded in learning such things of the resources and topography of the country as made it from that time forth part of the known and familiar world. He lost no lives and provoked no wars with the inhabitants. He discovered the Salinas, and brought away specimens of rich ores and precious metals which he says he found in the Indians' houses. This is a matter which wants some explaining. Something is due to the displacement of the reckless, lustful hope of gold, free gold, ready worked to the conqueror's hand, which had been the mainspring of Coronado's expedition, by a soberer appreciation of the nature and values of raw ores. But if the Pueblos had had no metal at all before the coming of the Spaniards, they could hardly have arrived at such a use of it, in the forty years' interval, as enabled Espejo confidently to assert that the country was as rich in minerals as it was already known to be rich in corn. What he brought away with him was the profound desire for the material mastery of that country which it provokes to this day in those who know it.

Espejo immediately applied for leave to colonize in New Mexico, as did many other Spanish gentlemen. And while he was doing it the whole village of Almaden made an exploratory *pasear* across the Rio Bravo and up the Pecos from which they were brought back under arrest by the authorities. Finally, by the devious course of Spanish politics, the choice of adelantado fell upon Don Juan de Oñate. Now mark how the note of high romance holds throughout the history of the Southwest. Oñate was married to a granddaughter of Cortés and of Montezuma, and he came for the founding of his first city to the very walls of that pueblo in which the fabled Poseyemo had taken refuge when his own town of Poseunge had denied him, from which he was finally driven in turn, drawing off with him all those rebellious youths, to found—so the Indians there believe to this day—the line of Montezumas and the Aztec nation.

Whether, among the numbers of Indian slaves and servitors, Oñate brought any of that blood to the land of their cradling, you may believe or not according to your disposition, for it was more than likely. At any rate, he brought the author of what was quite certainly the first American drama, a comedy relative to the conquest of New Mexico which was written by Captain Farfan and performed on the south bank of the Rio on the evening of the day of Oñate's formal *entrada*. The expedition had likewise its poet, one Gaspar de Villagrá, also a captain, to whose execrable but accurate epic we are indebted for much we know of it. Believe me, nothing of significance had been done in the land of Journeys' Ending but with something of the poet's largeness and the dramatists' gesture. Don Juan, himself, was, in an age of flourishes, distinguished for the magnificence of his own postures.

Arriving at El Paso del Norte, he took possession ceremoniously of all the country north, "In the name of the Most Holy Trinity, and the Undivided Eternal Unity, Deity and Majesty, Father, Son, and Holy Ghost . . . and of his most sacred and blessed Mother, the Holy Virgin Mary . . . Mother of God, Sun, Moon, North Star, guide, and advocate of humanity; and in honor of the Seraphic Father, San Francisco . . . patriarch of the poor, whom I adopt as my patrons, advocates, guides, defenders, and intercessors . . . I, Don Juan de Oñate, Governor and Captain General and Adelantado of New Mexico, and of its kingdoms and provinces, as well as those in their vicinity and contiguous thereto, as settler, discoverer, and pacifier of them and of the said kingdoms, by order of the King our Lord." In this fashion, with a very large company of soldiers and settlers, with seven thousand head of live stock and eighty unwieldy, solid-wheeled carretas, Oñate made his *entrada* the thirtieth day of April, 1595, and the long journey of Spanish exploration in the New World came to rest.

Poetry 10

From her earliest years as a writer, Austin published verse. Although her preeminence as a writer lies in her prose fiction and nonfiction, nonetheless her poetry was fine enough to appear in the leading literary magazines of the day along with the most well regarded American and British contemporary poets. She was especially fond of writing verse for children; a market for this was *St. Nicholas: Scribner's Illustrated Magazine for Boys and Girls*, edited by its energetic founder Mary Mapes Dodge.

Writing from New York to her confidante and frequent companion Dr. Daniel MacDougal, Austin refers enthusiastically to some editing on her recent Indian poems. "Not once did he [the editor, Ovington Colbert, of Chickasaw descent] fail to 'spot' the original Indian thought, and divide it from the things I had put in to make it intelligible to the white mind, or in the case of my earliest translation, to satisfy some editor's notion of form. I felt so relieved to know that I hadn't missed or mucked up the Indian idea, that it gave me courage to cut away all the frills and to leave them in their original simplicity."[1] Although Austin was referring to some poems written twenty years before, her ideas about getting "the Indian idea" right was key to her notion of "translating" Indian poetry. As Richard Drinnon notes, "She perceived that Indians *lived* that oneness with the universe she had experienced fleetingly as a child under the walnut tree."[2] Predisposed towards mysticism from childhood, as a poet she incorporated the beliefs of the ineffable and the mystic into her verse.

As much as she admired many aspects of Native American cultures, Austin never freed herself completely from Darwinian ideas of essentialism and the primitive. In short, Austin believed in the primacy of the Caucasian and the primitive or childlike qualities inherent in non-whites. Because of her beliefs (common in her day when the theory of eugenics was widely discussed as a way of breeding desirable characteristics into human beings), she held that non-whites, especially Indians and Mexicans, had certain essentialized ethnic characteristics that needed protection by interested Anglos like herself. She worked vigorously to "protect" their native folkways, believing them incapable of doing this for themselves. These attitudes are plainly evident in the introductory essay to her controversial book *The American Rhythm* (1923), about an indigenous rhythm—a basic beat common to humanity—which she argues underlies all poetic utterance: "What is the familiar trochee but the *lub*-dub, *lub*-dub of the heart, what the hurrying of the syllable in the iambus but the inhibition of the blood by smaller vessels?" (5). At the same time, however, she experimented with Indian rhythm in her writing, especially her poetry, and in so doing reexamined previously held cultural notions about Indians and their folkways.[3]

Austin preferred rhymed verse in her own poetry, and she asserted in *The American Rhythm* and elsewhere that rhyme appeals universally in all cultures beginning with childhood.[4] In her book of children's verse, *The Children Sing in the Far West* (1928), the only known collection of Austin's poetry, she acknowledges that children's poetry had interested her from the years that she had taught in Lone Pine. Like many poets of her day, Austin believed from experience that rhyme and repetition are key elements of verse, verse that appeals to both children and adults. She addressed her method of poetry making in *Earth Horizon:* "It had always been a knack of Mary's even as a child to reshape the familiar nursery jingles to [the] immediate interest of the play group" (213).

It should be noted that Mary Austin knew no Indian languages and thus, technically, cannot be considered a translator. However, she attended Indian rituals, ceremonials, and dances, and then used the words of the Sioux, Osage, Paiute, Cherokee, and other tribes as transcribed by ethnologists, to which she appended "additional material which [she] thought would bring out poetic values," yet remain faithful to the original form.[5] These interpretive creations, which re-expressed or gave impressions of the ethnologists' transcriptions, constituted what Austin called "Amerind" verse forms.

Harriet Monroe (1860–1936) and Alice Corbin Henderson (1881–1949), the founders of *Poetry: A Magazine of Verse,* published many of Austin's poems, as well as work by other notable American and British poets such as Wallace Stevens, Marianne Moore, William Carlos Williams, T. S. Eliot, Ezra Pound, and William Butler Yeats. Typically, Harriet Monroe would have suggestions for Austin, as in her letter of January 2, 1928, in which she advises her that she will take "Sounds," "Caller of Buffalo," and "Litany of New Mexico." On the buffalo poem, Monroe questions, "Don't you think *your* would be better than *they* in the penultimate line of *Caller of Buffalo?*"[6] Austin agreed. Monroe also advised Austin that her use of Indian and Hispanic words might confuse readers, advice ignored by the poet.[7]

Although Austin did not feel poetry was her strength, she did receive recognition for several poems. "Litany for New Mexico," published in the June 1928 issue of *Poetry,* received honorable mention in the November issue.[8] Henderson and Monroe also included Austin in their volumes of *The New Poetry.*

The poems included here are a sampling of early and late Austin. All seem suggestive of the lyrical prose she employed in her naturist prose.

Inyo

Far from the northward, from the cloven ridges
Pine-girt, deep drifted with bewildering snows,
Through ice-plowed gorge, the leaping river bridges,
Light span by span, from lake to lake below;
Through mountain meadow and the snow-fed hollow
Where birch and buckthorn thickets mark the trail,
Spurning the tawny hills in haste to follow
The long brown reaches of a desert vale.

To east and west roll up the purple ranges
Foot bound about with leopard-colored hills,
From east to west their serrate shadow changes,
From east and west stream down the tumbling rills
That mock the shadeless slopes and sullen ledges;
Through sunburnt wastes of sage and yellow sand,
Flow down to meet thy willows and thy sedges,
O lonely river, in a lonely land!

Foamless and swift thy winding waters follow
To find, unbosomed to the wind-swept skies,
The great lake lapping in a tideless hollow,
Wanton to each days changes as they rise;
Purpling to meet the splendor of the mornings,
Paling to catch their tender mid-day blue,

Trembling alike to smilings and to scornings,
Fleet light of loves, it cannot hold one true.

Like some great lioness beside the river
With furies flaming in her half-shut eyes,
Watching the light from heated sands up-quiver—
Untamed and barren, lone the valley lies.
Forego, O River, all the wrong you do her,
Hasting thy waters to the bitter lake,
Rise from thy reedy marges and subdue her!
So shall the land be fertile for thy sake.

Love Coming Late

Love came to me late,
    having sent on before him
    all his great company

Young love with his perfumed torch
    beguiling the senses
Passion, whose feet when I kissed them
    blackened my mouth,
Duty which galled me worst where the hurt was sorest.

Then with a sound of wings
    down edged for silence,
With a stir as of evening primroses blowing
    wide apart at the foot of the orchard,
Secret, contained and aware,
    Great Love came walking.

Came and sat down at the loom
    Where I stooped overwearied
And suddenly, as he wrought,
    Duty and Passion and Youth
    came back and served him.

Sounds

There is a sound of going
    in the tops of the mulberry trees,
The sound of a last breath.
In the cottonwoods also
And the willow-leafed poplars,
That a week ago were flame-pointed,
A sound as of bent blades clashing rustily.

There is a sound of going in the chamise
The sound of a besom sweeping, sweeping,
A sound of unconsidered things
Scurrying to brief corners of oblivion.

But with the spruce trees it is not so,
Nor with the balsam firs by the water borders.
A staying sound,
As of roots that strain but loose not
From the rock crevices.

I will go up to the evergreen pines,
To the blue spruces around Eagle Rock
And hearten myself with the sound of the star-built firs.

Caller of Buffalo

Whenever the summer-singed plains,
Past my car window,
Heave and fall like the flanks of trail-weary cattle,
When the round-backed hills go shouldering down
To drink of the western rivers,
And dust, like ceremonial smoke,
Goes up from the long-dried wallows,
Then I remember the Caller of Buffalo.

Then I think I see him,
Head-feathers slant in the wind,
Shaking his medicine robe
From the buttes of Republican River,
At Pawnee bluffs
Offering sacred smoke to the Great White Buffalo.
Then at dawn, between jiggling curtains, I wake
To the star-keen note of his deer-shin whistle.

O Caller of Buffalo!
Hunt no more on the ancient traces
Pale and emptied of going as a cast snake-skin.
Come into my mind and hunt the herding thoughts,
The White Buffalo
Of the much desired places.
Come with your medicine-making,
O Caller of Buffalo!

Rio Abajo

In Rio Abajo ghosts walk,
At Socorro I saw them,
Three and twenty brown gowns, rope-girt and sandalled.
By old Isleta ford,
Don Francisco de Coronado with his Spanish gentlemen—
Armor-rust on their satin sleeves,
Arrow-slits in their leathern greaves—
Rode all down the cotton fields
While the Tegua war-drums thundered.

Once in the dawn below Belen
Creaked the broad-wheeled carreta train
Whose single guttering candle showed
Where La Conquistadora rode
To reconquest and old pain.

Once by this saguan's ruined arch
Music its walls absorbed gave back again,
As in the dusk guitars were playing,
And on the stamped adobe floor
The dance still swaying.
Still is the Alameda sweet
With sun-steeped petals strewn
Where late the twinkling monstrance passed,
Mid gold more lucent than its own,
To bless the fields again.

Litany for New Mexico

Bless God for the day!

Bless Him for the wide clear-flowing
New Mexico morning,
Poured round the shadow pools,
Gilt on the cumbres.

Bless Him for the nooning,
When the white thunderheads with sails full bowing
Sleep on the three wind rivers.
Bless God and praise Him
For the west-sloping hour of siesta
Under domed cottonwoods,
That in a rainless land make ever the sound of rain.

Bless Him for the evening;
For the releasing cool hands of the wind
On the flushed headlands;
For the lilac and larkspur veils
Let down by the mothering mountains
Between the work that fails and the dream that lingers.
Bless Him for home-coming sounds—
The window-shine on the loma,

For the welcoming flame and the savory smell
And the snuggling cry of the children.

Bless God for the night!

Bless Him for the keen curled sickle that reaps
The saffron meadows of the sun's late sowing;
for the full-shaped globe of wonder,
Pacing the eastern ranges.
Oh, bless Him more than all
For the ever-recurrent orb that emerges
Between the light that goes and earth's oncoming shadow.

Bless Him for shared sleep,
For the midnight's healing fountain,
For the companionable cock-crow, warning
The sleeper back from dreams to the pastures of morning.

Bless God for the dawning,
For the earth collecting
Darkness again to her breast,
For the hills resounding
Clarion blue to the sun's relucence.

Bless God and praise Him
With exceeding thanksgiving
For His gift of the day and the night!

Love in New Mexico

It should have been there by the river,
By the Red buttes,
By the bridge of Ottowi,
Where the lion colored river fawns and gurgles;
Thin green the flames of sycamore unsheathing,
And the lifting, blossom cymes of the pear trees

A white wound at the heart.
It should have been there that you loved me.

Ah, heard you not the horns of color blowing
From the tall potreros,
Orange, scarlet, golden,
Or the brazen, bassoon-throated lowing
Of the earth, desirous for the plough.
If you were here by the river
It should be now!

It should be at the pear tree's rosy signal,
In the lost ecstasy of petaled orchards,
While in mid air the broody mountains
Stoop whitely on furled wings, as eaglets
Covering their mates in March, along the cumbres.
What then were youth or age between us,
Or wealth or pride, or any other creature;
What were comeliness of men, or woman's beauty
Who, lost in Beauty's self, need not the seeming?
It should have been there
In the Valle del Rio Grande!

11

Taos Pueblo

In 1929, Mary Austin entered into a collaboration with the young photographer Ansel Easton Adams (1902–1984) to produce a book about Taos Pueblo, near Taos, New Mexico. From the outset of the project, it was understood that Austin was the senior partner of the collaboration. Adams greatly appreciated the writer and was happy to accede to this arrangement, with the encouragement of Albert Bender, a wealthy friend and patron of southwestern arts. Indeed, it was Bender, Austin's long-time acquaintance and benefactor, who suggested the collaboration, which he largely underwrote. Tony Lujan of Taos Pueblo, Mabel Dodge Luhan's husband, secured the agreement of the tribal leaders to photograph the pueblo, and during the project Adams stayed with Tony and Mabel at her home, Los Gallos.

Bender's funding enabled Adams to arrange for the finest reproduction available of text and photographs; the printing paper was supplied by Dassonville, the book produced by the Grabhorn Press. The final edition of one hundred copies, with eight artist's copies, sold for the unheard-of (in the 1930s) price of seventy-five dollars, according to Adams' autobiography.[1] Although Austin expressed great fondness for Ansel and Virginia Adams, she nevertheless considered herself the principal author of the book, and Adams merely her illustrator. Adams treated Austin with the utmost respect, writing to their patron Bender that "with Mary Austin writing the text . . . I have a grand task to come up to it with the pictures."[2] When she learned the price of the book, Austin registered shock and encouraged Adams to seek some way of bringing out a "cheap edition," but for all her protestations, she liked what she saw when she obtained her copy, agreeing with the photographer that the book was beautiful.[3] In his autobiography, Adams pays tribute to Austin's text, quoting a section concerning women-controlled domestic arrangements within Taos Pueblo: "Every house is a Mother Hive, to which the daughters bring home husbands, on terms of good behavior; or dismiss them with the simple ceremony of setting the man's private possessions—his gun, his saddle, his other pair of moccasins—outside the door."[4]

Today the unusual collaboration that created *Taos Pueblo* is remembered more for Ansel Adams' photographs than for Austin's text.[5] Nonetheless, Austin's introductory essay did successfully capture in words the mystical aura of the place.

Taos Pueblo

Pueblo Mountain stands up over Taos pueblo and Taos water comes down between the two house-heaps, North house and South house, with a braided motion, swift and clear flowing. As you look at the south entrance to the valley, Pueblo Mountain, bare topped above, and below shaggy with pines, has the crouched look of a sleeping animal, the great bull buffalo, turning his head away and hunching his shoulders. Beyond him the lower hills lie in curved ranks of the ruminating herd. It is not so much the animal contours that give the suggestion as the curious quiescent aliveness of the whole Taos landscape, as if it might at any moment wake and leap. You look and look away, and though nothing has altered you are quite certain that in the interval the hills have stirred, the lomas have exchanged confidences. Far out, to the north, where Taos Valley ceases to be valley without having lifted again to hill proportions, there is a feeling of the all but invisible tremor of a sleeping sea.

From the air, looking down, there is the same sense of wild animality, but of a different creature; Mokiatch, my lord puma, taking his ease across all Colorado, but with his tail hanging down into New Mexico, a long flexile tail that crooks out to the east and then curls at the tip, far down at Santa Fe, into a cat coil, the final knot of the Culebra ranges. Culebra, snakey; that is how they curve about the eastern rim of Taos Valley, of which the upper cañon of the Rio Grande makes the western boundary, in the shape of a moon three-quarters full. Taos Pueblo lies close to the northern cusp of the moon curve and Taos water goes down in three parts to join the waters of Talpa Creek and Rio Chiquito, that with Taos water at the foot of the long hill making the final ascent into Taos Valley, becomes the east fork of the Rio Grande. . . .

. . . Taos is a Tigua possession, but as the Spanish came to it through Tewa country, with Tewa guides and interpreters, they learned to know it by its Tewa name of Tówih of which Taos (Towse) is a corruption. Oñate, taking possession of the country in 1598, in the name of the King of Spain and all the Blessed Personages, put the town under the protection of San Miguel Archangel, but early in the seventeenth century the Taiinamu, grown familiar with the Christian hierarchy, found a patron more to their liking in Saint Jerome, known to them in the Spanish form of San Hieronomo. . . .

. . . Only in the faces of the villagers, highnosed and proud, in the persistence there of an interest in dramatic entertainment and in the architecture of the old church, is there any reminder of its Indian origins. The church at Ranchos, more than any of those structures, has the deep rooted, grown-from-the-soil look of Pueblo buildings. So the villages of the Amerind aboriginals pass, they decay and disappear. In the North, only Taos the proud, Taos the rebellious, between Pueblo Mountain and the modern town of Fernandez de Tao holds its tribal integrity. . . .

. . . Out of the Plains contribution to their inheritance, the people of Taos have become taller, on the whole handsomer than their pueblo kin; their humor is sharper, more ironic; their pride—all Indians are prideful—has the touch of insolence characteristic of the free hunting tribes. Their history is explicitly marked with revolt, rebellion and resistance to White aggression.

. . . But it is the fact of Taos rather than its history which intrigues public interest. The fact of its persistence, sturdily unimpaired of its essential primitiveness, its vital pagan quality, gathering to itself the nostalgia of house-bred, book-fed peoples; this is the charm of Taos, its excuse and justification. There it stands like a tree, like the fabled tree of its Creation legend, whose taproot pierces to that underworld— the dark Womb-world of Becoming—from which man has ascended; a tree watered by hidden springs of whose waters our own sap is long untainted. . . .

. . . Always, for the most casual visitor at Taos, there is the appeal of strangeness; the dark people, the alien dress, the great house-heaps intricately blocked in squares of shadow and sunlight on the tawny earthen walls. There is the charm of aloofness: the absence of clamor, the soft voices, the motionless figures high on the flat roofs, secure in the impersonal privacy of the blanket. Or should you happen upon the pueblo in the one hour of evening bustle, when the men are coming in from the field, young people lingering on the bridge between the house-heaps, the *PREGONERO* draped and authoritative as any Roman senator, announcing the day's news and advices of the day to come, from North house or South house—Hlauuma, Hlaukwima,—you become aware of something subtly excluding in the unfamiliar speech rhythms, the alien tonality, and the utter want of revealing response in the listening citizens. You see them fixed by the voice of proclamation in whatever position it finds them, fixed as prairie dogs at the sound of a snapped stick, on the housetops, in the *PORTALES*, the women going to and from the creek, dripping water jars poised on their heads, the old men appearing automatically at the doorways, like those little figures out of wonder clocks, retreating as automatically. And in not one attitude anywhere a clue, a suggestion as to what it is all about. Everywhere peace, impenetrable timelessness of peace, as though the pueblo and all it contains were shut in a glassy fourth dimension near and at the same time inaccessibly remote.

And there is also the appeal of the beauty of wildness. Over North house, Pueblo Mountain looms, blankly, not linked with the valley even by the white line of an ascending trail. Behind South house the receding hills have the rounded contours of figures with blankets drawn for the isolation which it is the utmost of pueblo courtesy not to disturb. Between them the water of Taos creek lisps steadily; beyond the church it divides, going about and about the fields with a purling sound. Thickets of wild plums abound there, tangles of virgin's bower, meadow sweet, wild iris, blue bush lupines, and tufted grass. It is the wild plums that continue the note of aliveness, the sense of things going on, of contriving, which is so characteristic of the Taos Valley scene. In winter their twigged bareness is a bluish mist over the hidden *RILLITOS:* in the spring when the tinkle of melting snow raises the water noises a full tone, the plum mist reddens, it has a furzy look. Insensibly a downy whiteness comes over the thickets, the vast plumes of the cottonwoods. The hills have a wet blueness, the *PRADOS* are emerald, with silver flashes from the acequias. Suddenly the white fire breaks along the stream borders; white fire of plum-blossom, green flicker of cottonwoods.

By midsummer the plums begin to color, veiled red and yellow. In August the girls of Taos may be seen gathering them all up and down the irrigating ditches. Whole families of visiting Apaches from Jicarilla set up their peaked tents in the fields. Plums for drying and willows for basket making are harvested, medicine herbs from the water borders. Then the brown girls withdraw while the plum leaves redden; pure gold of rabbit brush burns slowly up and down the valley.

There is another sort of beauty playing always about the Pueblo country, beauty of cloud and rain and split sunlight. As Pueblo Mountain stands to the sun, any afternoon rain may enclose it in the perfect irised arch, doubles and reduplications of rainbows. Rains begin on the mesa beyond the Rio Grande, they come walking along the spidery beams, straight across the valley, they stalk one another up the cañons of the creeks, rainbow shine and aerial shadow. It is easy enough to take them as the Indian takes them, visible manifestation of the fructifying powers, People of the Middle Heavens, He rain, She rain; Thunderbird with his wings of dark cloud with his wing feathers edged with the fine cloud; Rainbow-boy. The contours of Taos Valley make always for surprise in the landscape. Nothing is ever twice the same; any turn of the road remakes the elements of the scene, any turn of the weather recolors it. And always the two fixed points from which it is most comprehensively viewed are Taos Pueblo—the top of Hlaukwima for choice—and a more ancient pueblo site, across the valley, on the far bank of Rio Chicquito, behind Llamo, close up under the hills. . . .

In its two and a half centuries of White contact, Taos has actually changed very little, except superficially. There are doors to go in and out of the storied rooms, to replace the hole in the roof and the descending ladders of prehistoric times. There is glass in the light holes, windows even, which were once filled by sheets of crystallized native gypsum, but still the rooms are warmed by the little three cornered fireplaces invented as long ago as Pit dwellings were in use, still the ladders come up from the Underworld of the sunken ceremonial chambers which are the transformed Pit houses of the Ancients, still from the house tops the creation epic is chanted by the appointed heads of the religious societies, in majestic rolling rhythms; still at the ceremonial times—not without sharp skirmishes with the Indian Bureau— the boys go into the kivas to be taught their tribal traditions, instructed in the ancient faith, and urged to make their hunger fast for the personal revelation, as it was in the Days of the New, the Days of the Unforgotten. . . .

. . . Perhaps the most stabilizing fact of Pueblo Constitution is its retention of the matriarchal formula for its social pattern. Every house is a Mother Hive, to which the daughters bring home husbands, on terms of good behavior; or dismiss them with the simple ceremony of setting the man's private possessions—his gun, his saddle, his other pair of moccasins—outside the door. To the wife—the soft voiced matron who trips about on small, white shod feet in fashions of three hundred years ago,—belongs the house, the furniture, the garnered grain, the marriage rights of her children. Peace and stability, these are the first fruits of Mother-rule. It is this peace and stability which makes in so large a part the charm of Taos for the restless Americano, all the more because it lies so deep, secret without being hidden, secure because undefended, loved,

"As a woman with children is loved for her power
Of keeping unbroken the life line of peoples"

says the Creation epic. Tap-rooted, the charm of Taos should endure for another hundred years, even against the modern American obsession for destructive change. But before that it will have fulfilled the prayer of the Rain Song of the Rio Grande pueblos,

"All your people and your thoughts, come to me
Earth Horizon!"

Earth Horizon

12

Earth Horizon, Austin's autobiography, was conceived as a statement of the influences that had shaped her life and literary career. As she writes in the introduction, "Long before that time it was clear that I would write imaginatively, not only of people, but of the scene, of the totality which is called Nature, and that I would give myself intransigently to the quality of experience called Folk, and to the frame of behavior known as Mystical" (vii).[1] She chose the title with care, defining the phrase "Earth Horizon" for the reader early in the book as being derived from the Rain Song of the Zia tribe, and "the incalculable value ring of sky meeting earth, which is the source of experience. . . . At the Middle Place, where all influences of the Earth Horizon come to equilibrium, experience explains itself, flowers and fruits to the holder" (33). At sixty-four, Austin felt that she had reached the Middle Place in her life from which she could panoramically survey her life experience.

Inventing her life in literary form, Austin used the technique of writing about herself in the third person—by referring to herself as "Mary" or "I-Mary"—a modernist device that Gertrude Stein used in writing about her life in *The Autobiography of Alice B. Toklas* (1933). Writing her life was the most difficult task she had ever undertaken, Austin admitted to her young friend Carey McWilliams, a California cultural historian and journalist. Perhaps it opened up again the early, painful remembrances of Hunter family life. She tells us pointedly: "I have never been taken care of; and considering what this has meant to women in general, I feel a loss in the quality of charm and graciousness which I am unable to rationalize" (351). Her mother, her brothers, her husband—all played their parts in the story of Austin's neglect as a girl and young woman. Yet she also describes friendships with those who appreciated her, including Presidents Theodore Roosevelt and Herbert Hoover, and many literary and artistic figures: Jack London, George Bernard Shaw, Joseph Conrad, Amy Lowell, Diego Rivera, H. G. Wells, May Sinclair, and scores of others.

The excerpts from "The Saga of Polly McAdams" foreground Austin's girlhood, on the one hand, and elevate the narrative to a history of foremothers on the other. Polly was the writer's maternal great-grandmother who emigrated from Ohio to Illinois in the mid-nineteenth century. For Austin, Polly was the essence of self-sufficiency, more of an idea than merely a relative. "Chief of the discoveries of the Polly McAdamses, as it was told to Mary, was the predominance of happenings of the hearth, as against what happens on the battlefield and in the market-place, as the determinant of events"

(15). Women like Polly McAdams reflect the importance of matriarchal presence in Austin's autobiography (although we sense the
writer's deep disappointment with her own mother, Susannah Graham
Hunter). Such women had the capacity to influence society, and to a
great extent, this is how Austin saw herself, whether she was informing
the public, "enlightening" literary New York, or carrying on her work
to preserve Native American crafts and Hispanic arts. She herself followed in the footsteps of Polly McAdams in retaining the abilities "to
coordinate society, to establish a civilization, to cause a culture to even-
tuate out of [her] own wit" (15). Austin conveys not only a golden time
of her female forebears in "The Saga," but more important, the tragic,
diminished years of growing up in the Hunter household. By the time
Mary turned ten, her father and sister Jennie had died. "She [Jennie]
was the only one who ever unselfishly loved me," the writer recalls.
"She is the only one who stays" (87).

Book 5, "The Land of Journey's Ending," narrates how the book of
the same title about the Southwest was born. *The Land of Journeys'
Ending* (1924) "gathered all the years of my life, all my experience; my
intentions; it determined the years that were left" (349). The Southwest became a source of inspiration for the writer—and her California
connections increasingly unimportant with the death of her daughter
and her divorce from Wallace Austin. New York, and ultimately Santa
Fe, absorbed her creative energies. In the last pages of book 5, Austin
accounts for how she managed to live—the sometimes menial material
circumstances in which she existed—before she marshalled the resources to build her home in Santa Fe, Casa Querida (Beloved House),
where she ultimately went into semiretirement, writing and lecturing
up to the end of her life. She concludes this segment of the autobiography by telling of Willa Cather's writing *Death Comes for the Archbishop*
(1927) while in Casa Querida, a story that Willa Cather vigorously
refuted. Cather insisted that she did write letters when she visited Casa
Querida during Mary Austin's absence, but never a word of her famous
novel.[2]

Austin's autobiography ends wistfully: "It is not that we work upon
the Cosmos, but it works in us. I suffer because I have achieved so little
in this relation, and rejoice that I have felt so much. As much as I am
able, I celebrate the Earth Horizon" (368).

EXCERPTS FROM
Earth Horizon: An Autobiography
Introduction

When first it was proposed to me that I write my autobiography, I anticipated great pleasure in the undertaking, for I thought it meant the re-living of my important occasions, the setting of them in their significant order, and so bringing the events of my life into a pattern consistent with my acutest understanding of them. It has always been a profound realization of my life that there was a pattern under it, which, though not always realizable when it occurred, explained and extenuated, in the end saved me from irreparable disaster. It was to appreciation of this inherency of design that I came as a child, reassured of its authenticity; felt it hovering in advance of moving to envelop me in its activities, advising and illuminating. So close it lay to my participation that the almost total incapacity of those about me to perceive its shaping, failed to put me at fault about it, never did put me completely out of touch until, by the giving of hostages of faith and affection, I found myself engaged against the pattern and so delayed of fulfillment.

I do not know how nearly it is the case with others, but of this I am certain, that the pattern was set for me, the main lines of it clearly indicated, the important evidences of it cleared, before I had lived the first third of my life. By that time the quality and function of my mind were revealed; the type and scope of my expressiveness indexed; the nature of my salient experiences declared, as you who have the patience to read what is written will discover. Long before that time it was clear that I would write imaginatively, not only of people, but of the scene, the totality which is called Nature, and that I would give myself intransigently to the quality of experience called Folk, and to the frame of behavior known as Mystical. Before I was able to name the events in which these tendencies were signified, or discriminate them from the sort of disposition that beset other people, these things came upon me. And because it turned out that what was so clear to me was not at all clear to the others, because I was repressed and misguessed in respect to my normal tendencies, because I suffered in the expression of them, it seemed to me the happiest of incidents that I should be able to release these early certainties, uncramp the scroll of my mind in autobiographical freedom.

What I thought was that, since the pattern of my adult endeavor was in no sense a made-up pattern, but one that arose through the surface index of Mary, myself, out of a deeper self, of which the umbilical cord which bound it to the source of selfness had not been cut, it in a measure justified all its behaviors, rid me of the onus of responsibility for those that failed to coincide with the current standards of success. I thought that the writing of an autobiography would involve primarily the detailed description of that dominance of my youth by the immanent Pattern, together with some account of the incidents that interfered with its eventuation, and then a few markers on the way of ultimate realization, and finally an estimate of the quality of accomplishment which had been arrived at. Always it was an item of my understanding of the task that the story of my youth, as being the most explanatory, would be the longest and most explicit chapters, taking as they do the stamp of ancestral influences. It has been my happy fortune to have been brought up intimately in touch with ancestral history, and so aware as few people are, of the factual realities of transmitted experiences. It has been my greatest pleasure, as well as the major importance of this writing, that this ancestral rootage should be so cleanly displayed.

But I found that there was more to an autobiography than that. There was the choice of incidents by the way, such as index the struggle of achievement. It is not enough to say that, since one has arrived at the point at which an autobiography is demanded, the pattern has not been wholly defeated. The difficulty has been that the incidents which have hindered and deferred the accomplishment have, in retrospect, appeared inconsiderable, have been overlaid with the firm lines of an accomplished destiny. I am not sure that I have hit in any case on the true obstacle or instrumentality, so that, although I have conceded something to the convention that demands of the autobiographer notice of distinguished personalities, I have not neglected the undistinguished from whom I have freely and frequently drawn. All that I have refrained from is multiplying their mention unduly, at the risk of omitting some of the most helpful. I have known and loved innumerably more people than I have mentioned. Also I have reacted widely and pointedly to contacts of the hour; I have lived in the exigencies of my time, even if I have not lived for them.

What has seemed important to me is to keep to what I began, the explication of the inherited pattern of an individual life, and to omit nothing that pertains to that essentiality. I have tried to account for the feeling of that pattern latent in my consciousness, for the inherent tendencies that produced it, the environmental influences which shaped it. I have given as succinct an account as possible of the contacts which helped or hindered, and dwelt, I hope not too insistently, on the rewards or the lack of them. It matters very little where, in a scale of achievement, I have arrived, or by what incidents. The totality of my experiences is that I have been faithful to the pattern, and it has not disappointed me.

BOOK I

The Saga of Polly McAdams

XI The world of change began to brood over the household the winter of '77. The new baby, named George, had arrived in August the summer before and had become Mary's the moment he was able to be taken about in the new-fashioned perambulator, which was accepted gladly in a nurseryless land, while in England it was still abhorred as "tempting the woman to roam," and even prophetic of the horrid spectacle of a male parent pushing his offspring about. The Hunter children welcomed it as extending the distance they could plan their play from the house without abandoning their young charge. They pushed and pulled and lifted it over obstacles, and confidently affirmed the superiority of their baby over all babies of the young clan. But in the winter nights there began to be hurried excursions of Mother to the girls' room with the sleeping child in her arms—"Take care of the baby, Mary, Pa's sick"—and Mary would hear, through sleep made uneasy by a sense of responsibility, the sounds of pain and restless pacing in the room across the hall.

The children had grown up accustomed to the labored, strangling rhythm of their father's asthma, the odor of burning pastilles, the night alarms, and their own helplessness about it, but this new illness came on so insidiously and intermittently that the only way the nine-year-old daughter had of estimating it was by the increasing pressure of responsibility, the moving of the baby's crib to her bedside, the agony of anxiety when he cried in the night, lest Father should be aroused by it; getting up in the morning thick with sleep, and, before she had anything to eat herself, preparing the baby's soft-boiled egg—her own unaccountably falling asleep in school after uneasy nights, and the hurried flight homeward after school to "take care of the baby."

Mary Austin consulting her dictionary. (Courtesy of the California State Library, Sacramento, California)

I never knew exactly what was the nature of my father's illness except that he suffered excruciatingly, and that it was agreed by all his physicians that it was the last phase of the trouble that had begun in the swamps of Corinth—I seem to recall a story of his being out posting pickets, running into a detachment of the enemy, and having to stand the better part of the night almost up to his neck in the cold ooze of the swamp. Whatever it was, the trouble proceeded in alternate movements of better and worse for a little more than two years. During the summer of 1877 there was an operation from which much was hoped, and nothing was accomplished. One of the singularities of child psychology I recall. It was that though my brother Jim and I admitted to each other after it happened, that we had known Pa's death might be expected, we never communicated it to each other, and never spoke to each other of our grief. It was to Jennie, old enough to understand though not to anticipate, that all Mary's confidences were made.

The end came in October, the 29th, 1878. But before that, Mary, strained with a vague distress, had twice taken alarm, and taking Jennie with her, without leave asked or given, had left school as the premonition overtook her, and trudged home in a fever of anxiety. So that when a day or two before his death the two sisters set out hand in hand, Mary apprehensive of the worse, nobody sent them back. Mary remembers how she tried to cry, as the most natural way of dealing with the sense of stunned alarm in which their flight had begun, and could not until they came to the place on Broad Street from which the white head-stones of the City Cemetery gleamed on the hill, where so often the neighborhood children had sat down to listen to a story, and coming herself suddenly to a more rational feeling about what her father's death might mean, Mary sitting down herself on the boardwalk in tears, and Jennie comforting her as if it were not her father also who was about to be taken. After that, the children were allowed to remain at home until the end—for years it gave the child a pained sense of dereliction that just at the last I-Mary came—there was Mary-by-herself apart and aside, seeing her father so frail and wasted in the bed, his hand straying always toward Mother, alternately moistening his parched lips and wiping her own tears—and the look on Susie's face, worn with grief and watching and luminous with love. Then there was I-Mary, and Uncle Otis with his arm around her, and she hiding her face against him lest somebody should see that she had no tears and think she did not care.

There is much that followed, never forgotten, but not necessary to set down here; all grief is so dreadfully alike. For once Mary had nothing to say; she laid herself dumbly against the sharp edge of sorrow, fearful that she would miss, as she thought she had missed her father's last moments, the least aching instant of loss.

It was indispensable for the family to stay on at the home place, there was livestock to be looked after and settlements to be made. Other members of the numerous kin were always about. Early in December, Mary was taken with a severe sore throat. It was one of those cases in which the doctor was not sent for because nobody knew what the trouble was. At night when her throat ached chokingly, Jennie would put her arms about Mary, stroking her face. So that after Mary recovered from her ailment, Jennie too came down with it. There was a little corner by the fire where she would sit, looking very ill, and trying patiently to respond to inquiry. There came a day when she could neither swallow nor speak. Aunt Effie came down that day and insisted that the doctor should be called, but it was then too late; probably in any case diphtheria was too little understood to have admitted of relief. The next day, in a belated recognition of the virulence of the disease, we buried her. I remember in the bleak little burying-ground looking up at my mother in her weeds and making toward her for the last time in my life the child's instinctive gesture for comfort, and being thrust off in so wild a renewal of Susie's own sense of loss, her rejection of what life had left for her, as leaves me still with no other comparison for appalling shock and severance of widowhood. From that moment on the hillside under the leafless oaks above my father's grave, and my mother thrusting me away to throw herself upon it, I have no instant of recovered recollection until early the next spring when, as we were about to leave the farm to a tenant, the livestock and farming implements were put up for sale, which marks the end of the life on Plum Street.

In time I recovered from my father's death. For a long time I could recall so minutely how he looked that the sight of a man wearing a shawl—always he wore such a shawl as you may see in early portraits of Lincoln—was a fresh thrust in the wound. As late as 1908, walking London streets, I could pick out the resemblances of type, but doubt if I could recollect them now. Mary Patchen, when I met her, could recall to me little traits and mannerisms which else had gone clean out of my memory. But with Jennie it is not so. She is not changed or gone; nothing is changed, not the bright blue of her eye, the cherry lip, the soft aureole of her hair. Still in the night—such times as when I have written a book and see it for the first time in the cold obscenity of print and know without opening the pages that I have failed, that I have sold myself to the delusion of a task for which I have no endowment, an adventure unrequited—she comes in the first sleep and strokes my cheek with her soft hands. The loss of her is never cold in me, tears start freshly at the mere mention of her name. I would not have it otherwise. She was the only one who ever unselfishly loved me. She is the only one who stays.

BOOK 5

The Land of Journey's Ending

V The journey I took before writing "The Land of Journeys' Ending" did more for me than simply to gather up the detailed presentment of the Southwest. It gathered all the years of my life, all my experience; my intentions; it determined the years that were left. California had slipped away from me. Sterling's death and other changes at

Carmel had made of it a faded leaf, pressed for remembrance. New York had failed to engage the exigent interests of my time. It was not simple nor direct enough; bemused by its own complexity, it missed the open order of the country west of the Alleghenies. It was too much intrigued with its own reactions, took, in the general scene, too narrow a sweep. It lacked freshness, air and light. More than anything else it lacked pattern, and I had a pattern-hungry mind. I like the feel of roots, of ordered growth and progression, continuity, all of which I found in the Southwest. Although I knew that I was probably putting much of my audience behind me, I knew that in electing to live there I was releasing myself to a larger scope. I knew that my work, which was essentially of the West, like "The Land of Little Rain," "The Flock," and "The Land of Journeys' Ending," had a permanent hold on the future. It could not be overwritten nor left to one side. After I came back from that journey, I began explicitly to put New York behind me.

I had already put my marriage aside, though I have put off telling about it because it is still a painful recollection. When I came home from Europe the first time, I knew that I could never take it up again. I had said to my husband when I left, when you can make a place for me, a background in which I can live with reasonable comfort and rationality, I will join you again. But that he never contrived. After a year of somewhat aimless clawing, he reverted to the desert, even deeper into its desolation, at Death Valley, and, although he had actually a competent income, he never managed it competently so as to make a frame of life secure for me and comfortably patterned. We would begin a plan as before, and suddenly it would be disrupted by alterations to which I was never a party. He was never able to make of our marriage a Thing, a planned, progressive arrangement. In the midst of an agreed-upon activity, suddenly I would be thrown upon my own resources, scrabbling for means, dislocated in my professional career. I was driven, in order to meet the uncertainties of professional life and my too easily shaken constitution, to live where I could live best, apart from him. And in that apartness, I was subject to the solicitation of other men, to the exigencies of being neither wife nor widow. Hopeless at last of effecting a more satisfactory arrangement, the proposal for a divorce came from me. I was grieved to find how grieved he was, but I thought there was still a chance that if he were free he might make a more satisfactory marriage. That expectation was never fulfilled.

I laid myself open to every possibility of an effective reconciliation, possibilities which he failed completely to realize; he had no capacity for concerted action, for coöperation. We remained friends, but we were neither of us very happy; I am stricken still to recall the impulses which held us together and the lack of coordination which drove us apart. It grew upon me finally that there is a male incapacity for re-patterning the personal life which is insuperable. It cropped up in other men whom I might possibly have married. Twice I was near it, but felt the happy arrangement inhibited by the incapacity of the men involved for making the adjustment. They could not come even halfway, as men of a younger generation have done. As was to have been expected, the men who might have married me were of the intellectual class, often involved in creative careers, and not financially secure. One or the other of us would have to make sacrifices; and it was always sufficiently plain that I should have to be the one. Once when I was younger, before I had thought of dissolving my marriage, I had talked with a woman who was bitter with the sense of being cheated of her own career to fatten her husband's. "But," said I, "when a man is really great like your husband..." Said she, "That does not count. You want your own, even if it is small." It never came to me to make a decision on that basis. There was no man who wished to marry me who carried the sanction of greatness in his hand.

I have had it in mind to give a more explicit account of my love life, but I am inhibited by considerations of fairness. A personal experience of that dimension is not exclusive to one member, but is the property of both partakers of the experience. If I tell all my truth, I know of no way in which the equation can be squared. I recall that a man who had lied about his relation to me excused himself on the ground that "You can tell this story so much more effectively." Men, I am convinced, do not volunteer information on their intimate experiences except when they are conscious of the necessity of exculpating themselves. I have never heard a man explain his love affairs without becoming aware that he is explaining himself away. I said something like that to Frank Harris before he had written "My Life and Loves," finding him disposed to agree with me. But I had no opportunity to talk with him after that book.

I came too late into the social scheme to have cared for love without responsibility. And of the men who so early accepted love without obligation, too many had rejected other things along with it, truth, integrity, intention, the shared sacrifice. Sometimes I think if I had had the wit to look for a Jew for a partner, I might have found both love and opportunity. Only the Jews are warm enough to tolerate art as a shareholder. But I didn't know that at the time. On the whole, what I regret is not the lack of a satisfying marriage, but the loss out of my life of the traditional protection, the certification of ladyhood. I have never been taken care of; and considering what that has meant to women in general, I feel a loss in the quality of charm and graciousness which I am unable to rationalize. The experience of being competent to myself has been immensely worth while to me. It gives clarity and poise. But without having had the experience of being taken care of, I am unable to realize the significance of that measure. I feel always a little at a loss.

There was a curious light thrown upon this problem of the essential relationships of men and women by a set of experiences initiated soon after my arrival in New York, and continued at intervals throughout my stay there. It began with an effort to know New York, the face of it, what went on in its streets and neighborhoods, its hours and occasions. As soon as my day's stint of writing was done, I would be out, going up one street and down another, observing, inquiring, and checking, and, where I found special quarters of interest, arranging to stay in them for days, even for weeks, in whatever character would get me closest to the quality of life there. Sometimes I simply rented rooms in the character of a typist; other times I sought employment and made myself part of the working community. What I was looking for was the web of city life, the cross-ties and interweavings which brought all classes into coalition, made the city unit. It was one of the complaints of my life there that it was too limited, kept within a narrowly circumscribed social round, so that with the immense mass of city dwellers I had no manner of contact. I had it in mind, of course, that I would make fiction of my feelings, fiction which would do what nobody was doing in fiction for New York, presenting a closely woven section of the life of the city. As a matter of fact, I never found it. There were cities; whorls of social contact and activity which went on within themselves apart and aside from the other manifestations, except as they were deliberately sought out as I was seeking them. I went down into the Cherry Street district and plied my typewriting trade, completely alienated from every other contact. I stopped in the neighborhood south and east of Washington Square and worked at artificial flowers. I went "partners" with a peddler of shoelaces and pencils. Over on the west side below Forty-Second Street, I boarded at a place which catered to railroad employees, and picked up a "steady" of the Brotherhood of Railway Engineers. I sublet two rooms in the Chelsea district, from a woman who told me her husband was "in the law business; at the City Hall, you know." It turned out that he was a hanger-on of the city courts, an "alibi" man, who, when an alibi or a witness was wanted, engaged to produce him. He was a friendly soul. I was ill with flu while there, and he used to bring me a comforting brown bottle and sit by my bed and tell me incidents of his practice. In the same house was a couple who had three sons in the police, who came home once or twice a week to play a game of pinochle with their old man and have a taste of mother's cooking, to which I was occasionally invited. In another place I made the acquaintance of a stranger from Chicago, an expert in cement foundations for skyscrapers, who taught me more about the city that is under the city than I could have imagined, the trend of the rocks, the underground waters. He was a clean and sober Irish-American, one who had fathered his widowed mother's brood and brought them to successful issues, and was now at forty-two alone and at loose ends. We went to the pictures together, and to a "show," which was all he knew of the drama, and to concerts in the social hall of Saint Patrick's Parish. And finally he began to tell me how cheaply one could live in Chicago, and about the butchers' picnic and the Sunday lakeside excursions, so that it became necessary for me to behave like a gentleman and—having on that occasion represented myself as a newspaper woman—get sent out of town, leaving no address behind. I worked under the Elevated at a hairshop, which specialized in dressmakers' show window dummies. The keeper of the shop was a middle-aged German Jewish woman, plain and harsh to everyone but her husband, younger than herself, a hunchback, and an artist in his trade. He used to go to the Opera House and to the streets of fashionable weddings to observe the hairdressing of the fine ladies, which he repeated in his dummies, working at them with an artist's concentration. He chose to make me the confidante of his raptures, so that his wife became aware of it, and I lost my job. For that was the one single item which held throughout the whole range of these experiences, that the men accepted me at face value, they never found me out, never so much as suspected me of a life of my own apart from what I showed. Sometimes the women were suspicious; the mother of my policemen friends, the wife of my alibi man. But no man ever discovered in me anything but the attraction of strangeness, the flattery of interested attention. My cement foundation worker never so much as inquired which paper I worked upon, nor did my Brotherhood engineer question my complete satisfaction with the scope and outlook of what he had to offer; so that it comes over me, when I think of the men who with more reason might have expected to mate successfully with me, that the failures grew out of an essentially male incapacity to realize what other factors than reciprocal passion entered into such mating. There were none of them able to make room for me, as a person, however much as a woman I might be desired; and on my part, love was not enough.

It was with the realization, however, of the limitations of experience that I settled in my mind that I would write the closing years of my life into the history of Santa Fe. I could be useful here; and I felt I could get back a consideration from the public that would in a measure make up for the loss of certified ladyhood. I do, in a measure, get taken care of here; I call on the community for help and coöperation—from the doctor, the lawyer, the banker, the artist, the business man—and the response is prompt and sure. It was an intuitive feeling for the reality of such response that led me, shortly after my return from the long journey, to purchase a plot of ground at the foot of Cinco Pintores Hill and later to build upon it.

Once having determined upon Santa Fe as my future home, I never quite let go of it. I returned from time to time; especially I visited Mabel and Tony Luhan at Taos. By this time they had brought their several affairs to the conclusion of marriage and a satisfactory social adjustment. Mabel had built a spacious house on the edge of the Pueblo allotment, and half a dozen guest-houses on the adjoining field, where one met people of interest and distinction. One meets there people like Robert Edmond Jones, a great favorite of mine, and Robinson Jeffers, D. H. Lawrence, Georgia O'Keefe, Agnes Pelton, Carlos Chavez. I went there often, for while there is practically no likeness between Mabel and me, very little consenting approval, there is the groundwork of an intelligent approach to problems of reality, and a genuine affection. There is about Tony a warm stability of temperament which makes him an acceptable third to all our intercourse, so that I count among the unforgettable experiences of New Mexico the journeys we have taken, journeys of exploration and recollection, laying ourselves open to the beauty, the mystery, and charm of New Mexico. Tony is an exceptionally good driver, not like the average American driver who constitutes himself merely the master of the car's mechanisms, the exhibitionist, but making it the extension of his personality. Tony puts the car on, and when he begins as he does usually, to sing the accentless melodies of his people which fit so perfectly to the unaccented rhythms of the machine, one has the sensation of sailing on the magic carpet along the floor of space. Time brings us all closer in these things, so that my life here is extended, practically and emotionally, by the inclusion of Mabel and Tony and the house at Taos.

When I finally withdrew from the East, and determined upon a house at Santa Fe, all the circumstances were favorably arrayed. I had a novel half-done, several good magazine commissions, and money on hand to accomplish the house as I had planned it. I rented a place at the top of the hill and engaged a builder. I had at the time one unresolved difficulty, which was the education of my niece Mary Hunter, my brother Jim's daughter. Mary's mother had died at her birth, and my brother had married again, and was now dead, so that the child had nobody capable of taking a genuine interest in her. From the first she had shown marked artistic and creative ability, toward the development of which I had worked as persistently and as wisely as I could, considering the opposition which the rest of the family imposed to me. It was not only that my family had never realized the quality of my artistic success, but that they had never forgiven me for succeeding against their advice. They still thought of me as failing of normal achievement, of being odd and queer, if not downright abnormal. Like most middle-class families, they resisted the idea of an artistic career for the child, and the stepmother in particular resented any movement on my part to further it. "I'll give her," she said, "a good practical education first."

Now, one knows that when the average middle-class person says that, he means exactly the opposite; not a practical training, but a dull one. Mary was not to be examined for salient traits, for speed and quality, fitness, but she was to be held down to the lowest and slowest levels, to the utterly commonplace and the absolutely standardized. And that had already happened to Mary; all interest and *verve* had been taken out of her schooling; she had been slowed down and inhibited. And no "practical" instruction had taken the place of what I had wanted to give her. The stepmother was not even an ordinarily educated person, but she was utterly unshaken in the conviction of the superior rightness of her decisions. Mary's father, before his death, had selected Wellesley College for her, and Mary was not doing well there. I had kept as close to her as possible and knew what the trouble was, and had done what I could to remedy it. What she needed was, not only to be released into creative work, but to have practical training, work with her hands; the business of spending her money wisely, the use of personal decision.

Mary came to me at Santa Fe, and there it seemed wisest to discontinue her college work and put her to the business of reality. The rest of the family was roundly opposed to it, and her Uncle George, who had acted as her guardian, took great umbrage. I don't know just what we should have done about it, except that I fell ill and needed her. I had let the contract for my house and was in the worst possible situation to endure a serious illness such as, on consultation, mine proved to be, and the decision that I must have an operation. The circumstances were such that it was impracticable for me to undergo anything of the sort unless someone could come forward and shoulder the situation. The doctor wrote to my brother George, himself a practicing physician, telling him what was necessary for him to know, and asking him to come. We waited a week, the doctor preparing to meet him at the train. Finally came a letter saying that he should not come, but that if I would come to him and put myself absolutely in his hands, he would do what he could for me. But that was, of course what I could not do. I could not leave my house, my literary commitments, nor this business of Mary. For Mary was beginning to develop a rather serious disability which derived from the years during which she had been under my brother's care. For myself, I could do nothing but suffer. I lay in bed in great pain for eight months, and in great anxiety about Mary, about whom my brother would take no steps. He was frightened and fell back on the family attitude. He did not believe my physician; he would not even consent to a physical examination of Mary; it was all my queerness. If Mary would abandon me and put herself absolutely in his hands, he might do something for her, but otherwise, not. In the end he sent a few hundred dollars, and when my house was completed so that I could leave it, I took Mary to a hospital, went myself to another, and had an operation from which I was a year in recovering. What I discovered was that not only had I been obliged to give up my commissions, but the manuscript of the novel which I had half-completed was missing. In the confusion of my illness and moving, it had been lost.

I do not know how I should have survived all this illness and disaster had it not been for that kindness and care which I had intuitively anticipated among my friends at Santa Fe. Particularly the Applegates. They were an Illinois family of old kin and kindness, and my nearest neighbors. Frank was an artist, and equally interested with me in the Spanish colonial arts and crafts. Alta reminded me of my sister Jennie, in appearance and in the quality of lovableness. She played a sister's part to me. By means of these things I began to regain my health, and Mary hers. She completed her education at Chicago University and is competently launched on a career.

After a time I began another novel, called "Starry Adventure," in which I gathered up the knowledge I had gained of the various levels of native life in New Mexico. About that time Frank Applegate and I had gone so far with the Spanish colonial arts that it seemed worth while to attempt their revival. I did not know that I should live to see the enterprise through, but I thought that if I had to leave it, somebody would be raised up to carry it on. Also I knew that if I could make a tolerable beginning, I should increase my own chances of living. I knew by this time that what had seen me thus far was the persistent character of my progressive activity. If something in me went on, I would go on with it. I got up from my bed and set the revival of the Spanish colonial arts in motion.

New Mexico is a bilingual country; the courts, the legislature, most public worship, is conducted in two languages. And in two languages everything made is expressed. The colonists who came here originally came direct from Spain; they had not much tarrying in Mexico. They brought with them what they remembered, and as soon as they began to create, they made things in the likeness of the things of old Spain, modified by what they found here among the Indians. For the first hundred years they made very little; they were simply being conditioned by what they found. They accepted the Indian house, but added a fireplace; they brought chests, but added tables and chairs in the Spanish pattern. They made *santos* and *bultos* in the pattern of the holy images of sixteenth-century Spain. When they began to weave it was in the pattern of Southern stuffs with a little suggestion from Mexico. They mixed with the Indians, the peon class, and brought into their blood an Indian strain, Indian capacity for making things, for design and color. These things had been beautiful, but the hundred years of American influence had broken them down and they had not learned to make much else. It takes more than a hundred years to destroy patterns in the blood.

Frank [Applegate] began to collect the old things, to sort them and put values on them. He bought an old house and began to restore it; he collected *santos* and old furniture and tin work. By this time I had begun to collect the folk literature, the plays, the legends and songs. We began our work of revival by starting a Spanish market, and an exhibition with prizes. It grew and grew. There was an annual *fiesta* at Santa

Fe which was attended by the natives, but not very successfully. There was a tendency to divert it to tourist uses. This grew to be an offense to the artists, so that Witter Bynner, John Sloan, Gus Baumann, Will Shuster, and a dozen other artists set out to create a *fiesta* that should be Spanish; they persuaded the natives and finally the rest of the community. It has grown to be notable, and thoroughly, alively native. We began a permanent collection of native arts; I collected scores of native plays and *corridos* and songs. There was, a little north of Santa Fe, an excellent example of an old private chapel, with painted reredos and altar and decorations. The family who owned it [Chapel de Chimayo] was dwindling and finally decided to sell it, made terms with a curio dealer. I was away from home when this happened, at Yale. Frank wired me, and I managed to raise the money to buy it in [to the Colonial Arts Society], to keep it for a religious memorial.

That was after Willa Cather came to write "Death Comes for the Archbishop," and I had to go to the hospital. Miss Cather used my house to write in, but she did not tell me what she was doing. When it was finished, I was very much distressed to find that she had given her allegiance to the French blood of the Archbishop; she had sympathized with his desire to build a French cathedral in a Spanish town. It was a calamity to the local culture. We have never got over it. It dropped the local mystery plays almost out of use, and many other far-derived Spanish customs. It was in the rebuilding of that shattered culture that the Society for the Revival of the Spanish Arts was concerned. It goes on; it broadens and extends itself; it penetrates the educational system. It gathers up sustenance for itself and supporters who will carry it on when I am no longer here. It has reached across the border and made liaison with kindred movements in Mexico. It touches the kindred arts of music, dancing, and poesy. And it has kept me going with it. I live largely by the living stream of creative artistry which it pours into New Mexico.

Notes

The abbreviation "HEH" indicates that the material is from the Mary Austin Collection of the Henry E. Huntington Library.

CHAPTER 1 INTRODUCTION

1. [Mary Austin], "Woman Alone," *Nation* 124 (Mar. 2, 1927): 228.

2. Almost all of her biographers have explored Mary Austin's marriage and maternity in some detail. See Stineman, *Mary Austin: Song of a Maverick*, 67–69; Doyle, *Mary Austin: Woman of Genius*.

3. Showalter writes in "Feminist Criticism in the Wilderness" how "the wild zone or 'female space,' must be the address of a genuinely woman-centered criticism, theory, and art, whose shared project is to bring into being the symbolic weight of female consciousness to make the invisible visible, to make the silent speak" (262–63).

4. See Doyle, *Mary Austin*, 53, 54; Fink, *I-Mary*, 61; Stineman, *Mary Austin*, 59, 148, 92. Personal conversations with Austin's niece, Mary Hunter Wolfe, also reveal the writer's concern about her eccentricity, a reputation that was perhaps not entirely undeserved but was nonetheless painful to her.

5. Mabel anglicized Lujan to Luhan. It was Tony Lujan who arranged with the tribe for Ansel Adams to photograph Taos Pueblo. See *Ansel Adams: An Autobiography*, 90–91.

6. Only the smallest sample of her critical writing is included here. See Austin's many articles and reviews during the 1910s through the 1930s in the *Nation*, *Forum*, the *Century*, *Saturday Review of Literature*, the *Southwest Review*, the *Yale Review*, and many other periodicals. For a full listing, see Dudley Wynn, *A Critical Study of the Writings of Mary Hunter Austin, 1868–1934*, 402–7.

7. See Austin, *Earth Horizon*, ed. Melody Graulich (Albuquerque: University of New Mexico Press, 1991).

CHAPTER 2 "ONE HUNDRED MILES ON HORSEBACK"

Reprinted from *The Blackburnian*, May 1887 (Blackburn College, Carlinville, Illinois).

1. For details of Austin's journey to the San Joaquin, see Augusta Fink's biography, *I-Mary*, to which I am indebted, especially p. 44, for details about the journey to the Hunter homestead.

CHAPTER 3   THE LAND OF LITTLE RAIN

"The Land of Little Rain," "The Basket Maker," and "The Little Town of Grape Vines" reprinted from *The Land of Little Rain* (Boston: Houghton Mifflin, 1903; reprint, Albuquerque: University of New Mexico Press, 1974). Other reprints exist.

   1. Scheick, "Mary Austin's Disfigurement of the Southwest."

   2. Page numbers cited in text refer to the 1903 edition.

CHAPTER 4   THE FLOCK

"The Flock" and "The Coming of the Flocks" reprinted from *The Flock* (Boston: Houghton Mifflin, 1906; reprint, Santa Fe, N.Mex.: William Gannon, 1973).

   1. Page citations in text are to the 1906 edition.

   2. Austin, "The Walking Woman," *Lost Borders,* 204.

CHAPTER 5   SHORT STORIES

"The Mother of Felipe" reprinted from the *Overland Monthly* 20 (Nov. 1892): 534–38. "The Mother of Felipe" was later reprinted in *The Mother of Felipe and Other Early Stories,* edited by Franklin Walker (San Francisco: Book Club of California, 1950), 17–26.

"The Conversion of Ah Lew Sing" reprinted from *One-Smoke Stories* (Boston: Houghton Mifflin, 1934), 96–109. The story was first published in the *Overland Monthly* 30 (Oct. 1897): 307–12.

"The Search for Jean Baptiste" reprinted from *St. Nicholas Magazine* 30 (Sept. 1903): 1024–27.

"A Case of Conscience" reprinted from *Lost Borders* (New York: Harper and Brothers, 1909), 26–41.

"The Man Who Lied About a Woman" reprinted from *One-Smoke Stories* (Boston: Houghton Mifflin, 1934), 7–15.

"The Woman at the Eighteen-Mile" reprinted from *Lost Borders* (New York: Harper and Brothers, 1909), 94–110.

"Frustrate" reprinted from *Century Magazine* 83 (Jan. 1912): 467–71.

"The Divorcing of Sina" reprinted from *Sunset: The Pacific Monthly* 40 (June 1918): 26–29, 74–75.

"The Coyote-Spirit and the Weaving Woman" reprinted from *The Basket Woman* (Boston: Houghton Mifflin, 1904), 45–58.

The following tales are reprinted from *One-Smoke Stories* (Boston: Houghton Mifflin, 1934):

"The Medicine of Bow-Returning," 131–35.

"The Spirit of the Bear Walking," 93–95.

"Wolf People," 175–76.

"The Shade of the Arrows," 87–89.

1. Austin, introduction to *The Basket Woman* (1904), vi–vii.

2. Austin, *One-Smoke Stories,* 7.

3. Austin, *Lost Borders,* 39.

CHAPTER 6   ARTICLES AND ESSAYS

"How I Learned to Read and Write" reprinted from *My First Publication* (San Francisco: Book Club of California, 1961), edited with introductions by James D. Hart.

"Sex in American Literature" reprinted from the *Bookman* 57 (June 1923): 385–93.

"Making the Most of Your Genius" reprinted from the *Bookman* 58 (Nov. 1923): 246–51.

"Woman Alone" reprinted from the *Nation* 124 (Mar. 2, 1927): 228–30.

1. Austin, *Earth Horizon,* 342.

2. [Austin], "Woman Alone," *Nation* 124 (Mar. 2, 1927): 229, 230. Reprinted in Showalter, *These Modern Women,* which includes other essays by notable "modern" women, including Crystal Eastman, Genevieve Taggard, and others.

3. Letter, Austin to Charles Battell Loomis, Dec. 11, 1923, HEH. During the 1920s, Austin considered the National Arts Club at 15 Grammercy Park in New York her home away from home.

4. Austin, "How I Learned to Read and Write," in Hart, *My First Publication,* 65. The book includes contributions by Gertrude Atherton and Jack London among others.

5. See Austin's series of articles titled "Making the Most of Your Genius"— "I. What Is Genius?"; "II. Training Your Talent"; and "III. The Education of the Writer," *Bookman* 58 (Nov. 1923, Jan. 1924, and Feb. 1924). Austin's best-known novel is *A Woman of Genius.*

CHAPTER 7   CACTUS THORN

"Final Chapter" reprinted from *Cactus Thorn* (Reno: University of Nevada Press, 1988), 95–99.

1. Lincoln Steffens (1866–1936) was an important progressive journalist, author of *The Shame of the Cities* (1904) and a friend of Austin's when she lived in Carmel during the 1910s. Their friendship eventually soured, supposedly because Steffens did not share Austin's romantic feelings.

2. Letter, Ferris Greenslet to Mary Austin, June 27, 1927, HEH.

3. Graulich, *Cactus Thorn,* viii.

4. A parallel situation occurs in *No. 26 Jayne Street* when Adam Frear is confronted with his duplicity by the New Woman character, Neith Schuyler, who shares with Dulcie Adelaid a similar, but rather less final, reading of the shabby treatment that women often receive at the hands of men, due primarily to their patriarchal perceptions of the world, one that operates on the principle of preservation by both men and women of male prerogative at any price. In *No. 26 Jayne Street,* Neith Schuyler is shocked to discover that Adam Frear believes that a man has the right to self-interestedly and without consultation terminate an amorous relationship.

5. Austin, *Earth Horizon,* 337. Austin goes on to say that she was so discouraged by the fate of *No. 26 Jayne Street* that for some twelve years, she decided to return to writing naturist works, chief among them *The Land of Journeys' Ending* (1924).

CHAPTER 8 STARRY ADVENTURE

"The Book of New Mexico" and "The Book of Eudora" reprinted from *Starry Adventure* (Boston: Houghton Mifflin, 1931), 38–45. The following translations of Spanish words appear in the 1931 edition.

1. Mabel Dodge eventually was divorced from Maurice Sterne, the modernist painter and sculptor with whom she came to New Mexico, and she then married Tony Lujan of the Taos Pueblo tribe.

2. Letter, Austin to Ferris Greenslet, Dec. 6, 1930, HEH.

3. Ibid.

4. Defined as "a porch" on p. 3.

5. A marsh, defined as "a miry place" on p. 4.

6. Defined as "a deep mountain gully" on p. 10.

7. Defined as "pine nuts" on p. 40.

8. Defined as *"The Shepherds,"* a Spanish Nativity play, on p. 40.

9. Defined as "rattles" on p. 42.

10. Defined as "the wish" on p. 44.

CHAPTER 9 THE LAND OF JOURNEYS' ENDING

"Journeys' Beginning" reprinted from *The Land of Journeys' Ending* (New York: The Century Company, 1924. Reprint, Tucson: University of Arizona Press, 1983).

1. Letter, Austin to Daniel Trembly MacDougal, Oct. 11, 1922, HEH.

2. Letter, Austin to MacDougal, May 13, May 16 [1923], HEH. Austin acknowledged his help by dedicating *The Land of Journeys' Ending* "To Daniel T. MacDougal of the Cactus Country."

CHAPTER 10 POETRY

"Inyo" reprinted from the *Overland Monthly* 34 (July 1899): 49.

"Love Coming Late" reprinted from the *Nation* 127 (July 11, 1928): 43.

"South-Western Poems," including "Sounds," "Caller of Buffalo," "Rio Abajo," and "Litany for New Mexico," reprinted from *Poetry: A Magazine of Verse* 32 (June 1928): 123–27.

"Love in New Mexico," an unpublished manuscript in the HEH Austin collection, is reprinted with permission from the Henry E. Huntington Library.

1. Letter, Austin to Daniel Trembly MacDougal, Apr. 1 [1922], HEH.

2. Drinnon, *Facing West*, 229.

3. Drinnon, *Facing West*, 230–31.

4. See Austin, "Poetry in the Education of Children," *Bookman* 58 (Nov. 1928), 270–75.

5. Austin, *American Rhythm*, 172–73, note 24.

6. Letter, Harriet Monroe to Austin, Jan. 2, 1928, HEH.

7. Letter, Monroe to Austin, June 6, 1932, HEH.

8. First and second prizes in 1928 went to Vachel Lindsay and Elinor Wylie. Austin's honorable mention placed her in the company of Robinson Jeffers, among others.

CHAPTER 11 TAOS PUEBLO

Excerpts reprinted from *Taos Pueblo*, photographed by Ansel Easton Adams and described by Mary Austin (Reprint, New York: New York Graphic Society, 1977).

1. Ansel Adams, with Mary Alinder, *Ansel Adams*, 90–91. According to Adams, in 1985 the first edition was priced in the auction houses at $12,000 (90).

2. Ibid., 90, from a letter to Albert Bender.

3. For details of publication, see the letter from Ansel Adams to Mary Austin, May 21, 1930, and the letters from Austin to Adams, Aug. 30, 1929; Apr. 9, 1930; Jan. 2, 1931, HEH.

4. Austin, *Taos Pueblo*, n.p., HEH. Also quoted in Adams, *Ansel Adams*, 90. The gender arrangements of Taos Pueblo's matriarchal society so appealed to Austin that when she felt its tenets violated, her reaction was vehement. Tony Lujan had left his Taos Indian wife, Mary, to marry Mabel Dodge. Austin angrily threatened her friends Mabel and Tony with the Bureau of Indian Affairs if "[Mabel] did not do right by Tony's former wife" (quoted in Adams, 90).

5. Ansel Adams also photographed the Owens Valley area and mated the

images with excerpted text from Austin's *Land of Little Rain* (Boston: Houghton Mifflin, 1950).

CHAPTER 12 EARTH HORIZON

The introduction, "The Saga of Polly McAdams," and "The Land of Journey's Ending" reprinted from *Earth Horizon: An Autobiography* (Boston: Houghton Mifflin, 1932). *Earth Horizon* was reprinted by the University of New Mexico Press (Albuquerque, 1991).

1. Page numbers cited in text refer to the 1932 edition.

2. Austin's autographed copy of *Death Comes for the Archbishop* is in the HEH rare books collection.

Bibliography

PUBLISHED BOOK-LENGTH WORKS BY MARY AUSTIN

The American Rhythm. New York: Harcourt, Brace, 1923. Reprints, Boston: Houghton Mifflin, 1930; New York: AMS Press, 1970.

The Arrow Maker. New York: Duffield, 1911. Rev. ed., Boston: Houghton Mifflin, 1915.

The Basket Woman. Boston: Houghton Mifflin, 1904. Reprint, New York: AMS Press, 1969.

Cactus Thorn. Reno: University of Nevada Press, 1988.

California: Land of the Sun. London: A. and C. Black, 1914; New York: Macmillan, 1914. Rev. ed., *Lands of the Sun*. Boston: Houghton Mifflin, 1927.

Can Prayer Be Answered? New York: Farrar and Rhinehart, 1934.

The Children Sing in the Far West. Boston: Houghton Mifflin, 1928.

Christ in Italy. New York: Duffield, 1912.

Earth Horizon: An Autobiography. Boston: Houghton Mifflin, 1932. Reprint, Albuquerque: University of New Mexico Press, 1991.

Everyman's Genius. Indianapolis: Bobbs-Merrill, 1931.

Experiences Facing Death. Indianapolis: Bobbs-Merrill, 1931.

The Flock. Boston: Houghton Mifflin, 1906.

The Ford. Boston: Houghton Mifflin, 1917.

The Green Bough. New York: Doubleday, Page, 1913.

Indian Pottery of the Rio Grande. Pasadena, Calif.: Esto, 1934.

Isidro. Boston: Houghton Mifflin, 1905. Reprint, New York: Gordon Press, 1973.

The Land of Journeys' Ending. New York: The Century Company, 1924. Reprint, Tucson: University of Arizona Press, 1983.

The Land of Little Rain. Boston: Houghton Mifflin, 1903. Reprints, Albuquerque: University of New Mexico Press / Zia, 1974; New York: Penguin, 1988; abridged version, with photographs by Ansel Adams, Boston: Houghton Mifflin, 1950.

Lost Borders. New York: Harper and Brothers, 1909, 1925.

Love and the Soul Maker. New York: Appleton, 1914.

The Lovely Lady. New York: Doubleday, Page, 1913.

The Man Jesus. New York: Harper and Brothers, 1925. Rev. ed., *A Small Town Man*. New York: Harper and Brothers, 1925.

The Mother of Felipe and Other Early Stories. Ed. Franklin Walker. Los Angeles: Book Club of California, 1950.

No. 26 Jayne Street. Boston: Houghton Mifflin, 1920.

One Hundred Miles on Horseback (1889). Los Angeles: Dawson's Book Shop, 1963.

One-Smoke Stories. Boston: Houghton Mifflin, 1934.

Outland (Gordon Stairs, pseud.). London: John Murray, 1910; New York: Boni and Liveright, 1919.

Santa Lucia. New York: Harper and Brothers, 1908.

Starry Adventure. Boston: Houghton Mifflin, 1931.

Stories from the Country of Lost Borders. Ed. Marjorie Pryse. New Brunswick, N.J.: Rutgers University Press, 1987.

Taos Pueblo. Photographs by Ansel Adams. San Francisco: Grabhorn Press, 1930. Facsimile reprint, New York: New York Graphic Society, 1977.

The Trail Book. Boston: Houghton Mifflin, 1918.

Western Trails: A Collection of Short Stories. Ed. Melody Graulich. Reno: University of Nevada Press, 1987.

A Woman of Genius. New York: Doubleday, Page, 1912; Boston: Houghton Mifflin, 1917. Reprints, New York: Arno Press, 1977; Old Westbury, N.Y.: Feminist Press, 1985.

The Young Woman Citizen. New York: Woman's Press, 1918.

ADDITIONAL SOURCES

Adamic, Louis. *My America, 1928–1938.* New York: Harper and Brothers, 1938.

Adams, Ansel. *Ansel Adams: An Autobiography.* Boston: Little, Brown, 1985.

Ammons, Elizabeth. *Conflicting Stories: American Women Writers at the Turn into the Twentieth Century.* New York: Oxford, 1991.

Atherton, Gertrude. *Adventures Of a Novelist.* New York: Liveright, 1932.

Ballard, Rae Galbraith. "Mary Austin's *Earth Horizon:* The Imperfect Circle." Ph.D. diss., Claremont Graduate School, 1977.

Bingham, Edwin R. "American Wests Through Autobiography and Memoir." *Pacific Historical Review* 56 (1987): 1–24.

Blend, Benay. "Mary Austin and the Western Conservation Movement: 1900–1927." *Journal of the Southwest* 30 (spring 1988): 12–34.

Bordin, Ruth. *Woman and Temperance: The Quest for Power and Liberty, 1873–1900.* Philadelphia: Temple University Press, 1981.

Brooks, Van Wyck. "Reviewer's Note-Book." *The Freeman*, June 9, 1920: 311.

Brooks, Van Wyck, and Otto L. Bettman. *Our Literary Heritage.* New York: Dutton, 1956.

Canby, Henry Seidel. *American Memoir.* New York: Houghton Mifflin, 1947.

Cassidy, Ina Sizer. "I-Mary and Me: The Chronicle of a Friendship." *New Mexico Quarterly* 9 (Nov. 1939): 203–11.

Cather, Willa. *Death Comes for the Archbishop.* New York: Alfred A. Knopf, 1927.

——. *The Professor's House.* New York: Alfred A. Knopf, 1925.

Chodorow, Nancy. *The Reproduction of Mothering: Psychoanalysis and the Sociology of Gender.* Berkeley: University of California Press, 1978.

Degler, Carl. *At Odds: Women and the Family in America from the Revolution to the Present.* New York: Oxford University Press, 1980.

Doyle, Helen MacKnight. *Mary Austin: Woman of Genius.* New York: Gotham House, 1939.

Drinnon, Richard. *Facing West: The Metaphysics of Indian-Hating and Empire-Building.* Minneapolis: University of Minnesota Press, 1980.

Field, Louise Maunsell. "Mary Austin, American." *The Bookman* 75 (Dec. 1932): 819–21.

Fink, Augusta. *I-Mary: A Biography of Mary Austin.* Tucson: University of Arizona Press, 1983.

Frank, Waldo. *Our America.* New York: Boni and Liveright, 1919.

Gelfant, Blanche H. " 'Lives' of Women Writers: Cather, Austin, Porter/and Willa, Mary, Katherine Anne." *Novel: A Forum on Fiction* 18 (fall 1984): 64–80.

Gordon, Dudley. *Charles F. Lummis: Crusader in Corduroy.* Los Angeles: Cultural Assets, 1972.

Graulich, Melody, ed. *Western Trails: A Collection of Short Stories by Mary Austin.* Reno and Las Vegas: University of Nevada Press, 1987.

Griswold, Robert L. *Family and Divorce in California, 1850–1890.* Albany: State University of New York Press, 1982.

Hall, Jacqueline D. "Mary Hunter Austin." In *A Literary History of the American West,* ed. Max Westbrook. Fort Worth: Texas Christian University Press, 1987.

Hammett, Dashiell. Review of *Everyman's Genius,* by Mary Austin. *The Forum,* Aug. 1925: 317.

Hart, James, ed. *My First Publication.* San Francisco: Book Club of California, 1961.

Henderson, Alice Corbin, and Harriet Monroe, eds. *The New Poetry.* 1917. Rev. ed. New York: Macmillan Company, 1923, 1932.

Hergesheimer, Joseph. "The Feminine Nuisance in American Literature." *The Yale Review* 10 (July 1921): 716–25.

Hill, Mary A. *Charlotte Perkins Gilman: The Making of a Radical Feminist, 1860–1896.* Philadelphia: Temple University Press, 1980.

Houghland, Willard, ed. *Mary Austin: A Memorial.* Santa Fe: Laboratory of Anthropology, 1944.

James, Edward T., ed. *Notable American Women, 1607–1950.* 3 vols. Cambridge: Harvard University Press, 1971.

Jaycox, Faith. "Regeneration Through Liberation: Mary Austin's 'The Walking Woman' and Western Narrative Formula." *Legacy* 6 (spring 1989): 5–12.

Lane, Ann J., ed. *The Charlotte Perkins Gilman Reader*. New York: Pantheon, 1980.

Langlois, Karen S. "A Fresh Voice from the West: Mary Austin, California, and American Literary Magazines, 1892–1910." *California History* 69 (spring 1990): 22–35.

——. "Mary Austin and Houghton Mifflin Company: A Case Study in the Marketing of a Western Writer." *Western American Literature* 23 (summer 1988): 31–42.

——. "Mary Austin and Lincoln Steffens." *Huntington Library Quarterly* 49 (autumn 1986): 357–82.

——. "Mary Austin and the New Theatre: The 1911 Production of *The Arrow Maker*." *Theatre History Studies* 8 (1988): 71–87.

——. "Mary Austin's *A Woman of Genius*: The Text, the Novel, and the Problem of Male Publishers and Critics and Female Authors." *Journal of American Culture* 15 (summer 1992): 79–86.

Lears, Jackson. *No Place of Grace*. New York: Pantheon, 1981.

"The Literary Spotlight: Mary Austin." *The Bookman* 58 (Sept. 1923): 47–52.

Martin, Anne. "A Tribute to Mary Austin." *The Nation* 139 (Oct. 10, 1934): 409.

Morrow, Nancy. "The Artist as Heroine and Anti-Heroine in Mary Austin's *A Woman of Genius* and Anne Douglas Sedgewick's *Tante*." *American Literary Realism, 1870–1910* 22 (winter 1990): 17–29.

Newhall, Nancy. *Ansel Adams: The Eloquent Light*. San Francisco: Sierra Club, 1963.

Norwood, Vera L. "Heroines of Nature: Four Women Respond to the American Landscape." *Environmental Review* 8 (spring 1984): 34–56.

——. "The Photographer and the Naturalist: Laura Gilpin and Mary Austin in the Southwest." *Journal of American Culture* 5 (summer 1982): 1–28.

Norwood, Vera L., and Janice Monk, eds. *The Desert Is No Lady*. New Haven: Yale University Press, 1987.

O'Grady, John P. *Pilgrims to the Wild: Everett Ruess, Henry David Thoreau, John Muir, Clarence King, Mary Austin*. Salt Lake City: University of Utah Press, 1993.

Olney, James. *Metaphors of Self: The Meaning of Autobiography*. Princeton: Princeton University Press, 1972.

Pearce, T. M. *The Beloved House*. Caldwell, Idaho: Caxton Printers, 1940.

——. *Mary Hunter Austin*. New York: Twayne, 1956.

——, ed. *Literary America, 1903–1934: The Mary Austin Letters*. Westport, Conn.: Greenwood Press, 1979.

Porter, Nancy. Afterword to *A Woman of Genius*, by Mary Austin. Old Westbury, N.Y.: Feminist Press, 1985.

Powell, Lawrence Clark. "Mary Hunter Austin: 1868–1934." *Arizona and the West* 10 (spring 1968): 1–4.

——. "A Prophetic Passage." *Westways* 65 (Feb. 1973): 61–65.

——. *Southwest Classics.* Tucson: University of Arizona Press, 1974.

Ringler, Donald. "Kern County Days, 1888–1892." *Southern California Quarterly* 45 (Mar. 1963): 25–63.

Ruppert, James. "Discovering America: Mary Austin and Imagism." In *Studies in American Indian Literature: Critical Essays and Course Designs,* ed. Paula Gunn Allen. New York: Modern Language Association of America, 1983.

——. "Mary Austin's Landscape Line in Native American Literature." *Southwest Review* 68 (autumn 1983): 376–90.

Scheick, William J. "Mary Austin's Disfigurement of the Southwest in *The Land of Little Rain.*" *Western American Literature* 27 (spring 1992): 37–46.

Sergeant, Elizabeth Shepley. "Mary Austin: A Portrait." *The Saturday Review of Literature* 8 (Sept. 1934): 96.

Showalter, Elaine. "Feminist Criticism in the Wilderness." In *The New Feminist Criticism.* First published in *Critical Inquiry* 8 (winter 1981): 179–205.

——, ed. *The New Feminist Criticism: Essays on Women, Literature and Theory.* New York: Pantheon, 1985.

——, ed. *These Modern Women: Autobiographical Essays from the Twenties.* Old Westbury, N.Y.: Feminist Press, 1978.

Sicherman, Barbara, and Carol Hurd Green, eds. *Notable American Women: The Modern Period.* Cambridge: Harvard University Press, 1980.

Smith, Henry. "The Feel of Purposeful Earth: Mary Austin's Prophecy." *New Mexico Quarterly* 1 (Feb. 1931): 17–33.

Spacks, Patricia Meyer. *Gossip.* New York: Alfred A. Knopf, 1985.

Starr, Kevin. *Americans and the California Dream, 1850–1915.* New York: Oxford University Press, 1973.

——. "Mary Austin: Mystic, Writer, Conservationist." *Sierra Bulletin* 61 (Nov.-Dec. 1976): 34.

Stineman, Esther Lanigan. *Mary Austin: Song of a Maverick.* New Haven: Yale University Press, 1989.

White, William Allen. "A Woman of Genius." *The Saturday Review of Literature* 9 (Nov. 12, 1932): 235–36.

Work, James C. "The Moral in Austin's *The Land of Little Rain.*" In *Women and Western American Literature,* ed. Helen Winter Stauffer and Susan J. Rosowski. Troy, N.Y.: Whitson, 1982.

Wyatt, David. "Mary Austin: Nature and Nurturance." In *The Fall into Eden: Landscape and Imagination in California.* New York: Cambridge University Press, 1986.

Wynn, Dudley. *A Critical Study of the Writings of Mary Hunter Austin, 1868–1934.* Ph.D. diss., Graduate School of Arts and Sciences, New York University. Ann Arbor, Mich.: University Microfilms, 1939.

——. "Mary Austin: Woman Alone." *Virginia Quarterly Review* 13 (Apr. 1937): 243–56.

About the Editor

Esther F. Lanigan has taught American literature and feminist studies at the University of Colorado, Colorado College, Yale University, and most recently in the Department of English at the College of William & Mary. She earned her doctorate in American studies from Yale University. Her biography, *Mary Austin: Song of a Maverick,* published by Yale University Press, is considered the definitive study of the writer. She makes her permanent home in Colorado with her husband, Charles, and considers the West the locus of her literary interests. Lanigan is presently at work on a book about couples whose artistic lives flourished in the West during the first third of the century.